Sport and Modernity

For Shelley, Dani, Char, Jesse, and Martin

Sport and Modernity

Richard Gruneau

polity

First published in 2017 by Polity Press

Polity Press
65 Bridge Street
Cambridge CB2 1UR, UK

Polity Press
101 Station Landing, Suite 300
Medford, MA 02155, USA

ISBN-13: 978-1-5095-0156-4
ISBN-13: 978-1-5095-0157-1(pb)

A catalogue record for this book is available from the British Library.

Library of Congress Cataloging-in-Publication Data

Names: Gruneau, Richard S., 1948- author.
Title: Sport and modernity / Richard Gruneau.
Description: Cambridge, UK ; Malden, MA, USA : Polity Press, [2017] |
    Includes bibliographical references and index. |
Identifiers: LCCN 2017006632 (print) | LCCN 2017033906 (ebook) | ISBN
    9781509501595 (Mobi) | ISBN 9781509501601 (Epub) | ISBN 9781509501564
    (hardback) | ISBN 9781509501571 (pbk.)
Subjects: LCSH: Sports--Sociological aspects. | Sports--Philosophy. |
    Civilization, Modern--Philosophy.
Classification: LCC GV706.5 (ebook) | LCC GV706.5 .G785 2017 (print) | DDC
    306.4/83--dc23
LC record available at https://lccn.loc.gov/2017006632

Typeset in 10.5 on 12 pt Sabon by Servis Filmsetting Ltd, Stockport, Cheshire
Printed and bound in the United Kingdom by Clays Ltd, St Ives PLC

For further information on Polity, visit our website: politybooks.com

CONTENTS

ACKNOWLEDGMENTS

This book owes a great debt to an extraordinary group of colleagues and students in the School of Communication at Simon Fraser University. Many of the book's ideas and arguments were first developed for lectures in an undergraduate course on Media and Modernity that I have taught at SFU for more than eight years. In several instances, student questions and discussion in this class helped to refine my thinking. I particularly want to thank the many graduate students whom I've had the good fortune to work with in my time at Simon Fraser. I have learned far more from them than they have from me. Special thanks go to Anouk Bélanger, James Compton, Mark Lowes, and Timothy Adcock Gibson, who were members of a reading group on "the politics of spectacle" that I organized in the late 1990s, held on a weekly basis in the Jolly Taxpayer pub in Vancouver. More recently, I want to acknowledge Dugan Nichols and Peter Zuurbier who were stellar graduate teaching assistants in the Media and Modernity course and always willing to sit down and talk about theories and histories of modernity.

A number of academic colleagues and graduate students either commented upon individual chapters or suggested valuable resources for research. I want to thank Doug Booth, Richard Martin, John Loy, Bill Morgan, Patricia Vertinsky, and Stephen Hardy for commentaries on the opening chapter, as well as Donald Kyle for bibliographic suggestions that helped me negotiate the terrain of Greco-Roman history. An early draft of chapter 2 was written at the invitation of Jonathan Finn as an Open Access article for the Canadian online journal *Amodern* 3 (2014). I want to thank Jonathan for his suggestions in revising an original draft of the article, as well as those of two anonymous reviewers. Doug Booth, John Loy, Patricia Vertinsky, and

Stephen Hardy also provided comments on the essay, as well as John Horne, David Whitson, Emma Griffin, Toby Miller, Alan Tomlinson, Robert Prey, Scott Timcke, Richard Holt, and Rob Beamish.

Chapter 3 owes an immense debt to John Horne, whose collaboration on another project was instrumental in developing my understanding of sporting "mega-events." The chapter also takes considerable inspiration from Ben Carrington, who has been pushing me for years to add a stronger postcolonial flavor to my work. This chapter was also influenced by comments raised in discussions of sporting spectacles and modernity with Scott Timcke, Shawn Forde, Gavin Weedon, Brian Wilson, Patricia Vertinsky, and Carolyn Prouse.

Chapter 4 began as a talk presented at the Sixth Rome Conference on Critical Theory in 2013. I want to thank Beverley Best and Enda Brophy for collegial support and attendance at the initial presentation. Some of the ideas in chapter 4 were also included in the Alan G. Ingham Memorial address that I gave at the annual meeting of the North American Society for the Sociology of Sport in 2015. My SFU colleagues, Shane Gunster and Andrew Feenberg, helped me rediscover an interest in the Frankfurt School. Andrew Feenberg and Jerry Zaslove also provided useful comments on the near-final draft of the chapter.

Chapter 5 evolved from a book chapter originally written in 2010 for a Festschrift for my friend, Bruce Kidd. That chapter was finally published in 2015 in a collection edited by Russell Field, *Playing for Change: The Continuing Struggle for Sport and Recreation*. I revised the chapter for a talk at Concordia University in the fall of 2011 at the invitation of Beverley Best, and many of the ideas arising from discussions after the Concordia talk are incorporated into the chapter in this book. I also want to thank John Horne (again) for ideas that came out of our numerous conversations as co-editors in 2015 of a book on *Mega-Events and Globalization* (Routledge). The chapter included here integrates ideas from the original essay from 2010 with arguments and ideas from an essay on the 1984 Los Angeles Olympics and neoliberalism that Bob Neubauer and I wrote in 2012, as well as some of the arguments that John and I included in our introduction to *Mega-Events and Globalization*. The chapter has also benefited from ideas raised by Anouk Bélanger, Rob Beamish, Mike Davis, Shawn Forde, Carolyn Prouse, Brian Wilson, Courtney Szto, Lyndsay Hayhurst, Kevin Fox Gotham, Jules Boykoff, Yuezhi Zhao, and Katherine Reilly.

Finally, I want to thank Amy Soo for help with manuscript

preparation, as well as the extraordinary patience shown by John Thompson and the Polity Press production team. I first conceived this project for Polity in the early 2000s but was not able to complete it for health and family reasons. When I finally did complete a working draft of the book at hand, in the summer of 2016, I was stricken with a near-fatal blood infection and forced to spend several months in hospital. It is impossible to thank the doctors and nurses in the ICU at Lions Gate Hospital in North Vancouver enough, as well as the teams of doctors and nurses at Saint Paul's Hospital in Vancouver, who nursed me back to health through the fall of 2016. Above all, however, I want to thank my partner, Shelley Bentley, for everything she has done; not only for supporting me steadfastly through my illness with such patience and grace, but also for tolerating the indulgence that this book represents. Our children, Danielle, Charlotte, and Jesse, also suffered through my illness but were always there to offer support when needed. I also want to thank my colleague Martin Laba for the unwavering support he offered my family and me in this difficult time, not to mention his frequent hospital visits and the mango sorbet he used to bring me. The book is dedicated to Shelley, Dani, Char, Jesse and Martin, whose love and care pulled me through an exceptionally difficult time.

Bowen Island, 2017

ILLUSTRATIONS

INTRODUCTION

In this book, I argue that the concepts "sport" and "modernity" share a roughly similar history. Both are conceptual abstractions, invented, debated, and refined between the seventeenth and twentieth centuries by upper- and middle-class individuals in Europe and the Americas. My goal is to provide a historical sociology of the making of these abstractions as well as of the competing narratives, struggles, ideologies, and changing practices associated with them. To narrow this very broad agenda, the book is loosely organized into snapshots of five moments in western history where sport and modernity can be conceptually intertwined: (1) the way ancient discourses, practices, and debates about athletics, body imagery, and spectacle selectively played a role in the making of modernity; (2) how sport became conceived as an autonomous "object" of modernity and as a distinctive field of practice within it; (3) how, along with international exhibitions, international sporting spectacles developed as part of the "staging" of modernity; (4) how sport emerged both as a " project" of modernity and of the critique of modernity; (5) how international sporting spectacles came to reference competing views of "modernization" and became significant features of "global" capitalist modernity – often resulting in increasing social and economic polarization in host cities and nations.

The study of sport and modernity is complicated by the fact that both terms have complex genealogies, multiple meanings, and contested histories. Some classical historians have argued that linguistic precedents for the word "sport" can even be found in Mediterranean antiquity, although this is not the majority view.[1] Most etymologies of the word "sport" trace its ancestry to a Latin root, *portare*, meaning to carry or to bear, and more specifically to *deportare*, to

1

carry away. The Latin root is evident in medieval French in the verb *porter*, to carry, and in the verb *desporter*, to carry or move from one place to another, to transport, or to divert or distract. The French word *desporter* resembles the medieval English word "disport," which was initially interpreted as the act of "carrying oneself in a different direction from that of one's ordinary business."[2] Disport thus connoted distraction in the pursuit of amusement, pleasure, or frolic. The actual word *sport* is evident in medieval English as early as the fourteenth century, with an initial emphasis on distracting amusements (by carrying the participant away from more serious daily tasks).

However, virtually from the outset meanings of the word evolved in multiple directions, referencing certain gaming practices and popular amusements, especially the field "sports" of the English upper classes, as well as a number of different social behaviors (e.g. the "sporting" behaviors of the betting gentleman; "sport" as a form of healthy exercise; being a good "sport;" making "sport" of something or somebody; wearing or "sporting" an item of clothing). By the early twentieth century, the word "sport" was emerging as a more coherent, but contested, category whose description often involved comparisons to (and contrast with) seemingly related practices such as play, games, leisure, and amusements.[3] Within three decades of the end of World War II, attempts to classify sport as a cultural practice with unique characteristics were widely evident in disciplines as diverse as philosophy, history, sociology, and psychology.[4] A notable concern for delineating sport as a distinctive category of analysis and evaluation continues in the present day. To cite just one of many examples, the classical historian Thomas Scanlon has recently argued that "sport" is a "culturally relative but universally present phenomenon, in local species difficult to define but in genus easy to recognize."[5] He goes on to cite his historian colleague Donald Kyle, who defines the genus – the overarching category – of *sport* as "public physical activities, especially those with competitive elements, pursued for victory and demonstration of excellence."[6]

Physical exercise and training regimes, ritualized games, and physical contests of varying types have been found in cultures around the world for as long as humans have kept records. Many cultures have also had important traditions of disciplinary knowledge in areas such as medicine, military training, and pedagogy, and have promoted a variety of physical training and dietary regimens. Medieval and Renaissance European scholars inherited and reinterpreted ideas about health and physical exercise from Greco-Roman thinkers,

Semitic, and Asian sources, as well as a variety of games and physical contests from the early Christian and Islamic worlds. Later European writers also resynthesized Hellenistic and Roman traditions of discussion and debate about the utility and morality of athletic contests and public spectacles, including considerations of their relations to commerce, culture, and politics. A number of these ideas were spread through colonial networks and influenced in turn by local customs and interpretations.

It took a unique conjuncture of events and social conditions in Europe and North America during the late nineteenth and twentieth centuries to prompt an interest among physical educators, philosophers, sociologists, and historians in defining sport and classifying its apparent characteristics. This project of definition and classification does not appear to have a decisive presence in European thought before the mid-1800s. For example, there is no entry for the word "sport" in the legendary *Encyclopedia* prepared in France by Denis Diderot and Jean le Rond d'Alembert in 1751–2. There are numerous references in the *Encyclopedia* to words that are often used today in association with the word "sport," such as "leisure," "pleasure," "games," "feasts," and "festivals," including occasional references to the Greek Olympics in entries pertaining to the "religion of the Greeks and Romans."[7] There are also references to individual activities that most people today would view as falling under the ambit of sport, such as athletics, gymnastics, pugilism, wrestling, hunting, and foot races.

Given their commitment to create a "universal encyclopedia," why didn't Diderot and D'Alembert commission a generic entry for sport? The obvious answer is sport was seen to be an English word and therefore outside of the linguistic reach of the *Encyclopedia*. There are no readily identifiable references to sport in French writing until the early nineteenth century. Moreover, even though the word was used in the title of a periodical magazine, *Le Sport*, as early as 1851, it was used inexactly, mostly with reference to activities associated with leisure and distraction. The first reference to "sport" in a French encyclopedia does not occur until 1872, where it is defined as an "English word to designate all outdoor exercise, such as horse racing, canoeing, hunting, fishing, archery, gymnastics, etc."[8] In Germany, as Jon Hughes points out, the word "sport" was not widely used until the late Wilhelmine era and tended to be "reserved for competitive Anglo-Saxon disciplines," such as boxing, athletics, and team games that tended to emphasize individual performance and quantifiable results. This was in contrast to *Leibesübungen*, a term that encompassed "Turner" expressive gymnastics and dance.[9]

3

Still, I think there is something else operating here beyond the perceived Englishness of the word. The absence of a reference to sport in Diderot and D'Alembert's *Encyclopedia*, or its restricted usage in Wilhelmine Germany, suggests that European intellectuals before the late nineteenth century did not yet have an agreed upon *single* category to describe, linguistically unify, and universalize a field of common qualities associated with physical exercise, game-contests, agonistic spectacles, or leisure pastimes. In this abstract and omnibus sense, sport had yet to be invented. In Pierre Bourdieu's phrase, it had yet to emerge "as its own object."[10] The actual linguistic sign used here is not the relevant issue. The *object* Bourdieu refers to might well have been called something other than sport. The key point is the emergence of an inclusive classificatory term as a conceptual "thing" whose meaning and content were meant to describe a distinctive field of practice. I shall argue later in this book that it was a very short step from the invention of sport as its own object to the argument that the object of sport had certain *inherent* properties or qualities. This initiated a struggle of sorts to assert *what* those properties and qualities are, or what they *should* be.

There can be little doubt that formal or operational definitions of sport as a distinctive area of human practice have enabled useful comparative discussion and evaluation. For example, like many other similar recent attempts at definition and classification, Scanlon's assertions noted above and Kyle's definition share the virtue of providing conceptual rigor to the study of very complex phenomena. Nonetheless, *any* formal definition of sport invites discussion about what it includes and what it leaves out. The beast hunts of Roman antiquity, and many of the "blood sports" of medieval Europe, such as ratting, bear baiting, or dog fighting, do not fit easily into Kyle's definition without stretching our understanding of concepts such as "physical activities" and the "demonstration of excellence" so broadly that they become analytically useless. Similarly, the concepts *species* and *genus* that Scanlon uses have the effect of constructing a falsely imagined analytical standpoint: an imagined "view from nowhere" closely linked to the empiricist dream of identifying concrete historical objects to be analyzed, in E. H. Carr's famous analogy, "like fish on the fishmonger's slab."[11]

Carr raises a major concern about analytic categories created in the present, but treated as if they were actually existing social objects; that is, the tendency to be insufficiently reflexive about the social and historical dynamics involved in their constitution. One of Karl Marx's most insightful observations was to note how the supposedly "objective" analytic categories used by bourgeois political economists – such as land, labor, and capital – were reified products of the very capitalist system they were meant to analyze. Pierre Bourdieu makes a similar point, by implication, when he invites his readers to consider how, and why, a distinctively modern *social* definition of sport came into being in nineteenth- and twentieth-century Europe and North America. The making of a modern social definition of sport, in Bourdieu's view, has never been a neutral or objective enterprise. Instead, it has been "an object of struggles, in which what is at stake is the monopolistic capacity to impose the legitimate definition of sporting practice and the legitimate functioning of sporting activity."[12]

When historians, sociologists, or philosophers have offered their interpretations and definitions about *what* sport is, let alone what it *ought* to be, or *how* and *why* it has allegedly changed from one state to another, their work becomes subtly implicated in such struggles. There is no pretense to academic objectivity that can disguise this. For instance, Johan Huizinga's Christian religious convictions strongly influenced his famous understanding of play as freely undertaken, meaningful, and civilizing activity.[13] He developed a view of play as a culture creating human essence in society that can be profaned through its association with excessive seriousness and constraint through the imposition of political and economic pressures. In contrast, Marxists of Huizinga's era viewed the romantic idealization of human "essences" as the well-meaning failure of idealist philosophy. Their preference instead was to try to realize the promise of such idealizations in *practice*, through the promotion of revolutionary struggle that opposed the reduction of human life to the objectifications of the capitalist wage form and industrial technology in pursuit of meaningful artisanal work and "free" leisure activity. The religiously inclined humanist, Huizinga, in turn, called Marxism "a shameful misconception."[14]

We can agree or disagree with Huizinga's designation, but we can't pretend that either Huizinga or the Marxists stood outside of history. Neither did the analytic categories they defined and preferred, nor the imagined content of these categories. This is why I am so interested in this book in the ideological dimensions of processes of definition, redefinition, and legitimation, not just in respect to sport but in respect to modernity as well. By using the term "ideology," I don't mean the attempt to identify "false" ideas in order to contrast them with "true" ones. Rather, like the sociologist John B. Thompson, I see the study of ideology as a social process wherein symbolic forms, and the institutions associated with their production, can be viewed to serve powerful interests and relations of domination.[15] I argue in this book that one of the most notable ways this occurs is through the process of *reification* noted above, viewed most simply as a confusion of socially created human relationships and representations with the seemingly objective world of "things. "

I make no claim to stand outside the ideological processes and forms that I discuss. The chapters that follow have a narrative character shaped by my own biography, intellectual training, and political concerns. Having said that, I've drawn on historical examples and supporting theoretical and philosophical literatures to make the stories I tell, and the arguments I advance, as plausible, compelling, and persuasive as I can make them. One unifying theme throughout the book is the influence of the twentieth-century tradition of *heterodox* "western Marxism." Proponents of this tradition argue that Marx's work contains methodological and analytical insights which continue to be important and useful in the analysis of western capitalist modernity. But writers in the tradition have typically rejected orthodox Marxism's teleological conception of history, pretense to science, and singular obsession with class struggle. Many years ago, I wrote an essay that criticized uses of the idea of "modernization" in the study of sport to make a case for Marxism – and especially the brand of Marxist analysis developed by Antonio Gramsci – suggesting this as a superior mode of thinking about sport and social development.[16] I haven't retreated completely from this view, but I broaden the perspective in this book to include ideas and arguments developed by Bourdieu and Michel Foucault, as well as research from certain branches of postcolonial theory, classical studies, literary theory, the history of art, critical urban geography, and a reconsideration of the "Frankfurt School" of western Marxism.

It was a reconsideration of the "critical theory" of the Frankfurt School, developed in parallel with some ideas from Bourdieu, which led me back to a consideration of modernity, as opposed to simply focusing on the critical analysis of capitalism alone. The Marxist tradition has mostly had little interest in the concept of modernity, seeing it as a bourgeois mystification that hides the dominating causal significance of capitalism behind an emphasis on the influences of secular rationality, science, or industrialism. In the 1980s, Marxist writers, such as T. J. Clark, Fredric Jameson, and David Harvey, some of whose ideas are discussed in later chapters, began to engage more creatively with the concepts of modernity and modernism. But a somewhat similar engagement was a feature of the Frankfurt School tradition as early as the late 1930s. I argue in chapter 4 of this book that writers associated with the Frankfurt School identified with Marxism, but they understood the task of "critical theory" to *fuse a critique of capitalism with a critique of modernity*. That dual focus is something I try to maintain throughout this book.

This is an appropriate point to return to a discussion of complications arising from diversity in the meanings of terms. For if "sport" is a term with a diverse and complicated history, the concept of "modernity" is arguably even more diverse and complicated. As Ulrich Beck, Anthony Giddens, and Scott Lash argue, the increasingly "reflexive" character of modernity that developed in the latter decades of the twentieth century is a large part of the reason for this.[17] In etymological terms, the English word "modern" has a Latin root, from the words *modernus* and *modernitas*, which simply referenced what was contemporary, new, or novel, often in an implicit and unfavorable contrast to what was older and venerable. In later chapters, I discuss how the idea of the "modern" began to change in medieval Europe to embrace the idea of *progress*. By the late nineteenth century, reflexive consideration of the nature, meaning, and character of modernity had become a notable trope within *modernism* – the cultural expression of modernity. It also began to develop as a significant feature of early twentieth-century sociology in the work of writers such as Max Weber and Émile Durkheim.

However, there is something undoubtedly distinctive about the intensity of critical reflection on modernity that developed in the 1980s and 1990s. This reflexivity was prompted by growing sociological interest in *globalization*, the apparent shift away from industrialism to a more knowledge-based economy, and the new importance of media and cultural industries across the world. During these years, revisionist discussions of modernity seemed to be everywhere, as were concepts that many people linked to modernity, such as "postmodernity" or "postmodernism." As this occurred, the term "modernity" was revised, stretched, reinterpreted, and sometimes rejected to accommodate what many saw as a new moment in human history.

By the end of the twentieth century, it was possible to identify at least six sometimes-overlapping conceptions of modernity. At the risk of immense simplification, I call these *epochal, epistemological, experiential, instrumental, relational*, and *discursive*. In the *epochal* conception, modernity is understood as a distinctive period in time and space, one most often associated with the advent of capitalist industrial societies in Europe and North America. Giddens summarizes this viewpoint concisely when he suggests, as a "first

7

approximation," that "'modernity' refers to modes of social life or organization which emerged in Europe from about the seventeenth century onwards and which subsequently became more or less worldwide in their influence."[18]

From this perspective, the major features of modernity are identified as a series of institutional and cultural transformations that are said to have "swept us away from all traditional types of social order, in quite unprecedented fashion."[19] A diverse range of ideas, practices, and values are alleged to have been be associated with these transformations, including the spread of individualism, liberalism, and universalism; the growth of industrial society and a belief in progress through the applications of reason, science, and technology. Many of the analyses of modernity that became popular through the latter yeas of the twentieth century were variations on this epochal perspective, suggesting a new set of transformative social, economic, and cultural dynamics in human life. Capitalist modernity was said to have entered a new phase, variously described as "postindustrial," "postmodern," "informational," "post-Fordist," "disorganized," "fast," and "liquid," among many other descriptors.[20]

A related analysis took a more *epistemological* turn, joining some of these sociological observations to the resurrection of critiques of modernity that had longstanding connections to older debates within modernism. These included arguments reminiscent of the anti-Enlightenment criticisms of nineteenth-century romanticism, and those of iconoclastic philosophers, such as Friedrich Nietzsche. A new "postmodern" culture had seemingly arrived, where the allegedly modernist pursuit of universal principles and ideals, essential identities, and totalizing classifications or theories was challenged by the breakdown of older forms of social and political association and identity; a widespread rejection of universal histories and metanarratives; a new celebration of difference and diversity; a collapse of distinctions between "high" and "mass" culture, often involving cultural recombination; collage, pastiche, playfulness, and preferences for "surfaces" over "depth."[21]

An *experiential* approach to modernity by contrast, focuses on the lived experiences of modernity in its various (including, for some, its so-called "post") stages. Marshall Berman's book from the early 1980s, *All that is solid Melts into Air*, is the work most commonly associated with this perspective.[22] In chapter 3 of this book, I discuss Berman's view of capitalist modernity as a Faustian world of constant, disrupting change: a world of "creative destruction" that enabled the formation of new subjectivities, freedoms, and new urban cultural forms, as well as new forms of domination. But I think any work that dedicates itself to the exploration of the phenomenology of modern life, or to shifts or splits in the subject positions that modernity in its various stages has created, can be described as an experiential approach. For example, Giddens identifies four "frameworks of experience" in modernity, and David Harvey tries to delve into the social experience of modernity in nineteenth-century Paris, using a diversity of documentary and literary sources.[23] Berman suggests that mapping the experience of modernity should also include literary representations, such as those provided by Goethe, Baudelaire, or Gogol, who developed fictional characters and scenarios meant to convey *what it feels like* to experience modernity.

It is also often argued that modernity can be understood as a range of *instrumental* projects of different types. Some of these projects are directly associated with readily identifiable economic, political, and cultural initiatives, such as the pursuit of free trade and empire, the colonization of parts of the word outside of Europe, the development of new forms and disciplines of work, and the pursuit of new technologies. Jürgen Habermas also proposes the idea of modernity itself as an overarching project aimed at the rational organization and improvement of human life.[24] Habermas suggests that the project of modernity can be criticized for its constraints on human action but, against the views of many postmodern critics, he argues it should also be acknowledged for the opportunities it provides.

In contrast to epochal or instrumental approaches that objectify modernity in various ways, Arif Dirlik argues "modernity is not a thing" but a *"relationship,"* where being "part of the relationship is the ultimate marker of the modern."[25] In Dirlik's view, and in the pioneering work of Samir Amin, the concept of modernity cannot be separated from western imperialism and colonialism.[26] That is, modernity cannot be conceptualized as a project without reference to the capitalist and imperialist projects led by the European powers and their colonial children in the Americas. Understanding modernity as a relationship rather than as a temporal object created by epochal change, or as a bourgeois project, created a meeting ground in the late twentieth century between *postmodern* theory's rejection of metanarratives; the emphasis on "difference" and discourse in poststructuralist philosophy; and the postcolonial critique of modernization as an ideological category.

In early postcolonial theory, modernization was criticized as a Eurocentric universalizing discourse based on an imagined separation between "primitive" and "advanced," or "undeveloped" and "developed" civilizations. Modernization, the argument ran, simply meant westernization. Yet, in one important line of thinking, the idea of modern subject positions had to be severed from earlier humanist and "essentialist" viewpoints. This set up a tension that still runs through postcolonial theory between poststructuralist writers who focus on difference, discourse, and culture, and who reject Marxist analysis as *inherently* totalizing and Eurocentric, and writers such as Dirlik or Amin, who want to retain a connection between the critique of modernity, materialist political economy perspectives, and socialist politics.[27]

From the 1960s through to the present day, many critical sociologists and political economists also endorsed a *relational* view of modernization, albeit with less attention paid to issues of racial and cultural marginalization, hybridities, and fragmented subjectivities than many late twentieth-century postcolonial theories. From the standpoint of radical political economy, modernization was a mystifying ideological category masking the core–periphery relations that had developed in the world system after the sixteenth (some argue the thirteenth) century. Socialist and postcolonial revolutionaries were first to unmask modernization as an ideological strategy that reproduced political, economic, and ideological conditions favorable to the imperialist regimes of nineteenth- and twentieth-century Europe and North America. Similar arguments were later developed in more theoretically and historically sophisticated ways in radical political economy during the 1960s and 1970s – especially in the "world systems theory" of Immanuel Wallerstein and the "dependency theory" developed by Andre Gunder Frank.[28]

Finally, modernity has also been viewed as a powerful *discursive* category central to the history that the "West" has written about itself. As Fredric Jameson argues: "The trope of 'modernity' is always in one way or another a rewriting, a powerful displacement of previous narrative paradigms."[29] This is another kind of relational perspective, but one where the discourse of modernity only achieves its meaning in relation to a discourse that preceded it. In Jameson's work, the discourses of both modernity and postmodernity are developed in the "superstructure" of capitalist societies, but are powerful enough on their own terms to act as determining features of social organization.[30] Other writers, especially those inspired by poststructuralism, have resisted the idea of reducing discourse to material determinants. Still, in each instance, viewing modernity as a narrative or discursive category lends itself to focus on the role played by representation in the "staging" of modernity as both an object and a project.

Epochal conceptions of modernity have arguably had the greatest presence in historical and sociological writing on sport. Allen Guttmann's discussion of modernization in his 1978 book, *From Ritual to Record*, is the best-known example. Drawing on a loosely Weberian model of ideal types, Guttmann views the modernization of sport as a reflection of broader institutional transformations associated with the decline of traditional societies and the advent of modern industrial societies. Most notable in his view are growing secularism, equality, specialization, rationalization, bureaucratization, quantification, and record keeping as defining features of modern sport.[31] Somewhat similar comparisons of the characteristics of traditional folk games versus modern sports are provided in Eric Dunning and Kenneth Sheard's work in the 1970s on English rugby, as well as in Melvin Adelman's work in the middle 1980s on the modernization of sport in New York.[32]

These early works stimulated considerable discussion and criticism resulting in more complex theories and more finely grained and historically nuanced understandings of sport's relationships to modernity in various social contexts. Critics also questioned the ideological underpinnings of such models of modernization, resulting in a dampening of enthusiasm in the late twentieth century about unreflective epochal approaches to sport and modernity.[33] Nonetheless, in a very different way, epochal conceptions were also widely evident during the late twentieth century in more critical work that sought to explore the nature of sport in societies where postmodernism was an emerging historical condition, supposedly leading to a new type of society.[34] Postmodern analyses of sport also drew on epistemological criticisms raised by writers such as Michel Foucault and, in some instances, by relational views of modernity associated with both radical political economy and postcolonialism. Some writers have also sought to explore postmodern experiences in sport, especially in respect to the fragmentation of modern subject positions and the play of differences associated with gender and race.[35]

At varying points this book is influenced by all six of the conceptions of modernity described above. However, the discussion that follows is especially influenced by epistemological, relational, and discursive perspectives on both modernity and sport. I am less interested in writing a history of either concept than in *historicizing* them while exploring their interconnections. Changing historical circumstances since the beginning of the twenty-first century have also shaped my perspective in the book. For example, in hindsight it is hard not to be struck by the breathless and sometimes tacitly celebratory character

11

of some of the writing on modernity, postmodernity, and globalization during the 1980s and 1990s. To an extent, this can be explained by the liberal triumphalism that crept into certain branches of social analysis after the collapse of state socialism in Europe.[36] In other instances, a positive and exuberant tone in the literature seemed related to the anticipation of a truly global economy and global public culture.[37] It should come as no surprise that this exuberant tone has occasionally found its way into writing on sport, especially regarding the role that sporting "mega-events" have played in creating global culture and their "legacies" for technological, economic, and social development in hosting nations. One of my arguments in this book is that the exuberance has been overstated, to say the least.

Something similar might also be said for many branches of postmodernism, whose obsessions with difference, discourse, and anti-essentialism in the 1980s and 1990s now seem far removed from some of the most pressing problems of the twenty-first century: environmental degradation and global warming; the persistence of regional, sometimes genocidal, conflicts; a striking gap between the world's rich and poor and the reassertion of patterns of "primitive accumulation" throughout many parts of the world; an unstable "financialization" of the global economy; a digitally networked world of instantaneous communication, extending knowledge, entertainment, and opportunities for self-expression, *but* also linking these to surveillance and capital accumulation in new ways; an upsurge in religious fundamentalist, racist, and politically reactionary thinking; a return to nativism and hyper-nationalism, and the ongoing domination and degradation of women.

The chapters that follow are loosely organized to address the selected historical snapshots of intersections between sport and modernity noted at the outset of this introduction. The opening chapter prepares the way historically and theoretically through a critical examination of practices and discourses surrounding athletics, body imagery, and spectacles in Greco-Roman antiquity. One of my objectives in the chapter is to reveal the complications, hybridities, and contradictions of "sport" in antiquity, in contrast to the often-polarized conceptions of idealized Greek athletics and "barbaric" Roman spectacles evident in the late nineteenth and twentieth centuries' "modern" discourse. The chapter concludes with a speculative commentary on the ways that these, and other related debates and perspectives from antiquity, played a role in later European formulations of modernity itself.

The second chapter turns to an examination of the objectification of sport in the making of English modernity. Throughout the chapter, I focus on the significance of linguistic and visual representations as constitutive elements in the processes whereby sport became disembedded from earlier European social and cultural logics to become viewed as an autonomous and universal cultural realm with its own distinctive set of practices and qualities. The chapter also examines how representations of sport became sites for articulating a range of instrumental discourses about English national character, appropriate moral behavior, and the legitimate uses of time, space, and the human body.

The third chapter addresses the "staging" of modernity in nineteenth- and early twentieth-century international exhibitions and international sporting competitions, with specific emphasis on their contradictions and ideological dimensions. Along the way, I discuss several relational aspects of the making of European modernity through the establishment of temporal contrasts between so-called ancient and modern civilizations, as well as spatial contrasts between allegedly "primitive" cultures versus modern ones. The chapter also explores how the making of European modernity was constitutively associated with colonial and capitalist creative destruction and accumulation by dispossession, and how international exhibitions and international sporting competitions both exhibited and displayed many of the most significant contradictions of the modern era

By the early twentieth century, there was growing concern in Europe and North America about both the possibilities and the limits of modernity. The fourth chapter explores the rise of German modernism during the Weimar era, including a growing enthusiasm for sporting practices. But the Weimar era was also characterized by debates about the social uses and values of modern sport, including a criticism of rationalization and a reduction of the body to the logics of the market and the machine. The chapter moves from a discussion of these debates to the rise of so-called Nazi "anti-modern" approaches to sports and sporting spectacles. At the same time, I discuss the critique of sport that emerged in the "critical theory" promoted by selected members of the Frankfurt Institute for Social Research. After World War II, Frankfurt School critical theory provided inspiration for some of the most trenchant critiques of sport to emerge during the 1960s and 1970s. The chapter concludes with a critical appraisal of the limitations and strengths of this tradition of social criticism.

The book's concluding chapter examines changing relations between sport, modernization, and globalization in the twentieth century, with specific reference to the challenges posed by escalating urban inequality and slums. The chapter begins with a discussion of postwar Keynesianism, liberal capitalism, and "modernization theory," then moves to consider the limits and possibilities of "civil society" approaches to sport and development to meet the challenges of urban inequality and slums in the early twenty-first century. The discussion then turns to a critical analysis of the factors that have led to the increasing size, scale, and economic importance of sporting mega-events in the era of neoliberal globalization, as well as their attraction to cities and nations outside the West. I argue that any consideration of these factors must rethink the widespread use since the 1980s of international sporting mega-events, such as the Olympics or the World Cup, both as claims to "modernity" and as vehicles for economic and social development.

— 1 —

ATHLETICS, BODY IMAGERY, AND SPECTACLE: GRECO-ROMAN PRACTICES, DISCOURSES, AND IDEOLOGIES

In a lengthy commentary on the nineteenth-century French writer Charles Baudelaire, Walter Benjamin remarks at one point: "among all the relations into which modernity enters, its relation to antiquity is critical."[1] The point is especially apt in describing modern European cultures in the late eighteenth and nineteenth centuries, whose promoters and critics frequently drew on classical references. As Marx argues in *The Eighteenth Brumaire of Louis Bonaparte*, just as modern thinkers seemed to "be occupied with revolutionizing themselves and things, and creating something that did not exist before," they conjured "the spirits of the past to their service, borrowing from them names, battle slogans and costumes in order to present this new scene in world history in time-honored disguise and borrowed language."[2] One of Marx's examples is how "the Revolution of 1789–1814 draped itself alternately in the guise of the Roman Republic and the Roman Empire."[3]

Conjuring an often mythic past to service modern projects in the present went far beyond the realm of revolutionary politics. Partly spurred by new archeological discoveries in the eighteenth and nineteenth centuries, enthusiasm for "classical" antiquity swept through Europe and North America, influencing areas as diverse as literature, art, political philosophy, education, and sport. In England in particular, a "classical" education became a key part of the curriculum of elite schools and universities.[4]

In sport, the idealized use of classical images and mythic narratives typically constructed a view of the timelessness of athletic competition and of toned male bodily symmetry as a universal standard of beauty. Philhellenic educators and historians such as Pierre de Coubertin, E. N. Gardiner and H. A. Harris imagined a "golden age" in Greek athletics which provided a *universal* moral and aesthetic standpoint, not only for evaluating athletic practices elsewhere in the ancient world but, more importantly, for assessing the nature, meaning, and value of sport in twentieth-century western modernity.[5] In this view, the cultural value of sport was seen to lie in the agonistic quest for excellence and honor for their own sake, as well as qualities of self-restraint, leadership and obedience, loyalty and cooperation, versatility, and the ability to take defeat well.[6]

However, these evaluations of sport were muddled by a deepening obsession with masculine physicality and vitality that swept across parts of Europe and North America in the late nineteenth and early twentieth centuries. On the one hand, what Harold Segel calls a "new thematics" of war and sport emerged to underpin a growing international enthusiasm for "physical fitness, the great outdoors, [and] blood sport."[7] In Italian futurism and Nazism, for example, the appropriation of classicism became linked to the celebration of bodily energies as part of an emergent critique of the decadence of European modernity, ultimately supporting a view of "war" as the world's "only hygiene."[8] On the other hand, this view fought it out with modern humanistic concerns about the elevation of raw instincts and emotions over reason; a one-dimensional obsession with specialized physical training over intellectual training; the potential degeneration of sporting contests into "bread and circuses"; and the belief that the growth of large-scale spectacles is an indicator of moral and social decline. Proponents of both perspectives claimed inspiration from athletics, body imagery, and circus spectacles in ancient Greece and Rome.

Since the 1970s, classical scholars have criticized such one-dimensional views of athletics and circus spectacles in Greco-Roman antiquity and have promoted more nuanced historical analyses.[9] A wave of new classical scholarship since the turn of the twenty-first century has revealed enormous complication, hybridity, social difference, and contradiction in the "sport" of antiquity. Partly inspired by this new wave of classical scholarship, my goal in this chapter is to provide a sociologically oriented summary of athletics, body imagery, and spectacle in the histories of ancient Greece and Rome. Through this summary, I mean to provide context for discussion in later chapters of the highly selective, often contradictory, social, cultural, and political uses of classicism in nineteenth- and twentieth-century Europe and North America. While there is considerable historical research on the role of classical narratives, images, and debates in the making of modern sport, I am more interested here in broader

16

sociological questions, including the ideological legacies of ancient Greek and Roman athletics, body cultures, and spectacles in shaping the nature of modernity itself.

Agon and the *vita activa* in Greek antiquity

Ancient Greek civilization developed over the course of many centuries through a series of migrations and conquests of territory, beginning in the Greek Peloponnesus and Aegean islands and expanding through much of the Mediterranean including the southern part of the Balkans and the western part of Asia Minor, Sicily, southern Italy, and parts of northern Africa. This led to hundreds of Hellenic city-states of varying sizes and influence, which lacked central mechanisms of unified political authority but typically shared a common body of linguistic, religious, and cultural traditions. Innovations in literature and art, athletic competition, and independent philosophical inquiry were notable aspects of these traditions.[10]

In the case of philosophy, classical Greek writers developed a level of critical reflexivity that was comparatively unique for their time. It was not enough to live in society unreflectively, what was required was to extend the goals of living to include reflection on the nature and meaning of life itself, including concepts such as representation, experience, justice, virtue, and politics. David Hawkes points out that, with the development of abstract speculation about concepts in ancient Greek social thought, "the veridical status of consciousness ceased to be connected to personal qualities" such as the status of the speaker, and "was instead equated with the ability to think rationally" and the ability to prove others wrong.[11] This not only helped to legitimate free argumentation in academies and gymnasia, it spilled into the central civic space of political discussion, the Greek *agora*.

Greek city-states developed complex systems of class and gendered labor that typically featured male aristocratic elites at the top of the social hierarchy, various occupational categories of "free men" and peasant-citizens in the middle and lower rankings – with women in more restricted positions within these hierarchies – and slaves at the bottom.[12] Slave labor accounted for the bulk of the manual labor force in agriculture, mining, craftwork and manufacturing, construction, and shipping, while female slaves made up almost all of the domestic labor force.[13] While technical/vocational knowledge was respected in Greek antiquity, it tended to be viewed by the aristocratic classes as a marker of lower social status. Advanced formal education

17

in letters (including poetry, rhetoric, and philosophy), music, and athletics was initially limited to the male children of wealthy families and was not available to laborers, slaves, or (notwithstanding some regional variations) women.

Over time, education in these activities became more widely available to free male Greek citizens in academies and gymnasia although, as David Pritchard notes in the case of Athens, even at the zenith of the city's experiment with democracy during the fifth century BCE, wealth determined how long boys would be at school and which of the disciplines any boy could pursue.[14] In classical Athens, athletics, letters, and music were prized as means for young men to display competence, win honor, respect, and glory; demonstrate the uniqueness of their personalities; and contribute to the political discourse of the polis.[15] At the same time, great value was placed on strengthening the male body for warfare and on the display of masculine physical appearance for social status and erotic intention.

Still, if the skills of letters, music, athletics, and warfare were prized in classical Greek antiquity, evaluations of the appropriate balance and value between them were more ambiguous. At first sight, this ambiguity isn't obvious, partially because the achievement and display of mental *and* physical prowess were influenced by an *agonal* conception of life. In her book *The Human Condition*, Hannah Arendt argues that this conception has roots in the heroic individualism expressed in Homer's epic poetry because the central concern of Homer's heroes was "to be the best and to rise above the others."[16] In the political realm, Arendt describes this striving as a commitment to "glory, fame and immortality."[17] Even Pericles, she argues, who is widely associated with democratic traditions in Athenian politics, notes in his funeral oration "that action can be judged not by moral standards but 'only by the criterion of greatness,' which earns 'everlasting remembrance.'"[18]

Agonistic striving lies at the core of what Arendt calls the *vita activa* in classical Greek antiquity, a category that includes labor, work, and action and which offers an idealized standard of how life should be lived. She makes an important distinction between technical activity involved in the fabrication of things and activity in pursuit of appearance, deliberation, and commemoration. For Arendt, the *vita activa* involves competitive striving, resulting in plurality of opinions, free debate, and their expressions in a political community. Critics have argued that Arendt's conception of the *vita activa* overstates the competitive display of autonomous speech as the ideal paradigm of public life and romanticizes the political realm as a space of freedom and deliberation.[19] The result is a view of Greek political life that underplays domination stemming from class and gender.[20]

While such criticisms raise important issues, Arendt's defenders suggest they misrepresent the subtleties of her analysis.[21] Some of these are evident in Arendt's discussion of relations between overt physical prowess and speech in the history of Greek civic life and politics. Arendt argues that in the *Iliad*, Homer describes Achilles as *both* "the doer of great deeds and the speaker of great words." In so doing, she claims that Homer viewed speech and martial prowess to "be coeval and coequal, of the same rank and of the same kind."[22] The battlefield is a place for heroic displays of physical prowess in ancient Greece, Arendt argues, but the Greeks believed that pure violence "is mute" on its own terms and for that reason can never fully "be great." It takes a combination of narration and the availability of spaces of appearance for political deliberation to cement the memories of great physical feats – to make them "permanent" through organized forms of remembrance – and these depend on modes of social activity far removed from physical violence. For Arendt, the strengthening of the Greek polis required an increasing separation of coercive physical action from speech: "To be political, to live in a polis, meant that everything was decided through words and persuasion and not through force and violence. In Greek self-understanding, to force people by violence, to command rather than to persuade, were prepolitical ways to deal with people characteristic of life outside the polis. . . ."[23]

In this passage, Arendt offers a glimpse of the earliest meaning of *agon* in Greek antiquity, a gathering of people, a *social* phenomenon.[24] She also clearly ties the idea of agonism to a *performative* public dimension. Here we see another side of Pericles who, in addition to insisting on the "criterion of greatness," implies the necessity of working through words and persuasion to create institutional forms of "everlasting remembrance." When agonism is conceived *only* in respect to physical prowess, an imbalance is created which risks destroying agonism's vital public quality. In making this point, Arendt invites us to consider physical agonism's potentially self-negating character.

Arendt's discussion of *agon*, and her interpretation of the separation of speech from action, provides a useful starting point to consider the contradictions of physical agonism and the ambiguous attitude that some ancient Greek commentators began to have of it. On this issue, Ryan Belot gives the example of the Athenian rhetorician Isocrates, who criticized the "latently destructive qualities" of

Sparta's celebration of agonism's "manly virtues" when they became "unhinged from a controlling ethical framework." For Isocrates, agonistic obsessions with male physical development and battlefield prowess could be noble and dignified "only if they squared with the requirements of justice and prudence."[25] Conceptions of justice and prudence were interwoven with an ideal of individual and collective *moderation*. According to Michel Foucault, an immoderate emphasis on physical desires or excesses, a "lack of control over the self," which included uncontrolled violence, could be criticized as imbalanced and therefore ignoble.[26]

Foucault goes on to argue that such imbalance also potentially undermined the ideal of virility in Greek antiquity, which valued the mastery of others secondarily to mastery of the self.[27] Yet I believe this formulation also provided legitimacy for a hierarchical and subtly moral distinction between those who demonstrate such self-mastery (typically men of the Greek upper classes) and those (barbarous, pre-political, feminine, slave- or animal-like) individuals or groups presumed to lack it. If this view existed among some Greek intellectuals in respect to questions of honor, restraint, and balance in the case of wartime violence – the most dramatically relevant and direct expression of the competitive display of masculine competence in Greek antiquity – we can find even more widely voiced concerns about immoderation with respect to the athletic games and contests that spread rapidly throughout Greek life from the archaic period (approximately 800 BCE to the Ionian revolt of 500 BCE) through Greece's "classical" period (approximately 500 BCE to the breakup of the Macedonian Empire in 323 BCE), and into the Hellenistic period (early 300s BCE to Greece's submission to the Roman Empire in 31 BCE) .

Ideologies and contradictions in Greek athletics

In the period between 800 and 500 BCE, most inhabitants of ancient Mediterranean civilizations were still involved in primitive agriculture, but dense networks of both short- and long-distance trade "for essential raw materials and manufactured goods, as well as luxury commodities," enabled the development of surprisingly modern looking economies and complex, sophisticated, urban cultures in a number of regions.[28] In this context, the process of creating new cultural initiatives could draw on an array of imported, remembered and imagined traditions. The famous Greek games at Olympia, officially begun in the eighth century BCE, provide a notable example. According to the first-century BCE traveler and geographer Pausanias, the Kouretes, Cretan protectors of Zeus, first staged races and later developed "a whole panoply of athletic contests" at Olympia.[29]

However, Pausanias suggests, "eventually 'there came a Pharaoh who did not know,' a king named Laias, and the Olympic contests which had long been hosted by the city of Elis were abandoned."[30] Later, another king "recalled that such contests had once been celebrated and determined to reinstate them."[31] In a commentary on Pausanias' account, Louis Ruprecht Jr argues: "the trouble was, at that great temporal remove, no one could remember what had been done at Olympia in the past." Gradually, other contests were added as later kings recalled other events "which had been orchestrated once upon a time." In other words, the ancient Greek Olympic Games were a cultural form built on a reimagining, recycling, and reworking of fragments and memories from the past whose relationship to their original predecessors was "complicated at best."[32]

Homer's epic poetry is the most notable source of information about the emergence of athletic agonism in Greece's so-called dark and archaic periods. According to Donald Kyle, athletic agonism is largely presented in Homeric writing as a "normal diversion of the aristocratic warrior class" where "prizes were given to exalt the dead and exalt the host."[33] From the Homeric period through the next several hundred years, regular participation in physical game-contests at tribal, clan, and religious festival occasions, along with physical exercise in gymnasia, became increasingly visible and popular features of Greek life, including the creation of a number of large Panhellenic festivals that combined athletic action with ritualized religious observances. In addition to the games at Olympia, held every four years to honor Zeus, similar Panhellenic festivals were also held at Delphi, Isthmia, and Nemea. There were also growing numbers of localized athletic contests in Greek antiquity, some of which were raucous affairs staged in honor of Dionysius, the god of the grape harvest, fertility, religious ecstasy, and theatrical performance.[34]

Prayers, sacrifices, and ritual feasting involving drink, music, and dancing were vital components of athletic agonism in ancient Greece. Indeed, Greek athletic festivals, or *agones* as the Greeks called them, became key venues for other forms of cultural recreation "including choral dance, literary recitation, commemorative statuary, and even tourism."[35] Religious sentiments were particularly notable at the large Panhellenic games where athletics were accompanied by elaborate rituals and animal sacrifices and the prize of nothing more than a crown made of leaves symbolized the dedication of individual displays of prowess to the gods.[36] The most prominent of these festivals attracted competitors and spectators from across the Hellenic world and were so prestigious that cities rewarded homegrown victors with special privileges.[37] Elsewhere, even though they were steeped in religious observance, localized athletic competitions featured prizes of money, food, implements of warfare, livestock, and oil and, sometimes, female slaves.[38]

As an extension of aristocratic warrior cultures, Greek athletic agonism initially symbolized connections between religious observances, male power, male eroticism, male heroism, and the ideals and aesthetics of upper-class nobility. This is not to say that women were completely excluded from physical exercise or athleticism, or from representations that spoke to female athleticism, martial prowess, or agonistic sensibilities. Greek mythology featured several formidable female Olympians; Spartan women were often encouraged to attend gymnasia and compete in athletic events; women competed in athletic events during festivals to honor the goddess Hera and in some local city events; and there is evidence of female participation in gymnasia and as athletic patrons in a number of Greek city-states after the sixth century BCE.[39]

Still, there is little evidence of any promotion of female athleticism that rivals that of the men.[40] Women were legally prevented from entering or watching the main athletic competitions at the major Panhellenic festivals, and a fusion of practices, traditions, and aesthetic motifs defined Greek athletic agonism as distinctively masculine. Representations of the nudity of male athletic bodies in the commemorative statuary and portraiture that became popular during the fifth century were particularly important in this regard.[41] At that time, representations of male nudity took on a highly idealized form, inspired by athleticism, the craft of armory, and the imposition of geometric symmetry on the male torso to transfigure the body in a dramatic and heroic way.[42] The much-copied statue *Doryphorus, the Spear Carrier* (Figure 1.1), sculpted by Polycleitus in the fifth century BCE is arguably the most famous and widely noted example of an emerging style of masculine "heroic nudity."

"Heroic nudity" in classical Greek statuary was not only a celebration of masculine erotic and physical power, but also equated the idealized heroic male body with an aristocratic habitus. Whether in public commemorative works or personal portraiture, bodily representations in Greek statuary combined ideologies of gender with ideologies that equated virtue and responsibility with social rank. As

22

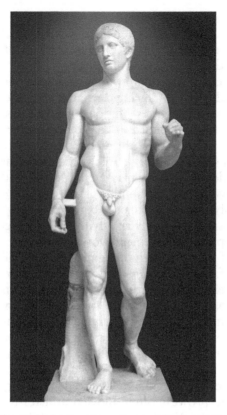

1.1 After Polycleitus, *Doryphorus (the Spear Carrier)*
(Roman marble copy of fifth-century bronze original)

Nigel Spivey points out: "Sex appeal was not absent from the postures of male nudity in Greek sculpture. But the essential motive for display was couched in terms of *noblesse oblige*. 'Nobility and dignity, self-abasement and servility, prudence and understanding, insolence and vulgarity are reflected in the face and the attitudes of the body whether still or in motion.'"[43] This trend found a powerful echo in Platonic philosophy. For Plato, there was a clear connection between *virtue* and "a body held upright" with "limbs running in a straight line," with sinews "finely taut." Plato goes on to contrast this "virtuous physique" with "all beggarly stooping and limp cowardice."[44]

Whereas male nudity and heroic musculature in Greek statuary blurred visual lines between heroism, godly, and aristocratic demeanor, sculptural representations of women were qualitatively different. There were notable instances of androgynous statuary in Greek antiquity, particularly in the case of representations of Dionysius, and it is clear that gender divisions and sexuality in Greek antiquity were extremely complex.[45] Nonetheless, representations of women in Greek art, and especially in sculpture, typically dramatized stereo-typical male/female differences in form and demeanor. Freestanding statues of female figures during the archaic period were always clothed, and while later representations of goddesses such as Athena or Artemis were often depicted in heroic poses, mortal women were always depicted in more demure repose. There is little evidence of female nudity in Greek statuary until the fourth century BCE, and even then female nudes did not display genital detail and often featured hand placements to cover genital regions. Female nudity in Greek statuary typically sought a balance between virtue, sensuality, and modesty, while simultaneously signifying the privileged class habitus of the person represented in the artwork.[46]

In the case of men, strongly imagined visual similarities between male gods and famous warrior-athletes were widely evident in vase paintings, bas-reliefs, and statues. Even if physical immortality was something impossible for humans to obtain, training in athletics enabled young men to literally resemble popular representations of the gods while simultaneously creating the possibility of "eternal remembrance" through the accomplishment and commemoration of great deeds.

As Greek athleticism became increasingly popular, the commemoration of athletic prowess often allowed athletes to achieve mythic status. For example, Nigel James Nicholson notes that the statue of Polydamas of Scotussa, victor in pankration at Olympia in 408 BCE, was a cultish "favorite with visitors to Olympia in the imperial period."[47] Many visitors believed that touching the statue could cure a fever, and the inscription under the statue narrated a series of godlike feats attributed to Polydamas, including killing a lion bare handed, stopping a speeding chariot by grabbing it, singlehandedly killing three of the Persian king's bodyguards who had challenged him to a three-on-one fight, and holding onto the hoof of a bucking bull until the hoof came away in his hands. According to Nicholson, any exaggerated narrative was permitted in athletic victory memorials, as long as it supported the prevailing "aristocratic ideology of athletics."[48]

There is little evidence that any of the athletic events practiced at major Greek festivals had ancestral connections to the spontaneous drinking games or rural game-contests that were popular among the peasant-citizen classes. According to Thomas Hubbard, "the

24

sort of contests practiced at lowly country gatherings like the Rural Dionysia (e.g. dancing on a greased wineskin)" never developed into public athletic events "of Panhellenic stature."[49] Still, some writers have argued that Dionysian rituals, and ritual animal blood sacrifices more broadly, were important in the development of theatrical forms of cultural performance in Greek life that formalized new relations between performers and spectators. Mark Pizzato makes this case in respect to the development of Greek theater as something that involved "a shift in the focus" of ritualized "collective aggression" drawing participants more directly into public rituals while simultaneously creating new conditions for spectatorship.[50] Theatrical forms emerged, in Pizzato's words, "as the embodiment of the Other while others watch."[51] The act of watching then became institutionalized as a *popular cultural practice*. Because athleticism was a vital part of the spectacle of religious ritual observance and sacrifice – and combined this with its own internal dramas of victory, life, and death – athletic contests arguably provided similar forms of embodied otherness, creating opportunities for popular (and often rowdy) spectatorship virtually from the outset, even as the aristocratic tenor and imagery in athletics remained strong.[52]

From the fifth through the fourth centuries BCE, participation in athletics also attracted groups outside the aristocracy because it created possibilities beyond the battlefield for the achievement of glory, fame, material rewards, sexual attraction, and the symbolic trappings of privilege.[53] While there are differences of opinion about the scope of democratization in the history of ancient Greek athletics, there appears to have been increased participation during the classical period by young men from the prosperous mercantile classes in Greek city-states whose parents could afford to buy specialized coaching and training.[54] Growth in numbers of gymnasia and greater opportunities for localized athletic competition created further openings for young men from the peasant-citizen and artisanal classes to become trainers, jockeys, and charioteers, although these professionals were most likely to be employed by wealthy patrons. Such opportunities continued to expand and develop through the Hellenistic period with the growth of widespread state sponsorship of athletic training, more athletic festivals with substantial prizes, grander venues, and larger audiences. Increasing professionalization in athletics led to the formation of athletic guilds and to the regularization of events in an informal "circuit" of interstate competitions, including *agones* in inland Asia Minor, Syria, and Egypt.[55]

Greek athletics developed a symbolic *representative* dimension virtually from their outset. Despite the absence of substantial prizes at the large Panhellenic festivals, early event winners, who were often wealthy on their own terms, were able to translate athletic success into further material privileges and advantages, including meal subsidies, privileged seating at theatrical and other festival events, and opportunities to train youth from other wealthy families.[56] Athletes' names, histories, accoutrements, and reputations or, in many cases, those of the patrons who sponsored them, referenced particular tribes, clan groups, home gymnasia, or cities. Symbolic capital could be accrued through athletic glory even at localized levels of Greek competition, leading to increased competition between wealthy patrons to gain status "by recruiting promising youths from their tribes to compete in the torch relay races or games at various deme-festivals (i.e. sub-local festivals celebrated within suburbs or districts)."[57]

More broadly, the representative features of agonistic striving in athletic competitions took on a symbolic political character in the context of Greek interstate competition. As Hubbard states:

> athletic victories were popularly regarded as a sign of divine favour on the part of the festival's patron god, a city's amassing victories at the great Panhellenic festivals like the Olympics and Pythian games would give it (and its rulers) a right to claim divine ratification of their justice and courage. The wider the field from which the city could recruit athletes and the better the training they received, the greater the city's long-term prospects for winning Panhellenic prestige.[58]

By augmenting a city's symbolic capital through athletic preeminence, wealthy oligarchs or other establishment figures could increase their status. At the same time, success in athletics, horse or chariot racing appeared to link the *arete*, the virtous excellence of the athletic competior, horse or chariot owner, to the *arete* of the city.[59] In this way, Greek athletics were drawn symbolically into competition for military and political hegemony within the Peloponnesus, as well as for status and recognition within Greek cities themselves. The scope of Greek influence across the Mediterranean also resulted in a number of Hellenized cities outside the Peloponnesus investing in athletic competition to enhance their status and recognition, including costly travel to major Greek athletic festivals.[60]

The Greek poet and balladeer Pindar suggested that *arete* is a moral quality inherited from ancestors, although he acknowledged the toils, resources, and dedication that went into athletic success. By the same token, defeat was a source of shame.[61] In fifth-century Athens, residents often expressed such sentiments in regard to *both* war and athletics. For example, they boasted "they did not have to practise 'toils', like the Spartans, to be courageous, since theirs was a natural *arete* which they had inherited from their mythical and historical ancestors." Yet they also believed that battlefield success, like success in athletics, involved resources and preparation, and that these were also responsible for Athenian military successes during the fifth century. Pritchard suggests that this "moral accounting" of military outcomes was culturally homologous with the ideology of Athenian athletics, and that the democratization of the Athenian military during the fifth century furthered the popularization of athletic agonism by creating a "new non-elite affinity with athletics." In this context, relations between war and athleticism were reconfigured as key elements in a more democratic Athenian popular culture.

Dialectics of popularization and critique

Greek civilization was characterized for hundreds of years by often fragile, fractious, and shifting coalitions of aristocratic/warrior states, with no single hegemon able to maintain dominance over the Peloponnesus for any sustained period, until the comparatively brief military hegemonies of Athens and Sparta in the fifth century and the later ascension of Macedonia in the fourth century, during the reigns of Philip and Alexander. Throughout these times, struggles for the growth and control of trade augmented the power of semi-aristocratic oligarchs.[62]

There was also longstanding tension between peasant farmers and aristocrats. For example, in Athens during the sixth century free artisans and peasants agitated with a measure of success for greater involvement in the political process. Subsequent reforms by political leaders such as Cleisthenes and Solon limited *some* of the power of the aristocratic classes in favor of broader political participation. Slavery was not ended, but it became restricted to non-resident and non-citizens, creating a mode of production based on "free" peasant and artisanal labor rather than on slavery alone.[63] Donald Kyle argues that in the search for new forms of social order in these transitions, Solon, in particular, became a strenuous promoter of new athletic festivals, thereby initiating an important transition from private to *civically organized* events.[64]

Other political and economic changes also had implications for the organization, practice, and meanings of Athenian athleticism. According to Max Weber, a combination of free labor and "property

27

as an object of trade utilized by individuals for profit-making enterprise" created an incipient form of capitalist production.[65] The ascendancy of Athenian democracy was built on an emerging mode of rationality that merged "primitive" social relations with economically instrumental ones. This accompanied and facilitated the formation of a new bloc of dominant social interests during the Persian wars and later imperial expansion. That bloc was subsequently challenged by regional competitors in the Peloponnesian War of 431 BCE, and by a devastating plague, leading to a highly chaotic political environment which saw Athens briefly subjugated by Sparta, followed by continued regional instability prior to the rise of Macedonian imperial dominance and the later division of Hellas into several regional kingdoms.

In this volatile economic, cultural, and political environment, it shouldn't be surprising that disagreements might arise about the importance, meanings, and uses of athleticism in Greek life; the appropriate degree of athletic specialization; and the balance that should be achieved between intellectual and physical development. These become particularly significant from the fifth through the fourth centuries BCE, attendant to the new intensity of internal regional warfare, increasing (technical) specialization in Greek societies, philosophical debates about new educational practices connected to Sophist philosophy, and the more widespread use of money, which made wealth portable and less tied to the land. Athletic agonism continued to express an aristocratic ethos, but that ethos was challenged by the ambitions and growing resources of groups in Greek societies who valued skill and success more than heredity as a basis for status and honor.[66]

Hired trainers, jockeys, and chariot drivers had been present virtually from the outset of Greek athletic competitions. According to Nicholson, as early as the late archaic period, there was already a "general perception that athletic services could be bought and sold."[67] The expansion of trade and monetary exchange in archaic and classical Greece, and increased public prominence of the largest religious/athletic festivals, transformed these festivals into *marketplaces*, where trainers and pay-for-service jockeys or charioteers could advertise their skills to prospective patrons. As aristocrats struggled with each other to secure both literal and symbolic victories in athletics, they became more reliant on paid professional/technical help, a trend that appears to have accelerated with the prospect of athletes and patrons recruited from the affluent merchant classes. Yet the resulting commodification and professionalization in athletics worked dialectically to threaten "the aristocratic tenet that victory, and, indeed all success, was largely determined by inherited abilities."[68] Widespread purchasing of athletic talent by aristocratic patrons had the unintended consequence of validating "a mode of exchange" that challenged aristocratic "control over society and sense of their own identity."[69]

The symbolic risk of commercialized and openly meritocratic athleticism to the aristocratic classes was the suggestion that excellence, and therefore honor and nobility, could be *learned* and *earned*. On the surface, this symbolic risk was offset by the ongoing power of traditional aristocratic interpretations of *agon* and *arete*, even as the presence of athleticism in Greek popular culture grew. Aristocratic commissioners of commemorative statues in the classical period rarely mentioned the roles of paid professionals who may have assisted in athletic victories. Moreover, aristocratic bodily habitus was repeatedly dramatized in representations of heroic nudity in popular statuary, and aristocratic patrons were most likely to invest in celebratory songs and poems by apologists such as Pindar, who elegized the rightness of "wealth patterned by prowess."[70] Yet there is little evidence of widespread public or popular disapproval of the aristocratic character of Greek athletic festivals or contests during the classical period.[71]

Still, there is no doubt that shifting social class, status, and political tensions in the classical and early Hellenistic eras contributed to criticisms of athletic agonism. One line of criticism was based on the extent to which aristocratic patrons continued to monopolize control over athleticism, to the exclusion of recognizing the abilities and skills of wealthy merchants, artisans, and intellectuals. According to Hubbard, this initial "tradition of class resentment may have diminished with greater inclusion of the intermediate classes in athletic training," but it set in place "a tradition of intellectual critique" that "tended to perpetuate itself among those who felt that social recognition of their skills and contributions was less than it should be."[72]

A related line of criticism focused more on issues of popularization, heightened specialization, and immoderation. The increasing numbers of athletic festivals, as well as a growing tendency for athletes to record all of the games in which they had won, instead of only their most prestigious victories, provided fodder for such criticism, much of which originated in a deep-rooted anti-democratic intellectual sensibility.[73] In the dawning years of the classical period, Heraclitus had noted disdain for "illiterates" and for "the failure of most people to follow the high and the noble," choosing instead to "follow the bards and use the multitude for their teacher."[74] Heraclitus went on to emphasize how excellence is always the province of "the few" in human life. "The bad" is the province of the multitude and Heraclitus saw the multitude as a regression from the noble individualistic principle (in his view) of "immortal glory among mortals" to an imagined herd mentality.[75] Moreover, he viewed that herd mentality to be both animalistic and barbarous. By this anti-democratic logic, *the nobility of the few* is contaminated when *the few become the many*. For some intellectuals, the proliferation of athletic contests in Greece, along with increased popularization, growing specialization, and the expansion of the cult of celebrity around athleticism, suggested both a threat to traditions of individual excellence and a distraction from more important things in life.

Concern about athletics as a distraction is evident as early as Homer's *Odyssey*, when Odysseus speaks disparagingly of athletic competition as being inherently trivial in comparison to the hardships of war.[76] The ideological linkage between athletics and war became strained because war was becoming more professionalized at virtually the same moment that athletes were becoming so specialized that they could no longer be relied upon to be good soldiers. Even at the height of the Athenian democratization of war and athletics, the playwright Euripides asked what athlete had "ever defended the city of his fathers because of winning a victor's crown?"[77] Similarly, the famous physician Hippocrates expressed ambivalence about the value of overly specialized athletic training.[78] Additionally, while athletics tended to be viewed positively in Athenian popular culture, such views were far from unanimous. Criticisms of chariot racing, and even chariot ownership, were evident in a widespread popular critique of aristocratic lifestyles. This included criticism of the aristocratic preference for military roles in the cavalry rather than as hoplites, as well as criticism of aristocratic pederasty, with its close connections to the cult of exercise.[79]

An issue of particular importance to Greek intellectuals, was the way that athletic obsession potentially distracted from agonistic traditions of rational argumentation and public intellectual engagement. During his trial for "corrupting" the youth of Athens, Socrates' famous claim that his "punishment" should be perpetual meals in the town hall – the award given in Athens to Olympic victors – was meant to be brutally ironic. Socrates satirized athletics as something that had achieved acclaim out of proportion to its actual significance. Similarly, while Plato occasionally had positive things to say about exercise and athleticism, he also suggested that the singular pursuit of physical training and athletic competition was immoderate and one dimensional.

Such views were consistent with the elevation of the ideal over the material world, and of mind over body, which were key aspects of Platonic philosophy. Plato questioned the reliability of the senses as a pathway to truth through his allegory of the cave, where what appears real to prisoners chained at the back of the cave proves to be nothing more than shadows on the wall. By this allegory, Plato "means to indicate that the visible world is made up of mere shadows of ideal forms, which are inaccessible to normal human perception."[80] The physical world may have its uses – the fire that throws the shadows is a human-made creation requiring technical knowledge – but knowledge available to the senses will always be inferior to knowledge that lies outside human experience.

This line of thinking is given a more distinctive political form in Plato's *Republic*, where ideas are held to be more authentic than the material world and the act of confusing the material world for reality is viewed simultaneously as a conceptual error and an ethical transgression.[81] A one-dimensional commitment to the physical/biological world through athletic specialization is an obvious manifestation of such a transgression. Thus, in the *Republic*, Plato discusses athletic training as a "narrow and monomaniacal pursuit that produces men with hard characters and little capacity for independent thought."[82] There are rough parallels here to Arendt's modern discussion of the necessary unity of physical *and* intellectual components in agonism, and of the invidious comparison she notes in Greek culture between the "muteness" of one-dimensional physical agonism and the deliberative, vocal agonism of the democratic polis.

Aristotle went on to develop and to refine Plato's emphasis on the inferiority of bodily sensory experience with similar negative implications for the evaluation of athletic agonism. For example, in the *Politics*, Aristotle notes:

> the soul rules the body with the rule characteristic of a master, while intellect rules appetite with political and kingly rule; and this makes it evident that it is according to nature and advantageous for the body to be ruled by the soul, and the passionate part (of the soul) by intellect and the part having reason, while it is harmful to both if the relation is equal or reversed.[83]

For Aristotle, intellect is what "rules appetite" and provides discipline to the body. He is suspicious of outright hedonism and emphasizes the need for *reason* as a regulator of the "passionate part of the soul."[84] Because he acknowledges the need for human beings to be involved in physical activities necessary to insure survival – such as work, diet, and exercise – he saw no contradiction in a well-rounded life focused on enriching the soul while enriching the body.[85] In Aristotelian thinking, mind and body form a unity, but the activity of soulful contemplation is of a higher form in this unity than activities undertaken out of social or physical necessity, or for simple amusement.[86]

For Aristotle, the ultimate goal of human activity is *schole*, leisure in the service of education, which includes learning how to use one's time freely and creatively in non-instrumental ways. Norbert Elias claims that Aristotle's intention here is to link the idea of *schole* with the pleasurable *experience* of leisure, and especially with the way that mimetic "hedonic" events, such as music and theater, have a curative effect on people through a "movement of the soul";[87] "Pleasure in the comparatively temperate form provided by mimetic events can have a curative effect. Without the hedonic element of enthusiasm, of the excitement produced by music and by drama, no catharsis is possible."

Elias goes on to extend the argument to include the enthusiasms and excitement of sports. But, in making this observation, and in drawing attention to Aristotle's interest in the embodied nature of pleasure, Elias downplays the significance of what the Romans later called the *vita contemplativa* in Aristotle, as well as traditions of rational intellectual asceticism and agonistic intellectual striving that run through Aristotelian philosophy. As Peter Sloterdijk rightly observes, the *vita contemplativa* in Aristotle is often nothing more than another form of agonistic conception, a *vita activa* of philosophical investigations.[88] This represents a distinctively rational, *intellectual practice*, far removed from, and superior in Aristotle's view, to any aspect of the embodied pleasures of mimetic events, let alone those of physical agonism. An even greater problem is the short shrift Elias gives to the inherent sense of social exclusion associated with Aristotle's views on leisure and entertainment. For example, in commenting on musical education, Aristotle states:

> we reject the professional mode of education (by professional I mean such as is employed in music contests) in which the performer practices his art not for the sake of improving himself, but in order to provide his audience with entertainment – and vulgar entertainment at that. For this reason we consider that the performance of such music is beneath the dignity of the freeman; it belongs rather to hired instrumentalists, who are degraded thereby.[89]

Aristotle's emphasis on education as a contemplative ideal directed toward "self-improvement" downgrades "hired" technical practice aimed at mere entertainment, seeing it as less than noble. This ideal was only possible in a class and slave system that relieved wealthy citizens from the responsibility of engaging in necessary labor. In such a system, "professional" practitioners of "mimetic activities" – whether in the realms of drama, music, or athletics – may produce a social good, but they cannot attain the "virtuous" status of the contemplative ideal. The professional charioteer, wrestler, javelin thrower or pankration champion would be no less guilty of "undignified action" from this perspective than the hired instrumentalist.

Aristotle's conception of the *vita contemplativa*, along with his contempt for "vulgar entertainment," was consonant with assumptions and prejudices of the Greek propertied classes. Still, his emphasis on the rule of the body by "the soul," and the rule of "the passionate part" of the soul by the intellect, existed in tension with hedonistic tendencies within the Greek upper classes and with the strength of the Dionysian elements in the broader culture of Greek antiquity. For example, as Pritchard notes, in classical Athens, popular Greek "symposia" were typically exercises in libidinal excess – where the Athenian upper classes "regularly took up drinking games, had sex with hired entertainers, and stumbled onto the city's streets" in drunken revelry in honor of Dionysius.[90]

In a late nineteenth-century discussion of the history of Greek tragedy, Friedrich Nietzsche drew attention to what he saw as a vital *union* of Dionysian and Apollonian creative impulses in classical Greek culture.[91] Nietzsche saw Dionysian revelry as a vital life force that affirms the sensuous range of human experience: joy and suffering, pain and pleasure. In ecstatic revelry, human beings are swept up by feelings of collective association that are much greater than themselves. By contrast, in Nietzsche's view, the Apollonian influence in Greek culture was evident in the Socratic legacy of individualistic comparison, rational structure, and skeptical argumentation, which Nietzsche believed had become rampant in the thought of the European "Enlightenment." The details of Nietzsche's particular interpretation of the history of tragedy, with its corresponding polemic against "negative" Socratic residues in western art, are scarcely worth reiterating here – Nietzsche himself retreated from them later in life. But the distinction he makes is useful insofar as it points further to the dialectical tendencies of social life and culture in Greek antiquity.

I make this point to emphasize the difficulty of trying to neatly compartmentalize or conceptualize ancient Greek conceptions of exercise and athleticism along any single axis, such as aristocratic or popular, sacred or secular, Dionysian or Apollonian, heterosexual or homoerotic. Aristocratic conceptions of agonism were certainly prominent in framing the cultures of leisure, exercise, and athletics and their assessments in both intellectual and popular cultures, but so were dramaturgical traditions of sacrificial religious ritual as well as the influences (and reactions to them) of aristocratic homoeroticism, ritualized violence, patriarchal sensibility, Dionysian revelry, the assumptions of idealist philosophies, and the dynamics of class and regional struggles. Moreover, the comparative balances between these respective traditions and emphases changed over time between the so-called archaic and Hellenistic periods as Greek and then Macedonian Empires grew and retreated.

This lent itself to shifting conceptions of acceptable or legitimate meanings of athletics and athletic training that appear to have varied between different groups and different times. There appear to be subtle differences in interpretation between aristocrats and intellectuals; intellectuals and the popular classes; intellectuals and civic or military leaders; men and women; and residents of established Greek city-states compared to residents of cities that could be viewed as part of Greek and Macedonian spheres of influence elsewhere in the Mediterranean. Similarly, if athletics and athletic training at the beginning of the archaic period in Greek civilization were already hybrid cultural forms, they continued to mutate and develop over the next 700 years. During the reign of Alexander, for example, Hellenistic traditions in exercise, medicine, and athletic training were brought into closer association with Semitic influences. More significantly, over the next several centuries Greek traditions of athleticism were rethought and reassessed through their encounters with the Roman Republic and Empire.

Appropriation, resistance, and the rise of spectacle in Greco-Roman antiquity

The early history of Rome is shrouded in myth but it is widely agreed that settlement on the banks of the Tiber River occurred sometime between the tenth and eighth centuries BCE.[92] A Roman Republic was formed in 509 BCE and after nearly 200 years of intermittent battles against neighboring tribes, the Republic achieved military dominance in central Italy. Roman republican military successes were consolidated through the annexation of conquered land and its redistribution among Roman citizens, the extension of citizenship to *some*

34

of their conquered regional rivals, the enslavement of many of its conquered enemies, and the creation of treaties of so-called "equals" involving substantial levies and taxation. Unlike Greek city-states, "which excluded foreigners and subjects from political participation," Rome rarely hesitated "to incorporate conquered peoples into its social and political system."[93]

Roman economic, military, and naval power eventually grew to challenge the wealthy Greek colonies that had existed in Sicily and southern Italy from the eighth century. After a series of treaty disputes, shifting regional alliances, and years of intense warfare, the Italian-Greek colonies succumbed to Rome in 275 BCE. But the conquest of Greek territories in Italy drew Rome deeper into fractious interstate struggles in several parts of the Mediterranean region, including ongoing wars with Macedonia, Corinth, and Carthage. In 146 BCE, Roman forces burned both Carthage and Corinth, pacified Macedonia, and created Roman provinces in Macedonia and the Greek Peloponnesus.[94] However, Roman subjugation of the Hellenistic world in the eastern Mediterranean occurred slowly and unevenly, and was not fully accomplished until the beginning of the Roman imperial period in the reign of Octavian/Augustus in 27 BCE.

During this time, Rome's encounters with Hellenistic societies resulted in a Latin appropriation of many facets of Greek religion, art, literature, and philosophy, including aesthetic ideas from Greek statuary, as well as engagement with Greek poets, dramatists, and philosophers, and a proliferation of Greco-inspired literary and educational works of various types. More importantly, cultural influences ran strongly the other way. As Ruprecht Jr argues:

> The Latinist appropriations of Greek literature and philosophy by the Romans also signal a great shift within the Hellenic, creating a curious hybrid only loosely related to the Greek original. When Horace says, *in Latin*, that "captive Greece has captured her conqueror," he is being too cute by half. And he knows it, I think. Captive Greece was just that – *a captive*. And with her capture came her deliberate and not-so-deliberate transformation.[95]

The precise nature of this hybrid Greco-Roman culture is much debated but, according to Christian Mann, there is consensus among historians about two clear lines of cultural influence. First, the eastern (largely Greek-speaking) provinces in the Roman Empire were "less affected" by "Romanization" than the western provinces were, for example, Germania and Britain, where Roman occupation brought "new urban patterns," including temples, aqueducts, theaters, and amphitheaters. Second, "gladiatorial games were among the few elements of Roman culture adopted by the Greeks."[96] In Mann's view, there is only scanty evidence of gladiatorial games in the Greek world during Roman republican times. But, in the imperial period, from the first through the fourth centuries CE, gladiatorial games became popular throughout Hellenistic cities in the Roman Empire, even in fabled Greek city-states such as Athens and Corinth.[97]

Mann suggests that nineteenth-century philhellenic scholars were reluctant to accept that the ancient Greek culture they admired so much had willingly embraced gladiatorial games, but more contemporary scholars agree that the Greeks adopted gladiatorial games voluntarily.[98] In his words, "the pull-factors outweigh the push-factors." Roman political power and the promotion of an imperial religious cult throughout the provinces undoubtedly provided the impetus for the spread of gladiatorial games through Hellenistic societies, but there does not appear to have been "diffusion by force." Instead, their popularity seems to have been influenced by a number of distinctively Hellenistic dynamics.

For example, the status competition between Greek cities, and between elites within cities, likely promoted the spread of gladiatorial games, just as it did with the earlier tradition of Greek *agones*.[99] Furthermore, while gladiators in the Greek east were from the lower classes, unlike aristocratic participants in *agones* of the classical period, they appropriated much of the classical era's language and symbolism and often depicted themselves as athletes. Thus, a "peculiarly Greek form" of athletic agonism framed "the self-presentation of eastern gladiators."[100] Greek intellectuals tended either to ignore gladiatorial games, or denounce them implicitly in criticisms of the spread of public spectacles throughout the romanized Hellenistic world. However, the broader public reaction to gladiatorial games was far more ambivalent, involving complex processes of "acceptance, appropriation and reinterpretation."[101]

In contrast, the spread of gladiatorial games does not appear to have substantially undermined existing Hellenistic festival *agones*. According to Mann, "gladiatorial shows were never integrated into the system of Greek agonistics. Neither at the Olympic Games nor at one of the numerous other *agones* did gladiators form a part of the spectacles."[102] Like other areas of Greek culture, Roman generals, and regional administrators tended to admire Greek *agones* and respected their sacrificial traditions. Nonetheless, the early Roman Empire put its stamp on Greek athletic festivals by creating a central mechanism for approving and coordinating them for the first time.[103]

Until the creation of the Roman Empire, Hellenistic athletic festivals had formed several local or regional circuits of competition. As the entire Mediterranean fell under Roman control, these festivals were reorganized under a central authority, and imperial measures began to affect the whole athletic circuit. As Sophie Remijsen points out: "if a city wanted a new contest, it no longer had to negotiate with numerous other groups to get it accepted, but could send an embassy to the emperor, and if he accepted the games everyone else did as well."[104] With central control, the timing of events could also be coordinated, preventing overlapping events and leaving time for travel. This enabled competitors to compete in as many *agones* as possible, further developing a model of circuit professionalism involving Greek athletic guild or "synod" members. The growth of gladiatorial games and their scheduling throughout the Greek colonies occurred as a largely separate enterprise.

The ancestral origins of gladiatorial contests – or *munera*, as the Romans called them – are a matter of considerable debate. The emergence of *munera* in Roman republican culture has been variously traced to several intersecting older social practices and symbolic traditions, such as Greek funeral games and Etruscan funerary ceremonies, early Latin religious festival games (*ludi*), training for military combat, wild animal hunts, and even Latin blood sacrifices. Alison Futrell argues that individual combats at funeral ceremonies are a particularly notable ancestral form of *munera* because of their ties to the idea of sacrificial obligation:

> The heirs of the deceased had a *munus*, or duty, to ease the transition between the world of the dead and the world of the living by providing the lubrication or sustenance of blood as a rite of passage. The blood spilt in ritualized combat guaranteed the community's continuity, despite the passage of its leaders. Thus, death is not an end but a transition . . . but continuously recreates itself anew.[105]

Futrell speculates that the tradition of funerary combat probably found its way into Roman settlements "in the context of the 'civilizing' process of the Etruscan kings," although the earliest record of *munera* in Rome occurs in 264 BCE, well after the expulsion of Etruscan rulers and the founding of the Roman Republic.[106] Accounts of gladiatorial combat in the Roman Republic continue to reference funerary rites through the first century BCE, during which time a subtle movement began to occur in the symbolic meanings of such combats through closer association with "the increasing publicization and politicization of the *fumus publicum* of the illustrious dead."[107]

As this occurred, gladiatorial combats moved from private to public spaces, including the Roman Forum. As part of this transition, "the sense of duty originally defined, as the duty owed the deceased by his survivors began to shift toward the duty owed the people of Rome by its leaders."[108] The Forum became the site for experimenting and testing designs meant to maximize "the impact of the *munera*," and these designs were later incorporated into the construction of Roman amphitheaters.[109]

This process occurred unevenly through the end of the first century BCE, with the private sponsorship of public gladiatorial combats remaining strong throughout the Roman provinces, even as gladiatorial combat in Rome developed closer relations with the state. Furthermore, the shift in symbolic duty that Futrell describes paralleled the growing association between *munera* and older traditions of festival *ludi*, involving theatrical entertainments, horse and chariot races, and athletic contests, such as foot racing and boxing. Attendant to this, the provision of gladiatorial contests to honor the dead as a sense of duty appears to have become more strongly politicized, inflecting already existing traditions of euergetism, as wealthy patrons jockeyed for status and political influence.

Large-scale gladiatorial contests were staged in a number of Roman venues in the waning years of the Republic, in two notable instances by Julius Caesar. Keith Hopkins describes these as follows:

> In 65 BC, for example, Julius Caesar gave elaborate funeral games for his father involving 640 gladiators and condemned criminals who were forced to fight with wild beasts. At his next games in 46 BC, in memory of his dead daughter and, let it be said, in celebration of his recent triumphs in Gaul and Egypt, Caesar presented not only the customary fights between individual gladiators, but also fights between whole detachments of infantry and between squadrons of cavalry, some mounted on horses, others on elephants.[110]

Hopkins goes on to note that, after 42 BCE, regular gladiator shows, "like theatrical shows and chariot races," were given "by officers of state, as part of their official careers, as an official obligation and as a tax on status." However, it wasn't until 20 BCE that Rome had its first permanent stone amphitheater. Six years after that structure was destroyed in the great fire of Rome in 64 CE, the Emperor Vespasian commissioned the Colosseum as a "gift" to the Roman people following the siege and bloody conquest of Jerusalem. Completed over the next ten years, the Colosseum opened in 80 CE with an extensive and ongoing program of executions, beast hunts, and gladiatorial combats.[111]

Although the brutality of the Colosseum is well reported, Hopkins and Beard claim that the scale of slaughter has been exaggerated because later Christian writers inflated the numbers of arena deaths.[112] Moreover, while spectacularly cruel executions were a frequent component of arena spectacle, a rationalization process in the business of gladiatorial training, and reductions in the supply of gladiators, appears to have added a measure of restraint to the numbers of deaths in actual gladiatorial combat. As gladiator shows became more popular, a "circuit" began to develop that operated on incipient market principles, with exchange relations in the buying and selling of gladiatorial labor power, fixed schedules, tours, and a hierarchy of training centers. These developments brought the Roman state more directly into the gladiatorial marketplace in an attempt to ensure competitive fairness, to regulate costs and prices, and to derive taxable revenues from gladiatorial schools and owners.[113]

Unlike arena executions and group massacres that sometimes took a vaguely gladiatorial form, the highest-status gladiatorial combats were overseen by religious authorities, refereed and conducted by strict rules, even to the point of insuring the sharpness of weapons and attempting to match the sizes of the combatants. Despite the possibility of death as an outcome, high-status combats were always conducted as a finale to a day's proceedings in the arena and were promoted as "fair" and "virtuous" fights between equals.[114] Even the Stoic rhetorician and philosopher Seneca, who was a trenchant critic of the arena and the circus, admired the *virtus* (exemplary manliness) of true gladiators. In contrast, he detested sword fights that sometimes occurred between "untrained convicted criminals without defensive armor."[115] For Seneca, such fights were examples of ignoble spectacle rather than displays of virtuous agonistic prowess.

There was undoubtedly something new about the theatrical displays of violence that emerged in arenas across the territories of the late Roman Republic and early Roman Empire. It wasn't the public display of the tortured deaths of "criminals," "traitors," or prisoners of war that was new, nor the bloodiness of beast hunts or the arresting drama of gladiatorial hand-to-hand combat to the death. Roman culture was no stranger to public displays of violence, including flogging, executions involving various forms of torture (such as crucifixion), extremely harsh military discipline, wartime brutality, and the cruel treatment of slaves. Moreover, older Greek athletic events familiar to the Romans, such as boxing, wrestling or pankration, often resulted in maiming or death.

The major difference in Roman gladiatorial combat lay in the direct involvement of the crowd in decisions about life and death. As Mann points out: "In most cases, a fight ended because one of the gladiators was wounded or exhausted. The decision about his life then lay in the hands of the spectators, who evaluated his performance in the fight. Had the defeated gladiator fought bravely, his life was spared; if not, his opponent was ordered to kill him."[116]

The Roman gladiatorial arena democratized spectatorship in a potentially lethal way. While it was a high-ranking official who made the final decision, the crowd's opinion was decisive. Gladiatorial games provided the audience, many of whom were citizens of modest means, with the dramatic thrill of an uncertain outcome, a sense of shared *public* membership in Roman society and, ironically, an expression of their privilege as Roman citizens in an environment that dramatized the coercive power of the state.

There are examples of male Roman citizens who fought in the arena freely, and of female combatants as well, although there were strong prohibitions against any form of upper-class participation by men or women in the spectacles of the arena, circus, or stage. Nonetheless, the immense popularity of male gladiators in Roman popular culture attracted occasional free citizens to the arena, although indebtedness often seems to have been the decisive factor in citizens' decisions to become gladiators.[117] Female gladiators and *venators* were not widespread and carried an element of novelty.[118] According to Steven Brunet, Romans saw such martial demonstrations as running contrary to "feminine nature." The presence of women in the arena was linked to the overriding concern in Roman culture with masculine martial characteristics and the subtext of female combatants was arguably to "teach the men who watched them to be more like men."[119]

Historians and archeologists have demonstrated persuasively that the majority of gladiators were "outsiders," usually recruited from the ranks of slaves, deserters, and political prisoners. Their weapons, armor, and fighting styles were often chosen to symbolize this outsider status, signifying fierce Samnites, Gauls, Thracians, or Phoenicians. In this way, gladiatorial games were a symbolic reminder of the wars in which Rome had acquired its empire and of the distant regions that were a home for wild beasts and exotic "barbarians." The human triumph over wild beasts arguably symbolized the triumph of Roman civilization over nature. Gory public executions and public decisions in gladiatorial combats between outsiders declared the inevitability of Roman justice for anyone who dared to challenge Roman authority.[120]

The possibility of redemption was a vital aspect of that sense of justice. If gladiators proved to be exceptionally brave or virtuous in the face of defeat and death, they could be "pardoned" after several fights, freed, and even granted citizenship. Peter Keegan argues that Roman graffiti typically celebrated gladiators for "their duty" and sought to provide a popular commemoration of "the dignity" of their honorable service.[121] Nonetheless, although famous gladiators often became iconic local figures, "even as free men, they still carried the social and legal stigma of *infamia*," a label they shared with marginalized "others," such as prostitutes and actors, involved with the provision of entertainment pleasures for the Roman public.[122]

The combination in gladiatorial spectacle of a ritualized sense of collective identification, matched with traditions of euergetism and the symbolism of Roman power over life and death, gave the amphitheater a special significance in early imperial culture. In Rome, the spatial placement of the Colosseum, virtually adjacent to the Circus Maximus and the Forum, created a vital civic hub centered on several different forms of spectacle, including chariot racing, gladiatorial combat, executions, military processions, political gatherings, speech-making, and monumental buildings in themselves. Of these ancient *spaces of spectacle*, the Circus Maximus, with a capacity of approximately 150,000 spectators, was by far the largest. As a longstanding site for chariot races, festival *ludi* and, later, gladiatorial contests, it predated the Colosseum by nearly 400 years.

Circus racing became increasingly professionalized in the late Republic and early imperial eras, and winners of events could earn substantial sums of money. The circus also became home to four distinctive "color factions" (Red, Blue, Green, and White) which provided intensely felt sources of personal and political identities, not only for Roman spectators but also for the owners of chariots and horses, including high-ranking officials and even Roman emperors. For example, Caligula, Nero, Domitian, and Commodus fervently supported the Greens, whereas Caracalla supported the Blues. Detailed records were kept of event winners, and the rivalry between factions often led to attempts to fix races, as well as to partisan disputes among spectators, frequently accompanied by violence.[123]

Roman cultural conservatism, "bread and circuses," and the politics of the popular

The early Roman Republic was a constitutional state with a Senate appointed from the patrician class and elected popular assemblies.

41

It also had a complex and sophisticated legal code that enshrined considerable rights of citizenship and ensured a degree of democratic participation in selecting local officials and in shaping local political decision making. However, the Republic was also divided by class hierarchies and was strongly patriarchal, based on a model of family relations dominated by fathers and husbands. Early Roman republican society also featured a deep tradition of patron–client social relationships and socially conservative values of masculine competence, self-discipline, moderation, public decorum, and religious piety.[124] Matched with a strong sense of ethno-cultural identity and civic duty – duty to the state was viewed roughly akin to a son's obedience to a father – these values were important in the Republic's ability to mobilize a formidable army of "free" peasant-citizens. Following the Roman defeat by Carthage at Cannae in 216 BCE, a puritanical martial asceticism appeared to root even more deeply in Roman culture.[125]

Suspicion that intellectual and artistic refinements were sources of softness and "effeminate character" was a notable aspect of Roman patriarchal martial asceticism. In this regard, the Roman culture of martial asceticism was different from the agonistic culture of classical Greece, even though both emphasized the importance of virtue and courage. For example, in the opening passages of his "Letters from Gaul," Julius Caesar worries that "Galli" tribes are "remote from the Roman Province [and] have infrequent trade contacts with its high culture and refinement, and thus remain unaffected by influences which tend to effeminate character."[126] Caesar worries that the Galli "barbarian" warriors may demonstrate a superior masculine martial asceticism to Roman troops who may have "softened" as a result of their connections to Roman "refinement." By contrast, in the Greek case, Thucydides cites Pericles, who ascribes a more multidimensional character to Greek agonistic culture: "Our love of what is beautiful does not lead to extravagance; our love of the things of the mind does not make us soft."[127] Roman traditionalists tended to be more aligned with Caesar's view than Pericles. Indeed, Kathryn Mammel suggests that many Roman traditionalists viewed Hellenistic culture as "morally dangerous" because it allegedly exposed Romans to "nudity, pederasty, effeminacy, luxury and degeneracy."[128]

This is not to say that social and cultural life in the Roman Republic was characterized by harmony or consensus. On the contrary, the early Republic was riven by internal struggles between patrician and plebeian classes for access to private and state lands, as well as political offices. These struggles lasted for more than 200 years, before the patrician nobility merged with certain factions of the plebeian classes and military leadership to form a new dominant class of large land-owners with extensive slave holdings. According to de Ste Croix, a new political and economic settlement in the final two centuries of the Republic gave greater political power to the wealthy, in proportion to their wealth, through new land ownership and taxation policies that pushed many peasant-farmers off the land in favor of large privately owned estates worked by slaves.[129]

These developments contributed to the creation of an urban under-class that was heavily dependent for their economic survival on crime, professional military service, and the largesse of affluent patrons and politicians, including "gifts" of spectacular entertainment. At the same time, new forms of individual status striving, conspicuous consumption, entrepreneurialism, and ambition began to rival older non-pecuniary conservative traditions that linked honor to modesty and collective duty. Eighteenth- and nineteenth-century historians tended to view these shifts largely as instances of moral failure – a lapse into greed and consumptive excess – among the Roman senatorial and equestrian upper classes. But it seems no less plausible to see this as a mutation of agonistic values of individual striving and achievement arising from new possibilities in a developing proto-capitalist market system. Capital accumulation and its display arguably provided new and seemingly "objective" measures of success and failure in the Roman Republic, including the ability to connect wealth to more traditional markers of status and power, such as political position.

This is the political-economic context in which "bread and circuses" arose as significant elements in political and popular cultures in the late Roman Republic and early years of the Roman Empire. The phrase *panem et circenses*, comes from Juvenal's *Tenth Satire*, in a commentary on the attempted coup by Sejanus, co-consul and powerful leader of the Praetorian Guard, against Emperor Tiberius in 31 CE:

> And what does the mob of Remus say? It follows fortune as it always does, and rails against the condemned [Sejanus]. That same rabble . . . if the aged Emperor had been struck down unawares, would in that very hour have conferred upon Sejanus the title of Augustus . . . the people that once bestowed commands, consulships, legions and all else, now meddles no more and longs eagerly for just two things – Bread and Circuses.[130]

Juvenal's commentary constructs an imagined history whereby the allegedly responsible *public* of the distant republican past is said to have devolved into a politically irresponsible *mob* that traded their duties cheaply "for doles of food and the lures of the racetrack and the arena."[131]

Every Roman ruler from Julius Caesar through the emperors of the late imperial period was involved in the provision of food as a form of welfare and entertainment as public spectacle. The largesse of Octavian/Augustus, for example, vastly exceeded even that of Julius Caesar. Augustus boasted how he gave 300 sesterces each to "never less than 250,000" of "the Roman plebs" in accordance with the will of his father. He adds that in his thirteenth consulship he gave "sixty denarii apiece to those of the plebs who at the time were receiving public grain: the number involved was a little more than 200,000 persons." In addition, Augustus claims "I gave a gladiatorial show three times in my own name, and five times in the names of my sons or grandsons, at these shows about 10,000 fought" and "Twenty-six times I provided for the people . . . hunting spectacles of African wild beasts in the circus or in the forum or in the amphitheaters: in these exhibitions about 3,500 animals were killed."[132] Even if we assume these numbers to be wildly exaggerated, Augustus's sense of pride is self-evident. The spectacular nature of such "gifts" to the Roman public was an expression of honor and reflected the pressure of social expectation for the scale of the spectacle to match the status of the provider.

Juvenal's vilification of the "mob" of spectators of such events as a fickle and decadent "rabble" bears a resemblance to some of the concerns expressed earlier by Seneca. Both writers were influenced by the philosophy of Stoicism, derived from a philosophical school of the Greek Hellenistic period. Stoicism provided a paradigm for self-reflection and living in harmony with nature, and its adherents valued individual autonomy and "freedom from passion" through the exercise of reason. The ultimate goal in Roman Stoicism was the pursuit of "virtue," through dedication to wisdom, justice, courage and temperance.[133] This is why Roman intellectuals who embraced elements of Stoicism, such as Seneca, Juvenal, Epictetus, and, later, Marcus Aurelius, viewed the arena and the circus in largely negative terms. In their view, if republican military, political, or religious festival displays of agonism once provided opportunities for the public performance of virtue, the arena and circus appeared to have reconstituted these as spectacles of vice and political distraction. The depth of Stoic disdain for arena spectacle is aptly summarized in Seneca's searing comment: "In the morning they throw men to the lions and the bears, at noon, they throw them to the spectators."[134]

Near the end of his *Tenth Satire,* Juvenal also suggests that people should pray for *mens sana in corpore sano* (a healthy mind in a healthy body). While the issue is certainly open to interpretation, I do not think he means the phrase quite in the way that sports administrators and pedagogues in nineteenth-century England later resynthesized it, as a plea for *physical* education in addition to education of the mind. Juvenal positions the phrase in a cautionary hymn to virtue and masculine asceticism, where "a stout heart" has "no fear of death," "knows neither wrath nor desire," and thinks the "woes and hard labors of Hercules" better than the pleasures of "loves, banquets and downy cushions."[135] Here, in a manner reminiscent of Aristotle, *rational asceticism* is linked to the virtuous life as "the only road to a path of peace." From this perspective, the irrationalities and excesses of the arena and the circus can only be seen as deviations from the realization of higher human possibilities.

In a somewhat different register, Plutarch, the Platonically inspired Greek essayist of the early Roman imperial period, extended criticism of the arena to the elites who pursued mass support through "gifts" of gladiatorial shows. In his view, such shows are "falsely attested honors" resembling "harlots flatteries, since the masses always smile upon him who gives them and does them favors, granting him an ephemeral and uncertain reputation."[136] Plutarch's criticisms elevated the concept of "bread and circuses" to an indictment of Roman society in general rather than the failings of the mob alone. For many critical intellectuals of the era, that indictment not only included the dole, the arena, and the hippodrome, it also encompassed pantomimes and theaters – indeed, all regions of Roman life that allegedly fell into the realms of distracting popular entertainment.

Still, these critical concerns about "bread and circuses" were not universally shared among Roman intellectuals, nor did they appear to represent the views of most Romans. For example, the Roman poet Martial wrote enthusiastically detailed descriptions of the Colosseum in passages meant to commemorate patronage and civic aggrandizement. His startlingly matter-of-fact discussions of the grisly cruelty of arena spectacle written for a popular readership are completely at odds with the condemnations lodged by writers such as Seneca or Juvenal.[137] Moreover, as Keegan points out, in addition to commemorating the duty of gladiators, Roman graffiti largely painted a positive, street-level view of spectacles as one part of "a class-inclusive common leisure culture" "which, at least in principle, even included the slave population."[138]

This leisure culture was sustained by a steady increase in the number of festival "holiday" occasions over the course of the Roman

Republic, and through the first few centuries of the imperial period. By the early fourth century, there were approximately 176 religious festival holidays in Rome, along with a number of other special events and occasions, such as funerals of prominent individuals.[139] Public games, theatrical events, and circuses accompanied most of these festival days, and gladiatorial combat was typically a feature of any sponsored funerary occasion. Furthermore, in addition to attendance at the arena or the circus, there was widespread participation in popular game and outdoor recreational pastimes throughout Rome and its provinces, including dice games, board games and ball games, physical contests (such as wrestling and boxing), and recreational activities in the countryside (such as hunting and fishing). Nonetheless, Keegan concludes, the Roman adulation of spectacle seems unique as "a culturally specific propensity to watch, rather than to participate" in organized physical competitions.[140]

Not unlike earlier Hellenic societies, a tension ran through Roman culture between the perceived legitimacy of activities that were popular, pleasurable or hedonistic, or instrumental, in economic or political terms, and those that were viewed as "dignified" and "virtuous." Yet the precise combination of polyvalent and often contradictory meanings and practices of the gladiatorial arena and the circus are extremely difficult to understand from the standpoint of the present. In addition to dramatizing the reach and power of the Roman state, while playing to a populist sense of justice, the Roman arena and circus were arguably forums where tensions between ideals of inherited rank and agonistic individual achievement, religion and secular markets, popular fandom and philosophical criticism, virtuous display and sadistic excess, public decorum and Bacchanalian revelry were all dramatized and presumably evaluated. No one really knows for sure what the majority of Romans made of all this. In the case of arena violence, the most reasonable conclusion, as Keith Hopkins suggests, is "we are dealing here not with individual sadistic psycho-pathology, but with a deep cultural difference."[141]

Difference, discourse, and the metamorphosis of spectacle in late Greco-Roman antiquity

The maze of difference in Roman culture becomes even more complicated by the juxtaposition of Roman identity with later tendencies of imperial cosmopolitanism, as well as by negotiations between Roman-ness and other strongly felt cultures, identities, and remembered histories. The culture of the polis in Greek antiquity had been decidedly *non-cosmopolitan* through most of the archaic and classical periods, as evident in the significant competitive tensions that existed between Greek city-states. The major Panhellenic festivals were arguably more significant as opportunities to display and dramatize these tensions than as opportunities to celebrate a cosmopolitan Hellenic culture. Indeed, Hellenism appears to have lacked any concept of a "world society" for much of its formative history.

However, in the fourth century BCE, the Hellenic philosopher Diogenes famously described himself as a "citizen of the world" (*kosmopolitês*), suggesting an emerging cosmopolitan sensibility among Greek intellectuals.[142] The idea of "citizenship" in a society beyond the individual polis gained further traction in the Hellenistic period through the brief imperial regime of Alexander, although it continued to be circumscribed by divisions within Hellenic cultures, for example between Greeks and Macedonians, and between Greeks and "barbarians." Centuries later, Roman Stoics imagined the concept of citizenship as something that could be extended to all human beings by virtue of their rationality, while simultaneously acknowledging obligations to Rome. Tension between a localized conception of Roman identity and an imagined cosmopolitan identity was increasingly reduced as the Romans began to conceptualize the "cosmos" in the image of their empire.

Roman assimilation of "others" under the empire's dominion was complex, and scholarship over the past two decades has noted the multiple and hybrid forms of identification that existed throughout the imperial period.[143] Despite the often brutal treatment of "barbarian" slaves, the empire was largely tolerant of its subjugated peoples, provided they did not rebel, oppose Roman gods as the Christians did, or otherwise act in a politically disruptive manner. While Roman acculturation occurred unevenly in geographical terms and was differentially embraced, rejected, or adopted by different groups at varying times, there was considerable political and economic mobility by colonials. By the end of the first century, chieftains from Gaul were serving in the Senate; Greeks, Jews, and Syrians held military commands; and recruits from outside the Italian peninsula had become a major presence in Roman military forces. Furthermore, during the second century CE, Africans and Spaniards were notable figures in the Roman upper class and intelligentsia, and nearly every Roman emperor after Marcus Aurelius was born somewhere in the empire *other* than Rome. In 212 CE, the Roman emperor Caracalla made cosmopolitanism "official" by extending citizenship to all freeborn individuals in the empire, although, as de Ste Croix points out, the rights of Roman citizens had been substantially reduced by this time, and Caracalla's edict arguably had more to do with enhancing the base of imperial taxation than any cosmopolitan impulse.[144]

Historians of Greco-Roman antiquity have long argued that there was little prejudice based on visible somatic traits, such as skin color.[145] In this view, it is extremely problematic to speak of "race," as we understand it today, at any point in Greco-Roman antiquity because the modern concept of "race" was created in the late eighteenth and nineteenth centuries. It is a point well taken, and one that speaks to the importance of acknowledging the point about "difference" noted by Hopkins above. Still, some scholars have argued that modern ideas about racism are foreshadowed by arguments in antiquity about such things as the "naturalness" of slavery; the sometimes xenophobic reactions to "barbarians" and belief in their inferiority; the simmering suspicion about the moral or cultural qualities of the "mob"; or beliefs about imagined differences in rationality between individuals and groups of different types.

In one well-known study, Benjamin Isaac suggests that Greco-Roman cultures contained elements of "proto-racism" based largely on inherited assumptions from Greek philosophy and medicine about how geography allegedly influences acquired human characteristics.[146] James Rosbrook-Thompson also notes the importance of assumptions about geographical determinism in Greco-Roman antiquity but chooses to focus more directly on the Platonic elevation of the soul over the body and on how assumptions of imagined rationality and control of bodily experiences and appetites were incorporated into a cultural hierarchy of difference.[147] Roman Stoicism gave priority to Hellenic cultural and philosophical traditions that valued rationality and control of the self over Dionysian traditions of affective revelry.

In addition, Rosbrook-Thompson argues, assumptions about relations between environment and rationality, and the elevation of mind over body, are evident in the "armchair ethnography" of Pliny the Elder in his monumental first-century work, *Naturalis Historia* (77–9 CE). Here, Pliny draws on Stoicism's reverence for nature's versatility and wonder to create an encyclopedic overview of everything from exotic plants and animals to "monstrous" races, including "primitive" and "subhuman" tribes, especially in the African interior.[148] Rosbrook-Thompson also points to similar assumptions about the "primitive" nature of certain peoples in the Christian thought of Augustine, and suggests how related ideas were later expressed by a host of apologists for subjugating "primitives" in the process of western colonization. He speculates that such ideas were resynthesized in racial stereotypes that developed in nineteenth- and twentieth-century modern sport, such as the allegedly "impulsive" character of black sportsmen.[149]

There is another point to make here, this time about connections between imperial power and the production of knowledge. Pliny's *Naturalis Historia* defined intellectual practice in a dramatically cosmological way, reflecting the self-positioning and self-presentation of Roman thinkers at the apparent center of the "world" of knowledge. As Jason König summarizes: "the political context of the Roman Empire often overflows into the metaphors used by knowledge-ordering writers to structure their work. Pliny's *Natural History* represents its own control over the world of knowledge as equivalent to the territorial conquest of the Roman Empire, using metaphors of mapping and the image of the Roman triumph."[150]

König goes on to argue that this promoted an agonistic "polymathy" that lent itself to the production of authoritative "compilatory" or "totalizing" projects in knowledge gathering: "for example by addressing a great range of subjects under the banner of overarching ethical aims ... by portraying one's own field of expertise as a central part of some overarching philosophical project."[151] He also gives the examples of Plutarch, and the second-century Greek physician/philosopher Galen of Pergamon, suggesting that some of their work drew on residual "images of Greek *paideia* as a cosmopolitan, universally empowering, unifying thread for the culture of the Mediterranean world under Roman rule, able to transcend local boundaries and particular specialisms."[152]

Galen had worked as a doctor to gladiators and he later served as a physician to several high-ranking late second-century Roman officials, including Emperors Commodus and Septimus Severus. As a physician, he believed in meticulous empirical observation, but he also engaged substantially in philosophy and became a fierce critic of Stoicism's methodological assumptions and elevation of mental rationality over the materiality of the body. He also resuscitated older criticisms of Greek athleticism's lack of social utility. He was especially critical of the intense and specialized character of athletic training for *agones* and he promoted "lighter" and "healthier" forms of exercise instead.

In a rather different vein, the second- and third-century Sophistic writer Philostratus evaluated the traditions of Greek athletic training and *agones* in far more positive terms in his book *Gymnasticus*, likely published in the early 220s CE. According to König, Philostratus writes with "many of the same sources and traditions as Galen in mind, although interpreting them very differently."[153] For Philostratus, the history of Greek athletic festivals, and the reinterpretation of Greek athletic training could be seen as valuable sources of knowledge for reevaluating educational practices in the third-century Roman Empire. König concludes that in the work of Philostratus, "thinking about the proper way to do athletics, is made part of a wider project of thinking about what elite Hellenic cultural accomplishment ideally involves."[154]

There was a notable revival of Greek cultural influences in the Roman Empire during the second century CE, promoted significantly from "above" by philhellenic emperors such as Hadrian and Marcus Aurelius. It was a time viewed by many writers of the European Renaissance and Enlightenment periods as a "golden age" in the empire, where armies were comparatively unified and restrained, important administrative reforms were put in place, few challenges of any lasting consequence were mounted against imperial power and stability, and emperors seemed considerably enlightened, especially in contrast to the tumultuous, arbitrary, and often cruel rule in the first century by emperors such as Claudius, Caligula, and Nero.[155] Still, this apparent "golden age" failed to resolve Rome's accelerating issues of class and political inequality. To make matters worse, a major plague lasting more than three decades in the late second century killed over five million people in the Roman Empire, setting the stage for a number of subsequent economic and political crises over the next several decades.[156]

These crises were accentuated by a combination of ongoing military expenses; the high cost of an expansive imperial bureaucracy, continuing concentration of wealth and power into fewer hands, accompanied by an intensification of the exploitation of slave labor and the increasing debt, and erosion of economic viability, of small peasant farms.[157] A marked decrease in the frequency of foreign wars in the first two centuries of the imperial era diminished the available pool of slaves, increasing the need for wealthy landowners to "breed" more slaves while simultaneously intensifying the means of exploitation on both slave and poor citizens alike. The need to breed more slaves initiated a subtle shift from an agricultural model based on what de Ste Croix calls "barracks slavery" on Roman estates, to an incipient, pre-feudal model of agricultural production based on the labor of slave families who were beginning to farm rather more like the indentured serfs of early feudalism.[158]

Furthermore, throughout the third, fourth and fifth centuries CE, taxes increased to meet escalating military and administrative costs. Runaway taxation, accompanied by coercive measures of tax collection, eroded popular support for imperial rule in many parts of the empire.[159] This was accompanied by a significant hollowing out of the curial class – the merchants, businessmen, and mid-level landowners who traditionally served as magistrates and regional senators across the Empire – precipitated by a withering of their rights, status, and wealth.[160] At the local level, outside of Rome itself, it was the curiae that provided or requested funds for public building projects, temples, festivities, games, and local welfare systems. In the Roman clientelist tradition, they would often pay for these expenses out of their own pocket, out of a sense of civic duty and as a means to increase their personal prestige. However, increasing numbers of the curial class felt pressured in both economic and political terms, prompting growing ambition to move upward into the senatorial class or face downward mobility into even more marginal economic and political positions.

In addition, notwithstanding the brief period of military expansion, bureaucratic centralization, and stability afforded by Diocletian in 284 CE, the Roman Empire continued to be torn by internal political struggles and significant external military crises. Amidst his reforms, Diocletian consolidated the power of the emperor and weakened the power of regional provinces, doubling their number and creating new layers of administration under a "tetrarchy" of regional "emperors" and regional diocese. After his death, a wide-ranging civil war broke out until Constantine was able to reunite the empire under a single ruler in 314 CE, moving the capital to Constantinople (contemporary Istanbul), furthering a monarchical style of rule, and adopting Greek instead of Latin as the language used in the royal court. Civil war broke out again after Constantine's death, leading to yet more rebellions, revisions and redivisions of the empire before the Eastern Emperor Theodosius I briefly became the single imperial ruler once more. When Theodosius I died, his sons inherited the Eastern and Western Empires respectively, with the eastern part of the Roman Empire developing an increasingly hybridized Greco-Roman (Byzantine) culture and the western part struggling to maintain itself militarily and economically, both before and after the collapse of Roman imperial authority in the West in 479 CE.

These events and transitions had significant implications, both for the Roman culture of spectacle and the continuation of Greek *agones*. By the time of the Severan dynasty in the 190s CE, approval from Rome had also become mandatory for any proposed public works in the provinces involving amphitheaters and "other spectacle

51

buildings."[161] Imperial control over spectacle buildings and events became even more bureaucratized through the chaotic third and fourth centuries, despite the unstable climate of ongoing military conflict and economic crises, including substantial inflation in the early part of the century. Still, Remijsen argues that "without exception all fourth-century emperors were supportive of Hellenic athletic games," with prominent games still existing in late century in Greece, Asia, Syria, Egypt, North Africa, and Italy.[162] Emperors and regional officials also continued to support the offering of gladiatorial games, although interest in gladiatorial games was declining. By the end of the century, Mann argues that they had ceased to be a part of civic culture in any area in the Mediterranean or in what is now northern Europe, even though beast hunts continued to be popular.[163] Similarly, and despite the support of local elites and the emperors, Remijsen notes "a clear decrease in references to games of all types" by the mid-fourth century: "no more mosaics, no more papyri, fewer references in literature."[164]

The elevation of Christianity to the state religion of the empire in 379 CE is the explanation most often given for the fourth-century decline in both Greek *agones* and gladiatorial spectacles. This isn't surprising, given how Christians had been persecuted throughout much of Roman imperial history and were often subject to tortured deaths in the arena. Persecution intensified during Diocletian's regime, especially in the period roughly running from 303 CE to his death in 311 CE. During this time, Christians were arrested in large numbers for their refusal to accept the imperial cult and many were condemned to death in the arena by burning alive, killing by wild animals, or in quasi-gladiatorial combat. If the arena was already unpopular among Christians, it appears to have become even more prominent as a killing field in the early fourth century.

Christian antipathy to Roman spectacle had been given a firm philosophical foundation over a century earlier by the Carthaginian monk Tertullian in his book, *De Spectaculis*.[165] Tertullian's book is noteworthy for its synthesis of discourses from Stoicism and early branches of Christian theology to provide a coherent theological rationale for the Christian rejection of spectacle. The issue is not simply that Christians had been killed in the arena for punishment and the amusement of the mob. Rather, for Tertullian – and not unlike Plato's allegory of the cave – it was the way that spectacle, with its emphasis on visual and aural sensation, had the ironic effect of *blinding* people to everything of true worth: "what are those things which eye hath not seen nor ear heard, nor ever entered into the heart of man? I believe, things of greater joy than circus, theater or amphitheater, or any stadium."[166] In Tertullian's view, all forms of spectacle – athletic and theatrical – can thus be viewed as examples of idolatry, deriving from pagan festivals and rites. Patrick Brantlinger observes that Tertullian "acknowledges that Saint Paul had referred not unfavorably to the Greek games at Tarsus, but he condemns boxing, wrestling and all athletic contests anyway."[167]

Augustine later developed somewhat similar arguments during the fourth century, again focused on how spectacle allegedly ignites bloodlust and the "savage passions" of the body instead of promoting the higher order of spirituality.[168] As Christianity became the official religion of the Roman Empire during Constantine's regime, this discourse was propagated widely. Yet the Church began to produce its own forms of spiritual theatricality in the promotion of religious observance, and these began to take on greater significance in popular culture, increasingly coming to rival the attention that had been devoted previously to popular amusement in many parts of the Greco-Roman world. Christian thought also produced its own mythology about how martyrdom had led to the end of gladiatorial spectacle in Rome, based on the attempt by a Christian monk, Telemachus, to stop a gladiatorial combat, resulting in his stoning to death by the crowd.

This incident is said to have led the Western Roman emperor, Honorius, to ban gladiatorial spectacles in Rome in 404 CE, although Honorius had already closed gladiator schools five years earlier.[169] More significantly, there is evidence that such spectacles remained in various forms in cities around the empire for at least another half century. For example, Brantlinger cites Salvanius, the presbyter of Marseilles, criticizing his fellow Christian citizens for demanding circuses in the city of Treves, even as the city was under siege by "barbarians."[170] Salvanius goes on to make a point that was later picked up and resynthesized in many eighteenth- and nineteenth-century accounts of the decline of the Roman Empire: that perhaps the coming of the "barbarians" is "preferable to the decadence and wantonness" of Roman civilization in late antiquity, or even that the barbarians might represent a heavenly sanctioned scourge of what many religious conservatives saw as lingering tendencies of immorality and idolatry in the Christian world.

At the beginning of the sixth century CE, the Roman Byzantine Emperor Anastasius abolished arena-centered beast hunts and pantomimes in Constantinople and elsewhere in the empire, leaving the amphitheaters and theaters empty. The last chariot race in the Circus

Maximus in Rome is said to have occurred in 549 CE; however, racing in the Constantinople Hippodrome, and in similar racetracks in the Eastern Empire, continued to be popular through the end of the millennium, and provided a major source of popular entertainment, intensely felt (and often violent) expressions of partisan political and religious identities, and publicly voiced political expression.[171]

Christian influences are also frequently noted as factors involved in the ending of the Greek *agones*, including the termination of a millennium of athletic competition associated with the festival at Olympia. The date most often given for the end of the ancient Olympics is 393 CE, based on the assumption that the end of the Olympics in the reign of Theodosius I was "connected to an imperial decree" against pagan religious festivals and celebrations. However, Remijsen claims that there is far greater evidence to suggest the Greek athletic circuit thinned and deteriorated more gradually, and that a final collapse didn't occur until the fifth-century reign of Theodosius II. The Isthmian games ended "sometime during the first two decades of the fifth century, the end of the Ephesus Olympics in the 420s and the abandoned headquarters of the athletic synod in Rome were donated to the Church shortly before 430 CE. The end of the ancient Olympics around the same time was just another step in this collapse."[172] The Antiochene Olympics survived longer, lasting until 520 CE.[173]

The reasons for the devolution and reevaluation of both circus games and Greek athletic festivals involved much more than the Christian prohibition of pagan festivals and rituals. Rather, they reflected many of the economic and social crises of late Greco-Roman antiquity. According to Remijsen, while religious factors were important in the decline of Greco-Roman athletic spectacles, "the main considerations continued to be financial and political."[174] For example, she notes how Constantine attempted to balance religious and political concerns by granting a request from the local elite in Hispellum, in Umbria, to stage circus games with plays and gladiator shows, on the condition that they would not be "defiled by the errors of a contagious superstition."[175] This probably meant a ban on religious sacrifices as a compromise that would allow the emperor to improve relations with elites in the city while maintaining a rejection of the overt celebration of pagan gods.

In this way, Remijsen suggests that imperial and regional administrations in late antiquity began to deny "the specificity of the agones," grouping them together with arena events and circuses, essentially as *secular* opportunities for the expression of civic aspirations and community enjoyment:

The main attraction of *agones*, however, which had caused them in the second and third centuries to multiply at a faster rate than amphitheatre or circus games, lay in their specific social and cultural role. Agones had served as a means to express the local identity of a city and had cultivated a privileged social class. By putting the *agones* in a generalized group of spectacles, the emperors sent out the message that the main assets of athletic contests were their festive atmosphere and spectacularity.[176]

Similarly, while urban elites continued in an effort to support their existing festivals, there were virtually no initiatives for *new* events. The hollowing out of the curial class, and declining resources of the cities, reduced the numbers of potential patrons for staging *agones*.[177]

In addition, while there were "many people still interested in watching athletics, few continued to practice it," other than a handful of members of local aristocracies who may have had exposure to the Greek athletic past through their educations.[178] As Constantinople emerged as the center of imperial power, Remijsen concludes, neither imperial nor regional administrators safeguarded "money for games when they took away civic revenues," nor did the athletic synods in Rome get new headquarters in Constantinople.[179] In this context, and like gladiatorial spectacles, the old Greek athletic circuit gradually disappeared. However, many other aspects of Greco-Roman practices, discourses, and debates on physical agonism, athletic training, spectacular display, and revelry remained to mutate and become resynthesized as they were absorbed into the Christian cultures of Byzantium and the emerging Christian world of feudal Europe.

Conclusion

With few exceptions, recent classical scholarship suggests no singular point of origin, no timeless field of ludic or agonistic inner logic, or deviations from that logic, to connect Greek or Roman athletics, body cultures, or circus spectacles to modern sport, or even to the culture of modernity more broadly.[180] Such practices in antiquity were highly complex, with contested, shifting, and sometimes contradictory meanings for different groups at different times. There is no doubt that fragments from the Greco-Roman past *anticipate* a number of contemporary developments: for example, the uses of athletics, arena, or circus spectacles to accrue symbolic capital for individuals or cities; the influence on competition by professionalization and commodification; the equation of athletics with class privilege and masculinity; the shaping of discourses regarding health and athletics by imperialist assumptions; or suspicions about athletic spectacle as violent "popular" culture, rather than practices that promote honor, virtue, or rational self-improvement.

However, the range of historically situated meanings of these fragments in the modern era is not something that can be fully understood by looking to the past. We cannot simply assume that modern sport has somehow "evolved" directly from these ancient practices. Indeed, it has become a matter of conventional sociological wisdom that the field of practices, discourses, and moral judgments that emerged to define modern sport and related celebrations of the body in nineteenth- and early twentieth-century Europe and North America is historically unique.[181] For example, in a commentary on the ethos of Victorian-era athleticism in England, Anthony Mangan sees a completely new pastiche of influences: "a marinated blend" of "Platonism, piety and practicality."[182] However, this unique blend of influences involved the selective conjuring of images, aesthetic motifs, and ideas from the past, reworked and pressed into the service of modernity.

Nonetheless, I do not believe that sociologists and historians have paid sufficient attention to such images, motifs, and ideas in the making of modernity itself.[183] Tensions between Greek and Roman emphases on mental rationality and self-mastery versus bodily indulgence, libidinal excess, and ritual efflorescence are particularly notable here. From the European sixteenth century through the European Enlightenments of the eighteenth century, debates about these tensions provided a basis for the classification of cultures into the categories of high and low, civilized and uncivilized, modern and primitive, western and non-western, deserving and undeserving. The modern period ushered in a host of new mechanisms, discourses, and institutions designed to promote rationality in bodily practice and bodily government.

In the so-called "higher" realms of western culture and civilization, these variously included: a modern resynthesis of ancient ideas associated with an intellectual *vita activa,* along the lines described by Arendt; an Aristotelian emphasis on contemplation as a marker of excellence; a celebration of polymathy and compilatory knowledge in the traditions of writers such as Aristotle, Galen, and Pliny; and a "rediscovery" of Greco-Roman artistic styles – particularly in statuary – as an imagined universal standard of aesthetic excellence. In the more practical realm of science, the emphasis was more on resynthesizing ideas that attacked the medieval belief in fate to promote a view of history as unfolding through the accumulation of knowledge.

In cases of sovereign power and politics, a modern rehabilitation of the performative traditions of *agon,* combined with Greek and early Roman ideals of civic duty, became notable features in the emergence of liberal democratic politics. In addition, deeply rooted traditions of physical agonism in the military were resynthesized with new hygienist ideas about the roles of human agency and the "health" and wealth of nation-states in the making of history. In the economic realm, classical traditions of agonism – seen as the quest for individual honor and achievement – mixed with new ideas pertaining to personal self-development to provide archaic inspiration for criticism of medieval religious proscriptions against excessive individualism and profit taking.

Furthermore, the critique of spectacle raised by Juvenal, Seneca, Plutarch, and others – mixed with Christian adaptations of these ideas in the work of writers such as Tertullian and Augustine – contained ideas that contributed to the making of modern western political theory, based on alleged irrationalities and distractions of spectatorship and the equation of hedonism and spectatorship with decadence, decline, and tyranny. This incipient political theory was reworked during the eighteenth and nineteenth centuries and inscribed into a broader critique of modernity, especially of so-called modern mass societies. This critique was often made with progressive intent but, as suggested at the outset of this chapter, it often took a highly conservative, even reactionary turn. A number of early twentieth-century critics of modernity began to argue that modern western societies were entering a cycle of decadence and decline that paralleled ancient Rome. This argument became particularly attractive to "revolutionary" anti-modern thinkers in the twentieth century who yearned for the return of an imagined culture of "barbarian" vigor to "cleanse" the apparent decadence of modernity, just as earlier barbarian invaders had supposedly cleansed the decadence of the Roman Empire. In later chapters, I discuss how disciplined physical education and athletic training, matched with spectacular displays of Apollonian bodies in ritualized celebrations of social solidarity, were taken up as part of this project by the propagandists of twentieth-century fascist governments.[184]

In a related line of thinking, the invention of modern sport in the nineteenth and twentieth centuries expressed a perceived need to better *balance* older Greco-Roman and Christian discourses about the values and virtues of rationality with "healthy" masculine energies, martial ambitions, and contemporary modes of collective effervescence. In the fifteenth century, Niccolò Machiavelli was inspired by his perceptions of the vital playfulness and intrigues of the Roman past, leading him to develop an early modern theory of politics as a balance of deceit and coercion, and to condemn Christianity as a stifling and effeminate force in human history. Machiavelli believed that the martial and ludic traditions of the Romans had been "taken hostage by the gray and depressing myth" of Christian passivity, "depriving humans from the enjoyment of the real Now for the sake of the fictional Tomorrow."[185] A new civilization would require recovery of these allegedly lost traditions of antiquity. There are echoes of this view in Friedrich Nietzsche's late nineteenth-century polemic against overly Socratic, rational, and Apollonian visions of modern societies, in favor of the need to acknowledge and recover vital Dionysian energies.

Roughly similar, yet noticeably opposite views were expressed in Edward Gibbon's influential eighteenth-century mapping of *The Decline and Fall of the Roman Empire*. Writing in the anti-clerical spirit of the French Enlightenment, Gibbon viewed late antiquity and the so-called "middle ages" that followed as dark times dominated by religious superstition. In Gibbon's view, this included a theological emphasis on life after death that fostered indifference to the problems of an emerging modern era. Gibbon advanced a broad range of economic, political, and cultural explanations for the so-called "decline and fall of the Roman Empire." However, among these, he argued famously that the Western Roman Empire "fell" because the Romans had become passive, effeminate, indolent, and overly devoted to the pleasures of the flesh and the spectacles of the arena.[186]

Imagined histories of Greco-Roman athletics and spectacle not only served as aesthetic and narrative framings of modern arena events, they also contributed to intense debates in Europe and North America about whether modernity itself should be seen as an instance of human progress or as regression. For many thinkers, the *project* of modernity included the idea of harnessing the power and popularity of human athletics, body cultures, and spectacles in a socially positive rather than a socially negative manner. Modern "sport" emerged as a distinctive field of practice in this context as part of a broadly imagined *progressive* struggle to construct a rational hygienic culture in place of an irrational culture of barbarism. The revival of neoclassical discourses and images became linked, sometimes breathlessly, to a range of new pedagogical or recreational projects, designed to promote types of physical activities that were both "healthy" *and* "civilizing."

Throughout this book, I argue that such projects were often

ideological because they implied that physical mastery, aesthetic appreciation, and duty in the development of the modern self could be conceived in universal terms. They were typically meant to create models of bodily governance, normalization, and disciplined spectatorship, consistent with the colonial and capitalist sensibilities of elites in modern western societies. These arguably included assumptions about the inability of the underclasses, of women, or of exotic "primitives" to achieve, or to fully appreciate, the values of reason, honor, and virtuous achievement. These projects also frequently remobilized ancient aesthetic prejudices of antiquity about the ideal of "virtuous physique," in contrast to what Plato had called "beggarly stooping and limp cowardice." The popularity of classicist imagery of this kind had the effect of reinvigorating a fusion of upper-class habitus and patriarchal somatic conceptions for the modern era and largely reproduced a discourse of disdain for the athletic bodies of women and the "imperfect" bodies of the poor or physically disabled. As I argue in chapter 4 of this book, in early twentieth-century Nazism these ideas were horrifically extended to include Jews and other "non-Aryans."

It seems apt to conclude here by mentioning the modernist legacy of Francis Bacon, who was strongly influenced by Galen's polymathy and empiricism. Bacon resynthesized antiquarian views of war as a mode of agonistic expression and moral training with new evolutionary and organicist ideas that linked the health of individuals to the health of social and political bodies:

> No boy can be healthfull without exercise, neither natural body nor politique: and certainly to a Kindome or Estate, a just and honourable warre is the true exercise. A civill warre, indeed, is like the heat of a feaver, but a forraine warre is like the heart of exercise, and serveth to keepe the body in health: for in a slothful peace, both courages will effeminate and manners corrupt.[187]

Bacon's views of the progressive accumulation of human knowledge were combined with his view of foreign wars as a necessary form of "health" to lay a foundation for an emerging conception of the cultural and moral superiority of the modern "West." But, before considering this idea in greater detail in a later chapter, it is useful to outline some key aspects of the "invention" of modern sport in England during the nineteenth and early twentieth centuries.

— 2 —

THE POLITICS OF
REPRESENTATION: ENGLISH SPORT
AS AN OBJECT AND PROJECT
OF MODERNITY

After the sixth century CE, while the Roman Empire in Constantinople was developing into a Christian civilization, many of the territories formerly governed as part of the Western Empire were reorganized by the Church in Rome and injected with an ethos of Christian universalism, sometimes in concert with large landed-estate holders and territory leaders, hereditary warlords of formerly "barbarian" invaders, and other times in conflict with them. Many of the legal and administrative structures of the Western Roman Empire survived, largely intact, for hundreds of years and, in many instances, Germanic invaders in the West were content to maintain alliances with the Roman Empire in the East. But the emerging pattern of governance across much of Europe was a patchwork of states of differing size and power, in conditions of near constant warfare, punctuated by brief periods of political, economic, and social stability.[1] Wars occurred between various state-like entities across Europe and the Mediterranean, between some of these states and the Roman Empire in the east, and between the Roman Empire and Islamic empires. Mongol invaders in eastern Europe in the fourteenth century introduced further divisions and cultural variations in types and modes of political organization.

In this chaotic environment, there was little possibility for any broad-ranging organization of athletic festivals or agonistic spectacles. In addition, even though Constantinople remained one of the largest cities in Europe, and prominent trading cities continued to exist across Afro-Asia, there was a substantial reduction in urban populations across much of the former Western Roman Empire after the seventh century. This was accompanied by a noticeable decline in the "microstructures and cultural values of urban civilization" in Europe in contrast to a more diffuse distribution of population centered in smaller towns, villages, and landed estates.[2] The scale of slavery that had existed in the early Roman Empire appears to have been noticeably reduced through the combination of Christian abolitionist tendencies and the transition of agrarian labor to serfdom, although a substantial trade in slaves continued throughout the Middle Ages in many parts of Europe, in the Islamic empires and Africa.[3] In the face of these changes, the economic surplus, and the imperial pattern of centralized allocation necessary to create large-scale urban spaces of spectacle, effectively dissipated. At the same time, artistic styles went through their own substantial modifications from the fifth through the thirteenth centuries, with the heroic nudity and realism of Greco-Roman classical styles falling out of fashion in favor of flatter and more static representations associated with Christian iconography, the ornate traditions of Islamic art, and a diminished interest in freestanding statuary in favor of mosaics and sculptured reliefs.[4]

The medieval patchwork in political and social organization across the Mediterranean and Europe was paralleled by a similar patchwork of athletic pastimes and agonistic spectacles. For example, in the western and northern parts of Europe, while amphitheaters and arenas fell to ruin, local and regional game contests of various types continued to be practiced periodically, often in association with village or community fairs and festivals. Hunting and fishing, for food or recreation, remained popular activities in areas where conditions allowed, and, in parts of what are now France and England, demonstrations of martial prowess, such as jousting, became increasingly popular and were organized in tournament form. In large ancient cities, such as Constantinople and Antioch in the eastern Mediterranean, chariot racing in large arenas remained a notable aspect of urban popular culture until the thirteenth century. Moreover, despite an antipathy to pagan festivals, contests, and games in Christianity and Islam, there was ongoing interest in both western and eastern Mediterranean societies in gymnastic exercises of various types; horse racing; game activities in which individuals used balls or other objects; as well as festival events which sometimes included demonstrations of various types of physical strength, speed, or skill.

All of these diverse practices were strongly shaped by the dominant social and cultural logics of their time. Gaming and sporting practices across northern Europe and the Mediterranean lacked institutional autonomy and were more characterized by regional cultural differences than by organizational or cultural coherence. In many instances, such activities were periodic, and they were more socially oriented than competitive. However, in other instances, competition could be extremely intense, involving detailed training regimes and often the gambling of substantial sums of money. Competition in many sporting or gaming practices could also involve significant emotional energy as well as levels of violence that would be found abhorrent today. Activities such as dueling, bare-knuckle boxing, wrestling with the intention of maiming, ratting, bear and bull baiting, cockfighting, dog fighting, fox hunting, and other blood sports were widely practiced across medieval and early modern Europe, as well as in European colonies. Even less overtly violent folk games involving teams of players kicking, handling, or using sticks to control balls of various types could degenerate into violent melees on occasion. Many of these activities were imbued with an aura of casual commercialism with little concern on the part of the players for their moral or educative aspects or for questions involving philosophical or aesthetic judgment.

The emergence of modern sport in Europe and North America involved the remaking of this jumble of diverse gaming and sporting practices, with their accompanying array of local logics and meanings, into a more unified, regulated, and purposeful social and cultural *field* of practice. The process occurred unevenly and incompletely in different European societies and throughout European and North American colonies. It was also accompanied by wide-ranging differences in regulation, cooperative association, repression, and conflict. Nonetheless, by the beginning of World War I, one can discern the clear outlines of a distinctive, and self-consciously modern, field of sporting practice, dominated by western nations.

Pierre Bourdieu argues that a relatively unified and legitimated field of modern sporting practice was consolidated through three broad structuring processes: autonomization, rationalization, and philosophical/political/moral justification. *Autonomization* refers to the (relative) institutional separation and disembedding of sporting practices from other logics of practice in social life, such as local folk cultures, economics, and politics. *Rationalization* refers to the increasing emphasis on predictability and calculation in the development of rules, and in the creation of self-administering governing organizations, as well as in the areas of training technique and tactics. *Philosophical/political/moral justification* refers to the structuring discourses that developed within sport in respect to such things as producing a "dominant social definition" of sport; establishing a set of universal meanings, purposes, and ethical principles associated with sporting practice; and producing an accompanying set of "definitions of the legitimate body and the legitimate uses of the body."[5]

Bourdieu never developed his analysis of these structuring processes in detail and as a result there is a great deal left out of his account. For example, while he makes suggestive observations about changes in bodily habitus and various forms of "capital" in sport, he has nothing to say about the roles of visual or linguistic *representation* in the production of modern sport as a distinctive field of practice.[6] In this chapter, I argue that the politics of representation are important aspects of the perception of modern sport "as its own object" and of the philosophical/political/moral discourses that linked this cultural object to an ostensibly *rational* "project" of modernity. The story I tell in the chapter is limited to events in England, the country often referenced as the cradle of "modern" sport as we know it today. I also focus more on the changing social conditions affecting representations of sport, and their apparent effects, than on a hermeneutic reading of sporting texts and images, or on the subjective interpretations given to these texts and images by individuals or groups at varying times in English history. Following Bourdieu, my goal is only to map a broad set of transitions and struggles associated with structuring the modern, western field of sporting practice.

Representation in early English sporting recreations

Folk games, martial activities, field sports and blood sports in England have ancestral roots that can be traced back well before the turn of the first millennium.[7] These activities varied by region and were differentiated by class and gender, although it was not uncommon for popular English recreations to bring together lord and peasant, men and women, albeit mostly in ways deemed suitable to the participant's rank and station. However, from very early on there were tensions between the needs, likes and dislikes of kings, queens, and lords and many of the activities popular among "the people." For example, in the case of hunting, as far back as the eleventh century King Canute commissioned the Archbishop of York to write strict game laws, and two centuries later the Normans imposed their own rigid set of forest laws and set up a network of forests with the right of chase (hunting) granted to certain lords and religious houses.[8] This is just one example in a long history where recreational pastimes of some types were accessible to certain people while being restricted to others and where popular recreations of certain types were frequently banned or regulated in secular law or by the Church. Yet, at the same time, there was also a strong tradition in the English countryside that embraced popular game activities alongside the traditional aristocratic pastimes of riding, hunting, and fishing. Moreover, the lines between work, leisure, and popular recreations in pre-modern life in England were blurred, with sporting pastimes often incorporated into fairs and religious festivals and with practices such as dice, word games, contests of strength, bowls, or quoits occasionally woven into the working day.[9]

In the dense oral culture of medieval England, accounts of courtly love, exploits in battles, and prowess in hunting or in physical contests found popular expression in storytelling, songs, oral poems, and various forms of street theater.[10] There appears to have been somewhat less mediation in fixed visual communicative forms until the late medieval period of English history. Still, there are notable examples of freehand sketches and wood-block prints outlining the technical aspects of martial activities in medieval England, and there are more than occasional artistic representations in tapestries and religious manuscripts of people hunting, fishing, engaging in blood sports, or playing ball games.[11] For example, the image in Figure 2.1, from the famous Luttrell Psalter, combines religious ritual themes with an illustration of medieval bear baiting.[12]

In a few instances, painted images or woodcuts of sports and games were on display in public spaces such as churches and churchyards. There were also occasional written descriptions of sporting pastimes in early medieval histories and descriptions of everyday life, as well as in the early development of English literature from the late 1300s

2.1 *Medieval Bear Baiting* (circa 1325)

through the fifteenth century; for example, Chaucer makes reference to fox hunting in *The Nun's Priest's Tale*.[13]

The spread of metal type printing into England in the late fifteenth century created new opportunities for more widespread written and visual representations of sporting pastimes. However, literacy rates in sixteenth-century England were low, and printing images was complicated and expensive. Only 20 percent of adult males and 5 percent of females were able to sign their own names as late as the middle decades of the1500s, although there were significant class variations within these percentages, with most aristocrats, gentry, and rich merchants fully literate by 1600, and most farmers and laborers in the countryside unable to read at all.[14] In conjunction with low literacy rates and widespread poverty, tight controls on publishing by both Church and state ensured that there was a limited commodity market for popular visual art, news periodicals, books, and pamphlets through most of the sixteenth and early seventeenth centuries.

Nonetheless, a market for printed works directed to the largely male and comparatively affluent reading public grew steadily through the 1500s, building on the popularity of writers such as Edmund Spenser, John Donne, and Shakespeare, as well as on increasing interest in continental Renaissance writing on religion and philosophy. There was also growth in the production and sale of illustrated calendars and handbooks of various types. During the Tudor era, English monarchs expanded the use of royal letters to promote writing, performing, and publishing. The Tudor court also promoted visual art by encouraging residencies from well-known Dutch and Italian painters, prompting an upsurge in public interest in imported European works and new techniques of portraiture and landscape painting.[15]

Kevin Sharpe argues that a growing enthusiasm for public representational practices during the Tudor era opened a door to new forms of dialogue between rulers and subjects. On the one hand, such practices typically offered powerful dramatizations of class power and royal authority. But, on the other hand, they also unintentionally promoted the view that power was perfomative and dialogical, something to be consumed, appraised, and discussed in an emerging public culture of consumption.[16] By the late 1500s, painting and engraving in particular were joining the growing book trade as publicly consumable art forms with small, exclusive, markets for portraits, landscapes, village, and city scenes. In this context, it shouldn't be surprising to find increased interest in sporting pastimes as subjects for artistic and literary representation. An early example

2.2 George Turberville (circa 1540–1597), *How a Man Should Enter his Yong Houndes to Hunt the Harte* (1575)

is George Turberville's *Booke of Hunting*, published in 1576, the first known manual published in English of hunting techniques, including an account of a hunt by the royal court.[17] Turberville's book is filled with depictions of hunting, dogs, and stags, similar to the image in Figure 2.2.

The *Booke of Hunting* is indicative of a growing recognition of sporting pastimes as practices to be singled out and objectified for discussion and analysis. Still, I think it is typical of the era to represent sporting pastimes as deeply rooted, and often undifferentiated, elements in the traditional social logic that surrounds them. Turberville dispenses technical advice about topics such as hunting strategies and the care and training of hunting dogs, but the book is heavily layered with references to behaviors appropriate to courtly life and to the medieval structure of class and gender relations. Sporting pastimes were emerging as notable objects of representation in English art and literature during the late sixteenth and early seventeenth centuries but, in my view, they were not yet *widely* depicted or assessed as autonomous or independent objects.

English sporting pastimes were not aestheticized on their own terms through art, literature, or philosophy until a unique conjuncture of conditions made this possible. Several developments are particularly notable. First, through the late 1500s, and increasing in political importance by the early years of the seventeenth century, Protestant reformers in England were outspoken in their criticism of violations of the Sabbath and of activities they deemed promoted idleness, diversion from "conscientious labor," or a lack of emotional discipline.[18] Inflaming the situation, James I published a *Declaration of Sports* in 1618 (also known as the *Book of Sports*), which listed sports and recreations that would be permitted on Sundays and other holy or festival days, and Charles I reissued this list in an expanded form in 1633. These royal declarations outraged Puritans and the effect was to bring the struggle over the regulation of popular sporting recreations into the center of the broader struggles developing in England between Puritan reformers and their bourgeois allies against the court, the established Church hierarchy, aristocratic culture, and, arguably, many of the rural poor who felt threatened by the Puritan attack on established ways of living.[19]

Mikhail Bakhtin has argued that the carnival spirit in pre-modern Europe had an earthy, coarse quality that provided an imaginative repertoire for the collective rehearsal of the grotesque and profane aspects of pre-modern folk cultures in Europe.[20] This allowed for ritualized dramatizations of the idea that "established authority and truth are relative," thereby providing a basis for imagined alternatives to existing hierarchies and dominant cultures.[21] In Bakhtin's view, medieval carnival cultures were both aesthetically and politically transgressive by representing the human body "as multiple, bulging, over- or under-sized, protuberant and incomplete. The openings and orifices of this carnival body are emphasized . . . (mouth, flared nostrils, anus) yawning wide and its lower regions (belly, feet, buttocks and genitals) given priority over its upper regions (head, 'spirit,' reason)."[22]

Bakhtin reads the profane, grotesque and often violent traditions of medieval and Renaissance folk cultures as the manifestation of an age-old collective tradition that has always provided a potential source of social opposition to official cultures. More recent commentators have challenged this transhistorical populism by suggesting that the meanings associated with carnival traditions in medieval and Renaissance folk cultures were always more ambivalent.[23] They celebrated a transgressive hedonism focused on the heterogeneity of human bodies, bodily over mental pleasures, and ritualized inversions of power. However, the carnival traditions associated with medieval fairs and religious festivals were events that the powerful *allowed* to

67

occur and were therefore tightly framed by the broader social logic of domination. Still, carnival traditions among the games and sports of "the people" were always potentially oppositional, especially when threatened with regulation from "above."

This qualification helps to explain how and why sporting pastimes became highly politicized in England through the 1600s. The Puritan attack on the pastimes of "the people" prompted a heightened level of political awareness by those whose practices were threatened by repression and regulation. In the Cromwell era, community feasting, drinking, and participation in traditional sporting pastimes, such as bull baiting or mob football, could easily be viewed both literally and metaphorically as a rejection of the values of the Protectorate. At the same time, this uniquely English politicization of "the popular" during the mid-seventeenth century was also subtly influenced by the changing dynamics of English political economy. Notably, as England's economic and political interests abroad grew stronger, local popular cultures became less culturally isolated and developed greater potential to become politicized along partisan, even utopian, lines.[24]

On this point, Linebaugh and Rediker have noted how new triangular connections were established through colonization and the slave trade with Africa, America, and Europe, and how such connections built fortunes for merchants and investors in cities such as Bristol, Liverpool, and London. These fortunes were not only built on the forced work of slaves, they also required strict discipline for the crews of merchant ships and the Royal Navy, who are described in one account of the era as "a motley rabble of saucy boys, negroes, mulattoes, Irish teagues and outlandish jack tars."[25] In the context of intense labor discipline, the pursuit of free activity, laughter, and pleasure through gaming practices of any type among this group could have a vaguely subversive character. Even more notably, the strengthening of arbitrary power and discipline promoted the emergence of radical egalitarian and utopian political movements. By the end of the eighteenth century, English ships not only carried a diverse group of sailors and slaves, sugar and tobacco, they were also a conduit for stories and rumors of events and conditions in far-off places – slave revolts, mutinies, revolutions, and the romantic vision of aboriginal groups seemingly living in a state of nature. The Atlantic world, opened up by a combination of patriarchal capitalist enterprise, colonialism, and slavery, sent slaves, prisoners, colonial adventurers, and exiled radicals to the New World, but also led former slaves, sailors, and colonials to resettle in England and brought cosmopolitan, sometimes revolutionary, ideas and identities into English plebeian culture.[26]

At the other end of the social spectrum, one of the most significant effects of new colonial wealth in English society during the seventeenth century was the strengthening of a bourgeois mercantile class, some of whom integrated with the English aristocracy after the Restoration in 1660 to create powerful gentry whose influences extended from the countryside to the city. Many of the moneyed entrants to the gentry joined with the older aristocracy in longing for a return to an older time, including what Emma Griffin calls "the idealized rehabilitation of popular amusements."[27] An important part of this idealization involved the celebration of nature, leading to greater interest in continental paintings of landscapes that might be customized to the leisured lifestyles of the gentry. The prospect of lucrative commissions for such work brought several influential continental sport and landscape painters to England during the late 1600s.

Yet, at the same time, the economic, political, and cultural changes transforming English society in the late 1600s were also working against the rehabilitation of popular amusements. For example, bull and bear baiting by dogs had long been favorite activities for royalty and peasantry alike and fixed venues for such events were well established in English cities by the 1600s. However, in many of the pits and "bear gardens" in English cities, formerly ritualized occasions for blood sport were evolving into commercial spectacles. Blood sports were becoming disembedded, albeit unevenly, from the traditional social logics that had long determined their meanings in community life and were re-embedded through the strengthening logic of markets. Whereas the spilling of blood often combined spectacle with deeply religious connotations in medieval England, the new combinations of blood and money, with increased opportunities for drinking, gambling, and the assembly of "unruly" crowds, renewed the criticism of popular sporting recreations – only now with greater reference to the importance of rationality, discipline, and *obedience* in social life. As English sporting recreations grew in popularity through the eighteenth century, bourgeois moralists tended to view them as more irrational, unproductive, and dangerous than ever. Set against the background of the eighteenth-century revolutions that occurred in North America and France, "irrational" popular customs and pastimes could be viewed as having a potentially dangerous political character. The issue, as William Pitt's moral lieutenant Wilberforce argued at the turn of the nineteenth century, was the recognition that

the "moral levity" associated with such customs and pastimes potentially carried the threat of "political sedition."[28]

Representation, objectification, and the emerging field of English sporting practice

The tension between the idea of sporting pastimes as an organic
aspect of rural and, indeed, of English life and the suggestion that
many popular pastimes were irrational, unproductive, and potentially dangerous was played out dramatically in visual and textual
representations throughout the eighteenth and nineteenth centuries.
The often contradictory nature of these representations was influenced by the expansion of two distinct but interrelated markets, one
in the countryside and the other in towns and cities. The rural market
was stimulated by the reestablishment of a culture of upper-class
conservatism, including implementation of new game laws in 1671
that restricted access to weaponry and reinstated property qualifica-
tions to hunt in rural areas.[29] While their numbers were small, some
radical groups during the revolutionary period had argued that the
land belonged to all the people as a right because God created all
men as equals. New late seventeenth-century game laws reaffirmed
the principle that "the people" had no such rights, although the
qualification imposed on the right to hunt was expanded, with a
nod to the growing significance of capital in English life, to include
anyone below the rank of esquire who owned freehold property
valued at more than 100 pounds or who held long-term leaseholds in
excess of 150 pounds.

By the early years of the eighteenth century, there was more demand
than ever in the countryside for visual works that dramatized the lives
lived by squires, including a fashionable interest in country houses
and other signifiers of rank and privilege. According to Henriette
Gram Heiny, England's relative prosperity and political stability
in the early 1700s allowed the landed gentry to develop a regular
routine of country sports which became an important part of their
lives: "Proud of their possessions and sporting accomplishments, they
prompted the creation of a new genre in art which, by the nature of its
imagery, became closely allied to landscape painting."[30] Depictions of
country gentlemen in the company of well-bred horses and hunting
dogs, along with stand-alone portraits of dogs and horses, were especially popular, highlighting the strongly masculine aspects of this new
genre. By the late 1700s, it was not uncommon to find country houses

with whole rooms dedicated to commissioned works and engravings devoted to landscape/sporting art.[31] The preference for paintings and engravings of dogs and horses, as opposed to farm animals, such as pigs or chickens, lay in the self-referential tastes of wealthy male consumers and in a vision of the countryside, as E. P. Thompson states, where "labourers have been subtracted."[32] Work was not the domain of country gentlemen, and images of pigs, for example, did not connote the imagined nobility of horses and dogs working in the service of their masters.[33]

In a discussion of this new genre of English art, Stephen Deuchar notes how paintings and engravings of rural sporting pastimes in the early 1700s were viewed as capturing the "soul of country life." Deuchar argues that sporting art became part of a class-based "rural ideology" reinforced by a parallel growth of pastoral works of poetry, prose, and other branches of landscape painting.[34] An emphasis on landscapes and animals was already well established in the works of seventeenth-century artists who addressed sporting subjects but, in the eighteenth century, a new generation of painters, such as John Wootton, Peter Tillemans, and James Seymour, began to reconstitute continental artistic traditions to pay greater attention to the everyday lives and recreations of the English gentry. In this emerging genre of painting, the rural sports of the gentry were idealized as healthy and natural activities, tacitly juxtaposed to the apparent "evils" of town and country life. As self-referential objects of decoration, the paintings were meant to testify to the wealth, knowledge, and tastes of commissioning patrons or purchasers.

One issue of importance in Deuchar's analysis is the tension in eighteenth-century works between a focus on gentlemanly participants and their animals in contrast to works where the practice of sport itself became the focus. According to Deuchar, early representations of people hunting, or of hunting dogs, and horses in rural landscapes, centered on the gentry by highlighting their social standing, property, wealth, and taste. An example is John Wootton's painting, circa 1733, of Viscount Weymouth and his hunting party (Figure 2.3).

Demand for such images continued through the eighteenth century, but Deuchar argues that subtle changes in the accessibility of hunting, shooting, and racing led to a shifting artistic focus away from overt displays of status and property ownership to a greater focus on representing sport stylistically "for its own sake." Here, the image was meant to capture the drama of the event, signifying the image owner's knowledge and appreciation of the sport. The trend toward this

2.3 John Wootton (1682–1764), *Viscount Weymouth's Hunt:*
Mr. Jackson, the Hon. Henry Villiers and the Hon. Thomas Villiers,
with Hunters and Hounds (circa 1733)

representation of sport as a distinctive visual object solidified after mid-century and became a staple feature of many late-century collections of English sporting art. Deuchar points to James Seymour's oil painting *A Kill at Ashdown Park* to illustrate the new focus on hunting itself as the *primary* object of representation, instead of the status of the participants (Figure 2.4).

The development of a more specific focus on sport as the *primary* object of representation broadened the audience for sporting art to include communities of enthusiasts outside the gentry. At the same time, refinements in printing and engraving technologies through the eighteenth century were enabling people of comparatively modest means to purchase inexpensive reproductions of well-known painted works as well as new series of prints in the "English country style." In this way, the country market for sporting art developed tighter connections to a burgeoning urban marketplace for other cultural goods, such as books, newssheets, newspapers, pamphlets, caricatures, and commercial entertainments.

In my view, the style of sporting art favored by the English gentry, and by those who used the gentry as a reference group, had an ideological character even beyond that which Deuchar ascribes to it.

2.4 James Seymour (1702–1752), *A Kill at Ashdown Park* (1733)

This is not simply because typical images in the tradition reproduced the patriarchal sensibilities of the era or "subtracted" workers from popular representations of the countryside, but also because the images reinforced a view of gentry-led country life in a fetishistic way, as an almost magical world with its own inherent logic. Early English sporting art represented gentry rule as a kind of theater, dramatizing the visibility of certain elements and functions of gentry life while rendering less savory aspects of power invisible.[35] Yet country and city were closely linked through institutions of law, finance, and trade, as well by as the drive for efficiencies in agriculture, enclosures of property, and the commodification of common property, all of which had been reorganizing both the English countryside and English city life from as far back as the fifteenth century. This process accelerated during the eighteenth century, during which there were more than a thousand acts of enclosure, prompting widespread social unrest and a steady flow of migrants to the cities.[36] According to E. P. Thompson, the new mobility of former rural workers, suddenly made "free" to sell their labor power for a wage, created a complex and chaotic environment in eighteenth-century English cities. In London alone, driven largely by in-migration from the countryside, the population grew from approximately 80,000 people in 1550 to more than 700,000 in 1750.[37]

The result was an environment filled for some with new cosmopolitan attitudes and freedoms in a social world brimming with vibrant markets, entertainments, and possibilities. This was a world of an expanding and comparatively affluent bourgeois culture, matched with a situation where many laborers had yet to experience the severe work and leisure discipline that would later be imposed on them by the time clock and the factory whistle.[38] But at the same time, for a majority of its inhabitants, the city was crowded, dirty, and filled with the uncertainties of poverty, disease, and desperation, a place where people often struggled in vain to make a hopeful life for themselves. Gangs, theft, and prostitution were widespread with substantial numbers of citizens involved in an underground economy that continually pushed the limits of the law and where imprisonment, floggings, and hanging were frequent public spectacles.[39] It was in this complex, unequal, and uncertain environment that many popular sport and gaming pastimes of the countryside were becoming reconstituted both as new forms of social association and as popular commercial urban entertainments.

Even in the countryside, one can readily overlook the sometimes chaotic and rapidly changing aspects of the social life of sporting pastimes. For example, game restrictions had always been difficult to enforce and hunting and poaching for food was a common feature of local folk cultures throughout the late seventeenth and the eighteenth centuries. Moreover, the longstanding command that the Church once had over the leisure of the poor, including their fairs and festivals, was breaking down, severing these activities from their anchorage in religious ritual and opening them up to new meanings and to new modes of regulation.[40] It doesn't strike me as a historical accident that a growing emphasis on sport as an object of representation in eighteenth-century England corresponds to early attempts by communities of mostly male enthusiasts to formalize and codify rules in sports such as cricket, golf, horse racing, and boxing, often through the formation of clubs and associations. The push and pull identified by Deuchar in artistic representations of country sport parallels the push and pull in the rationale and focus of early sporting clubs and associations, that is, between the aspiration to use a sporting pastime primarily as a social meeting ground for individuals of similar social rank and the growing desire to provide opportunities for association between men who shared knowledge of and passion for a particular type of sporting practice. We can identify this tension without assuming that the line between these rationales was ever clear cut. However, the focus on sport as a distinct object, which defines its own community of enthusiasts, grew far more obvious as formal associations developed around distinctive sporting pastimes and attempted to codify and to popularize formal rules. The objectification of sport was made even more concrete as sport increasingly took on a commodity form as promoters pursued audiences for the sale of sport as a form of commercial public spectacle.

One often noted index of the growth in cultural production in England from the mid-seventeenth through the eighteenth centuries is the rapid expansion of the trade in news. There were fourteen newspapers in London by 1645 and, while censorship tightened during the Restoration period, the trade in news exploded after the turn of the century.[41] By 1750, London had "five well-established daily newspapers, six thrice-weeklies, and several other cut-price periodicals, with a total circulation between them of around 100,000 copies per week."[42] Benedict Anderson has argued that new modes of representation in western life created experiences of "simultaneity" through which people who lived in geographically and socially dispersed spaces were able to feel interconnected. According to Anderson, the newspaper, along with the modern novel, created a sense of homogeneous time, allowing readers the possibility of imagining a modern national community.[43] We can surely expand this idea to include the new forms of visual representation that developed in close conjunction with the expansion of the popular press, such as caricatures, cartoons, and political prints, as well as other forms of art. In my view, this necessarily includes consideration of the growing numbers of paintings, engravings, and prints that featured sporting subjects.

Indeed, during the eighteenth and early nineteenth centuries, sporting pastimes became especially important as fields for articulating competing understandings of the kinds of people, the kinds of bodies, and the kinds of practices that ought to best define England as an imagined community. I am persuaded by Peter Burke to view this as part of an emerging modern project pursued by English elites from the sixteenth through the nineteenth centuries to differentiate an idealized English national culture from the allegedly "common" and "immoral" customs of the people.[44] The project is graphically evident in the textual and visual representations of popular sports during the eighteenth century that demonize the "barbaric" and "irrational" aspects of sporting practice, challenging any claim that these are "natural" or desirable features of English culture. The prominent trader, novelist, and journalist Daniel Defoe expressed this sentiment as early as the turn of the eighteenth century when he castigated the behavior of the "collected rabble of the people" who frequented the October Fair at Charlton. The "mad people," the "mob," he claimed, were given to "all sorts of liberties." Even the women, Defoe continued, "are especially impudent that day, as if it were a day that justify'd the giving themselves a loos to all manner of indecency and immodesty."[45]

The problem was that the expansion of a bourgeois cosmopolitan urban culture during the eighteenth and early nineteenth centuries in England was never fully at odds with more traditional expressions of class and gender in the countryside. Middle-class opposition to many urban sporting recreations was by no means new and neither was a concern for female "immodesty," nor a view of participants in blood sports as "the lowest and most despicable part of the people."[46] Still, the cultural lines between the rough and the respectable in English popular culture had yet to harden. Robert Malcolmson argues that "during the eighteenth century in particular, many gentlemen were not entirely disengaged from the culture of the common people," and continued to occupy "a 'halfway house' between the robust unpolished culture of provincial England and the cosmopolitan sophisticated culture that was based in London."[47] The longstanding country tradition that was open to the libidinal aspects of popular rural sports and pastimes was far from fully extinguished, and there were numerous points during the eighteenth and early nineteenth centuries where "genteel and plebeian experiences" for both men and women continued to mix. At the same time, by the middle stages of the eighteenth century there was a significantly divided view of the gentry among urban cosmopolitans. On the one hand, critics were growing skeptical of the gentry, seeing them as well-meaning and patriotic, perhaps, but also antiquated, foppish, irrelevant and, at their worst, as debauched and parasitic.[48] On the other hand, the gentry maintained a high degree of credibility throughout the century, prompting considerable emulation by those who had far less wealth and property.[49] In that sense, it was not only the gentry who occupied a "halfway house" in respect of their attitudes to the culture of "the people." There were also substantial numbers of the people who were attracted to the theater of rural ideology and the romance of class privilege.

This lent itself to a number of complicated political positions, where critics argued about which aspects of upper-class culture, morality, and rural ideology were valuable and worth retaining in a modernizing society, and which should be rejected. The issues were debated extensively in new journals such as *The Tatler* and *The Spectator*, with particular provocation introduced through the caricatures created by artists such as William Hogarth and, somewhat later, Thomas Rowlandson. For example, Hogarth had sympathy for what he saw as the traditional values of masculinity, honor, and courage in

2.5 William Hogarth (1697–1764), *The Cock Pit* (1759)

gentry culture; but he loathed the hypocrisy of the upper classes and their tendency to engage in activities that he viewed as irrational and filled with excess. He was particularly scornful of alcoholism, gambling, and cruelty to animals, and his series of paintings, *The Rake's Progress*, became a popular moral fable of the perils of gambling and the sporting life. A similar theme is evident in his well-known engraving of *The Cock Pit* (Figure 2.5), which parodies Da Vinci's famous painting, *The Last Supper*. But, in Hogarth's rendering, a blind lord gambles on a cockfight, unaware that his friend, Judas-like, is stealing his money. The crowd around the lord is far from healthy or noble and is represented as uncontrolled, violent, and dissolute.

Hogarth's ruminations on the modern English moral subject were on the forward edge of a veritable explosion in the eighteenth century of political caricatures, engravings, and commentaries critical of established class and power relations. The expansion of long-distance commerce and the growth of a wage-labor economy in the cities, along with increases in mercantile, clerical, and professional occupations, created larger markets for these representations and commentaries. In turn, these markets supported, and were supported by, a thickening web of new sites for social interaction, including salons, clubs, and coffee houses in which "private individuals could assemble for the free equal exchange of reasonable discourse, thus welding themselves into a relatively cohesive body whose deliberations may assume the form of a powerful political force."[50] The coffee house emerged as an important site for the development of what Habermas has called a bourgeois "public sphere," wedged between state and civil society.[51] The popularity of coffee houses was based in part on the alternative they provided to traditional alehouses, which, as one commentator of the era noted, were known for "vile obscene talk, nonsense and ribaldry," often combined with "the fumes of tobacco, belchings and other foul breakings of wind."[52]

Coffee houses were not without loud discussion, but they tended to have clear rules of conduct that referenced the emergence of what Stallybrass and White have called the bourgeois "will to refinement." Every coffee house had a list of rules usually reflecting a Protestant sensibility, including prohibitions on such things as swearing, cards, dice or gaming, drinking of spirits, or wagers over five shillings.[53] According to Stallybrass and White, by limiting opportunities for "intoxication, rhythmic and unpredictable movements, sexual reference and symbolism, singing and chanting, bodily pleasures and 'fooling around,'" the English coffee house emerged as a "de-libidinized" space for men interested in "serious rational discussion."[54] Women were typically marginalized in this masculine rational culture, although as Deborah Heller suggests, "blue-stocking salons" provided similarly sanitized sites for political discussion among educated eighteenth-century bourgeois women.[55]

If the English coffee house in the eighteenth century was a prime urban site for the "bourgeois will to refinement," the culture of sporting venues appears to have been more varied, providing spaces for gentility and social exclusion in some instances and a mixing of more diverse publics, with varying levels of commitment to bourgeois morality, in others. Research on the seamier side of eighteenth-century London has demonstrated that the cock pit, dog pit, bear garden, and prize ring were often closer to the libidinal culture of the alehouse than to the more refined culture of the coffee house.[56] As such, they kept alive some of the deeply rooted popular traditions of the English countryside, albeit increasingly repackaged in the form of urban commercial entertainment.

New networks of promoters, club and event organizers, property owners, and sporting enthusiasts took the lead in this process of repackaging, sometimes with aristocratic patronage. Through the eighteenth and early nineteenth centuries, this involved a wide range of strategies, including standardizing rules to allow sportsmen and, sometimes, sportswomen from different regions to compete against

2.6 James Figg trade card

each other; organizing gambling, building fixed venues for events, and scheduling regular competitions, sometimes moving activities to prevent closure by the police and making a public case in the media for sporting recreations as viable and necessary aspects of English national culture. There is even evidence in the early eighteenth century of the advent of pictorial advertising for commercial sporting recreations. For example, in an effort to popularize his pugilistic exploits and promote his London-based "school" for the instruction of various martial arts, the famous fighter James Figg promoted himself shamelessly, with titles such as the "Oxonian Professor" and "Master" of "the Noble Science of Defense." Figg also commissioned posters and developed a "trade" card (Figure 2.6) containing an image attributed to the young William Hogarth, known to be one of Figg's friends. Figg's school attracted a range of aristocratic and early nineteenth-century celebrity students, including Jonathan Swift and Robert Walpole.[57]

Notwithstanding Figg's connections to London society, fighting and dueling were illegal in early eighteenth-century England and often developed close connections to other illegal activities. On this point, Rictor Norton argues that the ambience surrounding many of the prizefights held in London throughout much of the eighteenth century was typically more rough than respectable, with audiences composed mostly of lower middle-class and lower-class individuals rather than the wealthy.[58] This was especially true in the early eighteenth century when pugilism appears to have had a strongly plebeian character. Yet pugilism became increasingly fashionable through the century, partly by marketing itself as the ultimate form of masculine self-improvement and partly by introducing new regulatory practices and equipment to control "excessive" brutality.

The changing, but always contested, status of fighting with fists provided ample fodder for eighteenth-century caricaturists. There were numerous prints that attacked the "barbaric" and "low" world of fist fighting in different ways and this theme continued well into the nineteenth century. Caricaturists also ridiculed the increasing fashionability of boxing among the wealthy and, by late century, many were using boxing motifs to criticize the gentry as "soft" in comparison to more heroic representations of the "common" Englishman. At the same time, there was a growing use of printed images ostensibly meant to *record* sporting contests themselves, as part of the continued growth of the popular press in the late eighteenth century including the emergence of specialist sporting publications, the first of which was *The Sporting Magazine* in 1792. Of course, there were inevitable tensions within such images between their functions as promotional vehicles, as alleged depictions of "real" events, and as vehicles for articulating partisan or moral judgment about them.

English sport as its *own* object and its connection to the project of modernity

After the sixteenth century, Europe was plunged into intense discussion and debate about theologies, philosophies, and sciences devoted to specifically abstracted objects of study – for example, God, human nature, justice, ethics, and mathematics. Renaissance scholars catalyzed an emergent modern debate about such things by popularizing, revisiting, and resynthesizing philosophical and scientific debates from Greek and Roman antiquity, drawing out implications for evaluating their own era. Through the 1600s, many of the key ideas initiated in earlier theological and philosophical debates became focused on questions about the nature and sources of human reason and the comparative importance of the senses in the apprehension and explanation of the natural world. Through debates initiated by writers as varied as Descartes, Kant, Hobbes, Bacon, and Locke, theological and philosophical discussion grew to include a variety of new abstracted objects for contemplation and study that would preoccupy

European intellectual life during the eighteenth and nineteenth centuries – human nature, the state, the people, wealth, language, society, and even history itself.

The philosophical and political debates associated with the European Enlightenments of the late seventeenth and eighteenth centuries contributed to the economic, social, and political struggles of the time. In this way, they set the stage for the production of discourses and images in England where representations of sporting pastimes would become something more than comparatively minor features of locally ritualized communication or simple objects of decorative pleasure. The most important transition in this regard occurred through two related processes of objectification: first, the trend toward sport becoming *an object of representation on its own terms*; and, second, the trend to make sporting pastimes into *self-conscious objects of contemplation and critical analysis*. Neither process was politically innocent. As Timothy Mitchel has suggested more broadly, the very act of representation in the emerging "colonial-modern" era "involved creating an effect" that people recognized "as reality by organizing the world endlessly to represent it." In this sense, representation "does not refer simply to the making of images or meanings. It refers to forms of social practice that set up in the social architecture and lived experience of the world, what seems an absolute distinction between image (or meaning, or structure) and reality, and thus a distinctive imagination of the real."[59] Through its representations in English society, sport became intimately associated with the development of new conceptions of the self and a struggle to articulate new collective imaginings of reality and community.

In constructing these representations, one of the most powerful mechanisms of legitimation was the claim to offer a transparent representation of the real. Popular images by artists such as Hogarth were only able to parody "real life" by making a self-conscious reference to it. Representations of rural sport by people such as Wootton or Seymour connoted similar references to social reality. In the case of print, there were sporadic attempts to describe and to classify different types of games in various parts of Europe as early as the sixteenth century, with similar initiatives evident in England by the mid-1600s.[60] However, such initiatives did not gain much momentum in English culture until the early years of the nineteenth century. Arguably, the best example is Joseph Strutt's book in 1801 on the *Sports and Pastimes of the People of England*.[61] In his introduction, Strutt claimed:

In order to form a just estimation of the character of any particular people, it is absolutely necessary to investigate the Sports and
Pastimes most generally prevalent among them. War, policy, and other
contingent circumstances, may effectually place men, at different times,
in different points of view but, when we follow them into their retire-
ments, where no disguise is necessary, we are most likely to see them in
their true state, and may best judge of their natural dispositions.

Strutt's key assumption here is the empiricist idea that it is possible
to "see" sports and pastimes "in their true state" and, indeed, to
discover the true state of men's dispositions. Yet he continually offers
moral judgments as statements of fact in his own attempt to reveal the
"true" and undisguised state of "men's dispositions" in sports, games,
and other pastimes. In this sense, his analysis is illustrative of a modern
Enlightenment sensibility. If a nation is known or judged through its
pastimes, as he suggests, then it behooves the modern scholar or artist
to identify what pastimes and behaviors best fit a society's preferred
future. Strutt saw himself as an antiquarian scholar but, more broadly,
I see his book as an example of the developing tendency in the eighteenth and nineteenth centuries for the bourgeois intellectual elite to
rediscover and analyze elements in the popular culture of the nation
as part of a widespread attempt to determine what should be retained
from pre-modern social life and what should be left behind.

As the nineteenth century progressed, this process was connected
to a second level of abstraction wherein sport was represented
not so much as an indicator of the "true state" of men, but with a
view to identifying and discussing its *own* true state – its apparent
inner logic as a cultural form. It took the influence of the European
Enlightenments to create conditions where the representation of sport
was able to move to a point where it could be understood fully as its
own object. In this way, the European Enlightenments of the eighteenth century created the philosophical opportunity to position sport
as part of an emerging "project" of modernity. According to Jürgen
Habermas, that project involved the use of human reason to develop
"objective science, universal morality and law, and autonomous art
according to their inner logic." Enlightenment philosophers, and the
scholars, educators, jurists, and new middle-class moral reformers
who drew inspiration from their ideas, wanted "to use this accumulation of specialized culture for the enrichment of everyday life – that is
to say, for the rational organization of everyday life."[62] Through the
late nineteenth and early twentieth centuries, the belief that a form
of socially improving sport could, and, indeed, *should* be understood

as having an "autonomous" cultural character emerged as a unique feature of the making of modern sport as a distinctive field of social practice.

To a great extent, a very invested and partisan form of *representativeness* that was spreading through English sport challenged this idea. The cultural terrain of English sport was reshaped by the formation of clubs and organizations in an increasing number of sports; the development of standardized rules and fixed venues, along with improvements in transportation; the strengthening of English nationalism; the continued popularization of commercial recreations; anxieties about class, racial, ethnic, and gender differences and a growing sense of economic and political competition between communities. The idea that an athlete or team might represent local communities, ethnic groups and races, and more importantly, the nation meant that the results of competitions were coming to matter more than ever. Newspapers, magazines, and sports promoters sought to cash in on the passions that became increasingly associated with representative sport, and, not surprisingly, visual representations of sport often reflected the deeply felt ideas and prejudices of the era.

Two famous prizefights in the early nineteenth century, between English "Champion" Tom Cribb and a visiting American fighter Tom Molineaux provide a fascinating example. The Cribb–Molineaux fights were widely covered in English media, prompting editorialists to worry that the English nation had "lapsed into frivolity" instead of addressing itself to more pressing concerns. However, the fights were compelling for their dramatization of several complex and powerful tensions. As Daniel O'Quinn notes, Molineaux was a freed slave who had become a successful prizefighter in the United States, whereas Cribb was celebrated not only as a champion pugilist, but also as the epitome of English national character. Textual and artistic representations of the fight were varied, complex, and coded in multiple ways.[63] These included overt racial prejudice, evident in racist language and public hostility to Molineaux, to a point where the crowd forcibly intervened in the first fight when Molineaux had Cribb on the ropes. At the same time, O'Quinn argues, racial representations of the two fights also referenced liberal views associated with an abolitionist political stance that had become more pronounced in England in the latter third of the eighteenth century. Racial representations were also strongly mediated by nationalist identification, with Molineaux widely referenced as "American." At a time when England was at war with France, Molineaux's threat to Cribb's supremacy was both palpable and generalizable. The "Black," the "Moor," the American, was not only physically imposing, he was younger than Cribb, a skilled fighter, and trained by another ex-slave, Bill Richmond, who had been one of Cribb's toughest opponents. In this context, Cribb's eventual victories in both fights *mattered* to a great many people. Indeed, Joel T. Helfrich argues that the fight played a pivotal role not only in reinforcing racist sentiment in England, but in the refinement and intensification of early nineteenth-century English nationalism.[64] The print shown in Figure 2.7 below, by George Cruickshank, ominously suggests the threat posed by the imposing Molineaux. Figure 2.8 shows a print by Thomas Rowlandson which dramatizes "the action" of the second fight as Cribb knocks Molineaux to the ground in front of a cheering crowd.

By making the results of sporting competitions important to whole communities, the growth of "representativeness" in English sport through the late eighteenth and nineteenth centuries added to earlier concerns about the lowbrow character of many traditional sporting recreations. It was seen to provide new sources and levels of passion to sporting spectacle, presumably leading to increased violence, gambling, and cheating. In one sense, concerns about such things drew on very old criticisms of the "mob" or the "rabble" that had roots in Greek and Roman antiquity and had been resynthesized in eighteenth- and nineteenth-century Europe to include the folk cultures of popular recreations. But I think there was something new in these concerns. At the very moment that sport was increasingly acting to represent the imagined interests of different communities, it was filled

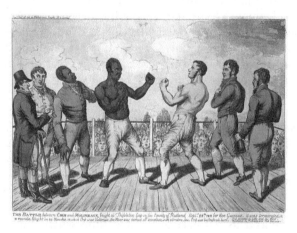

2.7 George Cruickshank (1792–1878),
The Battle between Cribb and Molineaux (1811)

Rural sports: a milling match between Cribb and Molineaux. 28 September 1811.

2.8 *Rural Sports: A Milling Match* (1811)
by Thomas Rowlandson (1756–1827)

with contradictions, loathed for its capacity to inflame passion and
to inspire cheating and violence, but also celebrated as a force for
social integration, especially in its capacity to extend the realm of
representativeness to the nation. By the late nineteenth century, when
social Darwinian attitudes were strongly felt, sporting prowess was
developing a new currency as a basis for national comparison. Yet
at the same time sport was also beginning to reference an imagined
community all its own, with its own sense of homogeneous time
and membership in a geographically, socioeconomically, and demo-
graphically diffuse population of enthusiasts. By the end of the second
decade of the nineteenth century, the English sporting "world" had
developed its own specialized chroniclers – well-known writers such
as Pierce Egan who had a large following of readers. Over the next
several decades, the proliferation of sporting magazines continued
to subtly reinforce the idea of sport as a world of practice defined
through temporal and spatial separation from the rest of society.

At first, this dawning recognition of temporal and spatial separation was not directly connected either to an implicit moral framework
or to an implicit theory of society. For most of the medieval period
through to the eighteenth century the union of the Christian idea
of an organic society was melded in most of Europe with a view
of the naturalness of social hierarchy – like beehives or anthills, a
natural pyramid with the deserving few at the top and the many at
the bottom. Debates about the health of the social body and about

85

the rights of the few versus the obligations of the many were framed by these assumptions. However, during the eighteenth century, these debates were influenced by an emerging idea of progress based on the human capacity to understand and to control nature. A newly imagined rational public interest lay in defending and advancing the health of the social body through the creation of rational institutions – institutions primarily associated with markets and governance, such as mercantile organizations, accounting and banking organizations, insurance companies, parliaments, and the judiciary.

These institutions also included hospitals, schools, barracks, and prisons, which required intimate knowledge of the populations they served and promoted the individual's internalization of the discipline required to make these institutions work. All of these institutions became elements of an emerging project of modernity because they sought to extend the regime of reason in the pursuit of progress.[65] Habermas has little to say about the actual operation of such institutions. Here, one looks to Michel Foucault, who emphasizes how the imagined need to protect and to advance the social body operated through a combination of segregation and integration and the deployment of new techniques of administrative power. Contagions were increasingly monitored, the sick segregated and treated, criminals and delinquents isolated and disciplined, and students educated both technically and morally.[66]

Foucault pays scant attention to sporting pastimes in his writing, although he does make several observations about bodily practices and physical exercise in Christian monasticism and extends them to a consideration of gymnasia as disciplinary sites and spaces similar to those associated with schools, barracks, hospitals, poorhouses, factories, and asylums. In the creation of modern sites and spaces for exercise, the deployment of categories, classifications, regulations, instruction, and surveillance is geared toward making potentially unruly bodies disciplined and more docile. Like all emerging institutions of modernity, the ultimate aim of the process is for individuals to become responsible for their own normalization and to develop new understandings of their identities that enhance the "health" of the social body.[67]

This movement toward control of the self and the normalization of bodies was closely intertwined with the bourgeois will to refinement, and it required a wide-ranging campaign of repression, regulation, and reform of seemingly irrational and rough popular leisure activities. In a very obvious sense, this campaign also emerged as a matter of economic and political necessity. From the late eighteenth through the nineteenth centuries, the hardening of capitalist market principles in England meant that the drinking, merrymaking, and sometimes disorderly recreations popular among the new working classes not only carried the whiff of potential political sedition, they were said to disrupt the daily routines of business by encouraging absenteeism, debt, and insubordination. In early nineteenth-century England, Jeremy Bentham expressed the utilitarian concern that even normally rational individuals effectively lost all reason in "deep play" and could not help themselves from financially beggaring their families or from engaging in other disruptive behaviors.[68] The repression and regulation of such activities was therefore viewed as the imposition of rational order for the greater good – the strategic deployment of reason in the pursuit of modern progress. Throughout the nineteenth century, and in the spirit of both economic pragmatism and bourgeois moral reform, play in English streets was declared illegal, tavern locations and hours became heavily regulated, alcohol consumption was controlled at public events, and there were campaigns against sports where maiming an opponent was the primary goal. Set against the background of a broader movement against animal cruelty – the Royal Humane Society was founded in 1774 – there was also a systematic attempt on the part of middle-class reformers to ban sports that encouraged the suffering of animals.

But enthusiasts continued to reference sport's capacity to build energy and physical strength and to fight "effeminacy," claims that struck a chord in the context of growing English nationalism, the social challenges of a new industrial civilization, and the perceived demands of an expanding British Empire. In addition, sporting pastimes maintained strongly residual connections to health and to rural ideology. The major question for sports enthusiasts, especially among the late nineteenth-century middle class, was how could English sporting pastimes be defended against widespread criticism, remade, and given moral utility as orderly, healthy, and socially improving practices? In other words, how could sport be organized to make claims to social hygiene, health and "culture" versus decadence, illness, and "barbarism?" The pursuit of answers to these questions never developed as a coherent master cultural strategy; rather, it unfolded in an uneven and fragmented way, mediated and complicated by subtle shifts in class, gender, and racially based cultural preferences, as well as by the fact that games and sports themselves were finding greater purchase in the marketplace as economically productive enterprises.

One of these fragments was the development of a new culture of "gentlemanly" athleticism in British public schools that drew on older notions of aristocratic pedigree, privilege and duty, but mixed them with newer bourgeois ideas about the importance of self-help and self-improvement.[69] On the playing field, young men were taught that sporting contests, in order to proceed fairly, had to be momentarily set apart – given a degree of autonomy – from the broader rules of social privilege. The goal was to create a community of peers who recognized and agreed to be bound by higher rules of regulative authority. It was obvious in football, for example, that there could be no "fair" demonstration of prowess – no fair result to the game – if the son of a bottle merchant was prevented by his lower rank in social life from tackling the son of a lord.[70] At the same time, the idea that sporting contests were valuable training grounds for virility and courage became subtly integrated with new ideas about self-development and the educative and moral value of games.

Still, while many proponents of English public-school athleticism were evangelistic in their promotion of the social usefulness of sport, there were serious questions about the appropriate limits of that evangelism. Almost from the outset, there was a significant split in the vision of moral entrepreneurship associated with nineteenth-century English sport. On the one hand, controlled, rational, achievement-oriented sport was beginning to be viewed evangelistically as something that promoted distinctively English and, largely, masculine virtues: self-reliance, modesty, an appreciation of the importance of fairness, control of one's emotions, politeness and respect for one's adversary. During the nineteenth century, this manifested itself in a globalizing moral entrepreneurship preaching the virtues of an ostensibly rational modern British culture throughout the empire. The most committed moral entrepreneurs believed that no one should be formally excluded from participation in the community of sporting enthusiasts on the basis of their social origins, as long as they demonstrated complete devotion to sport as a fair and morally grounded area of cultural life. Simply stated, the idea was that sport might teach anyone to act like a gentleman.

But, on the other hand, schoolboy athleticism reinforced the view that only existing gentlemen were capable of grasping and developing a vision of sport as a civilizing and character building enterprise. During the late nineteenth and early twentieth centuries this idea found expression in the restrictive concept of amateurism.[71] Amateurs by definition were gentlemen. Ladies might play sport if it was undertaken with appropriate decorum but there was a strong sentiment that the "object" of sport was properly masculine. There was also a strong view among members of prominent amateur sports clubs and associations that amateurs would be contaminated if they played or competed against *non-gentlemen*, a category that initially included artisans and laborers, "colored" colonials, and "Indians." While the philosophy of amateurism expanded to become less overtly restrictive through the twentieth century, it nonetheless specified a rigid behavioral code associated with the idea that sport could *and should* serve a purpose beyond mere amusement or crass commerce. Games should be fun, but they were also a serious matter to be undertaken in the spirit of self-improvement, sobriety, and the promotion of what Anne McClintock calls the "predominantly male agon of empire."[72]

The advent of photography in the nineteenth century spoke more than ever to the notion that representation allowed the viewer to glimpse reality, as news magazines and periodicals rushed to get dramatic photographs of athletic triumphs and failures. Photography also created a seemingly endless rehearsal of sober solemnity in sport through the emergence of the "team photograph" as a distinctive cultural genre. The late nineteenth century witnessed the production of thousands of staged team photos, usually involving a group of young men, serious and confident, often with arms crossed, and looking somehow improved by their having participated in the sports team. The static, somber, and staged character of the team photograph was undoubtedly due in part to the necessity of having to sit still for the long exposure times needed to take successful photographs. However, the style remained in place, even as the technology of photography advanced.

Any sport that made a claim to culture more than barbarism during the Victorian era was tied to a very narrow understanding of the legitimate definition of sport as an object of practice as well as of legitimate sporting behaviors and preferred forms and uses of the body. By the end of the nineteenth century, a clear distinction between sports as a form of rational recreation, rather than seemingly irrational amusement, had become fully institutionalized in England and across England's colonies. Rational recreation and "civilizing" sport were promoted in amateur sports organizations, schools and municipal parks, libraries, and even in many trade unions. Irrational leisure – typically associated with drinking, gambling, low levels of self-control and "rough" sport – was patrolled by the police.[73] Professional sports still carried the stigma of an earlier attachment to rough leisure. However, through the early twentieth century they began to occupy a cultural position that sometimes moved fluidly between the two poles of rational and allegedly irrational recreation. Despite their exclusion from amateur organizations, promoters of professional sport in the early twentieth century didn't hesitate to adopt some of the moral entrepreneurs' rhetoric about sport as a socially valuable builder of masculine and national character and as a timeless feature of western culture.

I think this latter conception of sport as a timeless cultural form is an underappreciated aspect of the process of winning consent in English society for a view of sport as a socially improving cultural activity. The development of a social/philosophical basis for sport as a distinctive field of practice was built on a self-conscious reference to the past; but not so much on the past history of English sporting pastimes than on a resynthesis of ideas from classical antiquity. One of the modern benchmarks for this view became John Locke's reinterpretation of Juvenal's reference to "a sound body and a sound mind." This dictum became a mantra in the "muscular Christian" movement that grew in England throughout the nineteenth century, preaching the combined virtues of Christianity and rational sporting competition. Tony Mangan has argued persuasively that muscular Christianity, in turn, fused the idea of Christian morality with social Darwinian thinking and British imperial ambition. It was the presumed right and duty of "gentlemen" sports enthusiasts to aid in the defense and expansion of empire, either through military service or by helping to "civilize" the allegedly "backward" and "less fortunate" races within the British Empire.[74]

In keeping with the muscular Christian's backward glance toward classicism, one of the most important aspects of visual representation of sport during the nineteenth century was the increasing use of images from Greco-Roman classical antiquity. The trend had begun in the context of a booming interest across Europe in Renaissance histories of Greece and Rome and in ancient sites and artifacts uncovered by eighteenth- and nineteenth-century explorers and archeologists, including the original site at Olympia itself. By the late nineteenth century, the effect was dramatic and it strengthened the claim that sport could be understood as part of an imagined lineage of western culture that stretched from ancient Greece and Rome to modern Europe. In the next chapter, I discuss the numerous attempted revivals of "Olympic Games" in various parts of Europe during the nineteenth century, but it is worth noting an example or two here. One of the most notable English Olympic revivals was implemented by the physician, magistrate, amateur botanist, and moral entrepreneur William Penny Brookes in Much Wenlock, Shropshire, in 1859, which was followed by a larger event organized in London, at Crystal Palace, in 1866, among others. Brookes was fascinated by ancient Greece and was also an early champion of muscular Christianity, arguing that "as Christians . . . we should, on moral grounds, endeavor to direct the amusement of the working class."[75] Coubertin shared Brookes's fascination with antiquity and was influenced by Brookes's moral entrepreneurial vision. His own proposal for a modern Olympic Games was never simply an attempt to recover the past. Rather, he intended to advance an emerging modernist vision of sport and the healthy body as means to solve the problems of excessive militarism and "social and psychological equilibrium" that he felt plagued modern Europe.

I believe that the project taken up by the new proponents of socially improving sport in the late nineteenth century was as an *aesthetic project* in addition to an educative and organizational one. The fusion of imagery from Greek antiquity, with ideas taken from English movements for rational recreation and the tradition of English public school athletics, lent a transhistorical aura to a set of historically and culturally specific practices. It also lent itself to the promotion of Greek traditions of "heroic nudity" and harmonious bodily proportions as key elements in an idealized bodily aesthetic. In English visual culture, this bodily aesthetic stood in implicit contrast to frequent representations of the bodies of the English gentry by caricaturists, such as Rowlandson, as bulbous and gout-ridden. A classical "virtuous" bodily aesthetic also provided a basis for criticizing the plebeian, carnival body as profane, undisciplined, and undesirable. One of the most famous images of this classical athletic body is the *Discobolus* by the Greek sculptor Myron in the fifth century BCE. An excellent copy of the sculpture, taken from Hadrian's Villa in Tivoli, Italy, was auctioned to an English art dealer in 1790 before it was acquired by the British Museum in 1805. While the *Discobolus* was only one of many images of idealized athletic bodies circulating in English literary and artistic cultures in the early nineteenth century, it became an extremely influential reference for the production of other representations of idealized male bodies in nineteenth-century England (see Figure 2.9).

The growing reference in English sport during the nineteenth and early twentieth centuries to images of idealized bodies taken from Greek classicism was an important further dimension of the incorporation of sporting practice into an imagined project of modernity. As Stallybrass and White argue: "the classical body was far more than an aesthetic standard or model. It structured, from the inside as it were, the characteristically 'high' discourses of philosophy, statecraft, theology and law, as well as literature, as they emerged from the Renaissance. In the classical discursive body were enclosed those

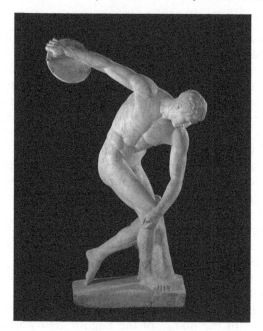

2.9 After Myron, *The Townley Discobolus*

regulative systems which were closed, homogeneous, monumental, centered and symmetrical."[76] The project referenced classicism as a way of differentiating an imagined transhistorical sporting ideal from ongoing corruption of that idea evident in the growth of popular sporting entertainments, undertaken for commercial rather than educative purposes. As Susan Brownell points out, classicism also tacitly constructed an imagined linear history of "western civilization" that contrasted "modern" western "civilized" societies against allegedly "primitive" societies.[77] In addition, classicism subtly reproduced a view of the straightened, strong, and proportioned body as a manifestation of upper-class habitus and patriarchal sensibility.

It is important to understand that the modern project of integrating diverse sporting practices, and of particular images of sporting bodies into an allegedly civilizing western cultural tradition in the late nineteenth and early twentieth centuries was never something that won universal approval. It has never been possible to have consensus over which practices count as "legitimate sport" and which do not. For the most part, sporting enthusiasts were far more interested in match results and in the drama of sporting spectacles than in philosophy. There was also continued resistance among elites to the idea of any type of sport as a form of socially improving culture, based on sport's apparent elevation of the body over the mind, and on a belief that the growing thirst for sporting spectacle shown by the modern industrial masses exemplified the spread of frivolous, or dangerously irrational, tendencies in western cultural life. Like the Roman Circus in antiquity, the argument ran, the widespread popularity of modern sport should be understood as an indicator of a growing malaise of modernity, a symptom of civilizational decay.

In this sense, the appeal of classicism as a legitimating discourse in sport was complicated by the powerful negative image of the Roman Colosseum, home to bloody gladiatorial contests and the tradition of "bread and circuses," ostensibly associated both with the aristocratic manipulation of the plebeian classes and the irrationalities of spectacle directed to the "mob." Undoubtedly, in some quarters, the power and grandeur of Rome made an appealing historical reference point, but the project of highlighting the allegedly "civilizing" qualities of sport compelled nineteenth- and early twentieth-century moral entrepreneurs to prefer Greek over Roman signifiers.

The idea was to aestheticize sport in the traditions of *positive* rather than *negative* classicism.[78] In its imagined "true state," early twentieth-century "amateur" sport, in particular, was tacitly promoted as the legacy of Pericles rather than Nero, of Olympia and the Athenian gymnasium rather than the Roman Colosseum. Early Olympic proponents insisted that the modern Olympics would stage sporting competitions side by side with artistic demonstrations. At the same time, Hellenic signifiers and classical representations of sporting bodies became widely evident in the late nineteenth- and early twentieth-century promotion of sport as a transhistorical, and thereby autonomous, form of culture. The tradition of positive classicism was reinforced in 1896 by the choice of Athens as an initial site for Pierre de Coubertin's proclaimed project of Olympic revival. However, the tradition soldiered on after Athens as a noticeable aspect of early twentieth-century modernism, even as it mutated in various ways through the first third of the twentieth century.

Conclusion

In this chapter, I've argued that the social production of modern English sport as a distinctive field of practice by the early twentieth century involved complex processes of representation, objectification, and abstraction. In my view, the changing features and significance of

93

visual and written representations of sport were important constitutive elements in the processes whereby sport became disembedded from earlier European social and cultural logics to become viewed as "its own object." In the eighteenth and nineteenth centuries, in particular, representations of sport became sites for articulating competing discourses about English national character, appropriate moral behavior, and legitimate uses of time, space, and the human body. With this, there was also growing recognition of sporting pastimes as independent empirical *objects* whose classification and scientific study might be pressed into the advancement of a broader *project* of western modernity. That recognition developed in parallel with the desire of sporting enthusiasts to rationalize and to standardize their enthusiasms, either in the pursuit of commercial interests, class, gender, or racially based exclusivity, or more broad-ranging programs of educational or moral reform. Simultaneously, there was a subtle, but increasingly significant, movement toward recognition of the "separateness" and, indeed, the imagined "autonomy" of sport. In order for competitions to be truly meaningful and fair, they needed to be insulated momentarily from obvious constraints of external privilege. There was also growing specialization in the uses of time and space to set sporting activities apart from everyday life and communities of enthusiasts developed a strongly subcultural sense of sport as a distinctive "world" with its own important events and issues.

Additionally, based on a fusion of Enlightenment thinking with the increasing availability of information about sporting pastimes in Greece and Rome, there was an emerging belief that sport could be thought of as a transhistorical, indeed, a universal *form* of culture. I have argued that this idea became intertwined ideologically with the broader "civilizing" impulses of an English imperial social order. Through the nineteenth and early twentieth centuries, representational practices in various forms of literature, philosophy, and visual art began to articulate a set of distinctively western, class, gender, and racially based perceptions that were then imagined as *universal* meanings, purposes, and ethical principles in sport. By promoting and representing sport as an imagined form of civilizing culture, with roots in western antiquity, sporting enthusiasts in England, and increasingly, across Europe, North America, and other English, or formerly English, colonies, were able to strengthen their case for sport as a modern cultural practice with the potential to reconcile robust "manly" physicality with respectability and restraint; passion with controlled discipline and order; individualism with social solidarity.

The effect was not only to reinforce the idea of modern sport as its own object, but also to connect the very idea of sport closely to a project of western modernity with very distinctive understandings of idealized body imagery, "civilized" corporeal dispositions, and delimitation of culture into high and low, rough and respectable.

In mapping these processes in England, it is important not to isolate representations of sport from the material conditions that produced them. Yet it is also important not to see these representations and their ranges of cultural and ideological meanings as a kind of superstructural icing on a separately existing material foundation. Representations of sporting practices and of sporting bodies in English history are better understood as constitutive features of the production of the modern sports field and, in this way, as elements in the social production of English capitalist and colonial modernity from the seventeenth through the early twentieth centuries. I recognize that by focusing on the English case I have risked distorting an understanding of events in other geographical places where there have been alternative understandings of the changing social and cultural roles of physical exercise, athletic agonism, or sporting spectacle. Still, if the goal is to understand and to analyze the historical formation of globally *dominant* elements in the field of "modern" sporting practice, there is much to be learned by studying the history of representation in English sport.

— 3 —

"STAGING" (CAPITALIST/ COLONIAL) MODERNITY: INTERNATIONAL EXHIBITIONS AND OLYMPICS

Modernity, Timothy Mitchell argues, is always constituted through representations of "rupture or separation, whether of a rational self from a disenchanted world, of producers from their means of production, or of nature and population from the processes of technological control and social planning."[1] The "act of representation," he continues, "constantly repeated" creates a "world as picture" that makes certain "referents – nation, people, economy – appear as an object that exists prior to any representation, something given, material, fixed in its unique time and space."[2] In Mitchell's view, modernity is "not so much a stage of history but rather its staging."[3] His particular interest is how visions of modern life have been constructed to form a distinctive time-space in the "homogeneous shape of the West and characterized by an immediacy of presence that we recognize as the 'now' of history."[4]

This is a view that makes representation, discourse, and ideology central themes in the history of modernity. In this chapter, I undertake a brief overview of that history, addressing what I take to be its contradictions and ideological dimensions. I then consider the emergence of international exhibitions and Olympics as key elements in the staging of modernity in what Eric Hobsbawm has called "the long nineteenth century.[5] The discussion that follows is strongly influenced by Mitchell's critique of Eurocentric objectification in representations of the "now" of history.[6] But, whereas Mitchell tends to inflect the textual/discursive aspects of modernity, I am somewhat more concerned with the social conditions of discursive practice. This involves a critique of ideology, not simply as representation, but as part of a "whole material social process."[7]

The "modern idea of modernity" and its contradictions

Writing in the seventeenth century, Francis Bacon argued that gunpowder, the compass, and the printing press could be viewed as indicators of a new age.[8] Bacon's obvious pride in these inventions typified a growing self-confidence in Europe about the human capacity to understand and to improve the world. In contrast to earlier views in late Greco-Roman antiquity of *modernus* or *modernitas* as "the time of now," or of "novelty" which paled in comparison to what was old and venerated, European intellectuals between the fifteenth and seventeenth centuries began to develop what Krishan Kumar calls the "modern idea of modernity."[9] Kumar connects this idea to the teleological character of the Christian sense of time that had become dominant across the Roman Empire by the fifth century CE. Instead of a cyclical view of time and history as equivalent to the rhythms of the days and seasons, or the life spans of human organisms, Christianity was responsible for introducing the idea of organizing history into periods (e.g. BCE and CE) building to a final purpose – the Second Coming of Christ.

However, in the debate that arose in Europe about the comparative value of the thinking of "ancients" versus "moderns," some writers began to argue that history has a secular purpose – *progress* through the accumulation of knowledge and its application. In the early seventeenth century, Bacon exemplified this view in his suggestion that the modern European world stood in contrast to Greek and Roman antiquity as an adult does to an infant.[10] The invention and widespread use of mechanical clocks in Europe after the fourteenth century suggested an expanded human capacity to subject time to practical purposes.[11] Similarly, the apparent accumulation of goods and wealth suggested new abilities to improve the human condition. Additionally, advances in medicine and science seemed to culminate in 1687 in Isaac Newton's apparent "discovery" of a rational, homogeneous, and infinite universe.

Armand Mattelart claims that in this intellectual climate the "inertia of dogma" was challenged by a new belief in "movement" and in the human capacity to master nature.[12] As this occurred, both the medieval acceptance of fate and the celebration of fixed ideals, such as honor and piety, were challenged by a growing emphasis on reason, experience, science, and technological innovation: "The world came to be seen as perfectible."[13] A Promethean vision of human progress developed slowly and unevenly throughout the seventeenth and eighteenth centuries as an emerging ideological template for modernity. However, it continued to be rivaled by a powerful and popular counter-discourse that saw "decay and degeneration were as much part of the human story as growth and progress."[14]

There is considerable irony in the fact that all three of the technologies that Bacon saw as key indicators of a "new age" in Europe had Chinese antecedents. Still, from the standpoint of seventeenth-century European colonial expansion and economic development, his confidence in technological innovations as indicators of a new age seemed warranted. The compass expanded the capacity for European exploration, colonization, and trade; gunpowder provided means for creating large-scale European states with monopolistic control over the delivery of violence in the territories they claimed, and it assisted in the subjugation of less technologically developed societies; the printing press provided new independent realms of symbolic production associated with a growing trade in books, opinion, and "news of the world" that helped to separate the production and dissemination of knowledge from the dominance of religious and political authorities.[15]

These changes were constitutive elements in the breakdown of European feudalism, the growth of capitalist enterprise, and the spread of new forms of administration over human beings. They were accompanied by intense competition between emerging states and between religious authorities; a seemingly perpetual race for military advantage and the wealth to sustain it; and the exploitation of colonies and their peoples as sources of wealth and geopolitical advantage. By the end of the eighteenth century, new understandings of individualism, individual rights, human potential, and achievement contributed further to a developing view of western history as a forward march of progress. The American Revolution had created what its founders believed to be "the first New Nation" of the modern age, and the French Revolution reinforced new ideas of liberty and equality as the fruit of modernization.

This understanding of modernization emerged between the seventeenth and twentieth centuries in tandem with the spread of European economic and political dominance over much of the world. With these changes, the self-defined modern West was increasingly seen in binary contrast to its own "traditional" past – its imagined historical "childhood" – as well as to an exotic, but allegedly primitive, culturally stagnant, or childlike non-West. As noted in the opening chapter of this book, the stage was set for differentiating "primitives" from "moderns" in the legacy of ideas from Greco-Roman antiquity about the "naturalness" of slavery and the importance of reason in the mastery and development of the self. These ideas were resynthesized in sixteenth- and seventeenth-century accounts of pagan "primitives" and "savages" who populated the "new worlds" opening up to Europe through exploration and colonization. A wave of evolutionary social Darwinian thinking in the nineteenth century tightened the link between the idea of modernity and that of western progress, now seen to lie in evolutionary conceptions of "development" through the progressive features of individualism and free markets, innovations in technology, new systems of government and administration, and the advent of liberal democratic political rights and institutions.[16]

However, this conception of modernity as the historical path followed by the social, economic, political, and cultural development of western nations was filled with contradictions. Bacon's obliviousness to the non-European sources of the technologies he so admired is particularly notable in this regard. Indeed, as John Hobson points out, a large part of the "rise" of the West from the sixteenth through the nineteenth centuries lay in the European appropriation of the "resource portfolios" of non-western civilizations in Asia and Africa.[17] These included long-distance sea navigation aided by the compass, iron and steel making, printing and papermaking, military technology, and financial institutions. Hobson follows Andre Gunder Frank in claiming, even with these appropriations, that Europe lagged behind many of the non-western societies, especially China, until the end of the eighteenth century.[18] It was only through a combination of enrichment from the gold and silver resources in the Americas, African slavery, colonization, militarily secured "free" trade, and factory-based industrialization that Europeans were finally able to surpass Asia in the sphere of overall economic development and international commerce.[19]

Marx understood the immense cost of "progress" in modern societies and cultures, not only at the expense of the white European and North American proletariat, but also of slaves and dominated colonials. In Volume 1 of *Capital*, he argued that the "rosy dawn" of the capitalist mode of production lay in the "discovery of gold and silver in America," as well as "the extirpation, enslavement and entombment in mines of the aboriginal population, the beginning of the conquest and looting of the East Indies," and "the turning of Africa into a warren for the commercial hunting of black skins."[20] Elsewhere, Marx references slavery "as much the pivot on which our present-day industrialism turns as are machinery, credit, etc." For Marx, slavery and colonialism played decisive roles in the creation of "world trade" as a "necessary condition for large scale machine industry."[21] In *The Communist Manifesto*, Marx and Frederick Engels also summarize how the national and international dynamics of capitalist competition led to a constant revolutionizing of the means of production as a condition of modern civilization. "Wherever the bourgeoisie has got the upper hand," they argue, it has "pitilessly torn asunder the motley feudal ties that bound man to his 'natural superiors,'" and has "drowned the most heavenly ecstasies of religious fervor, of chivalrous enthusiasm, of philistine sentimentalism, in the icy water of egotistical calculation." This occurred unevenly, but also inexorably, as the bourgeoisie devoted itself to the pursuit of what Marx and Engels call a "single, unconscionable freedom – Free Trade."[22]

As a political pamphlet rather than an in-depth scholarly analysis, the *Communist Manifesto* can be accused of dramatic overstatement. It is certainly fair to say that aristocratic elitism, religious fervor, and sentimentalism have proven far more resistant to "drowning" than Marx and Engels suggested in 1848. Still, I agree with Marshall Berman that Marx and Engels' focus on capitalism's constant revolution of the means of production captures an important dynamic of modernity.[23] There are two key aspects to this in Berman's view. The first is the emergence of a mode of modern subjectivity centered on a rejection of community life as backward-looking, closed systems, in preference for communities whose collective resources enable individuals to become autonomous and freely creative. Drawing on Goethe's *Faust*, Berman suggests that the emergence of "the modern" is associated with the advent of a new form of individualism, based on the free pursuit of "intensely felt action, life, creativity," and of the political, social and economic means to make this happen.[24]

But, secondly, Berman sees a Faustian contradiction at the core of this modern conception, due to capitalism's need to continually revolutionize its means of production. He references Joseph Schumpeter's description of capitalism as a force of *"creative destruction"* to explain the experience of modernity as uncontrolled, constant change, creatively positive in many instances, but only through the often horrific destruction of what came before it.[25] The strain of modern thinking that emphasizes reason and perfectibility suggests humans have nothing to fear from capitalism's forces of creative destruction.[26] However, according to Marx and Engels, this is an excessively optimistic vision of bourgeois power. In their view, the bourgeoisie "is like the sorcerer who is no longer able to control the powers of the nether world."[27] So-called "free" bourgeois subjects undertake projects of creative destruction – for example, the creative technical and economic advances of the West, built on the destruction of the cultures of European feudal serfs in the advent of industrialism, or of indigenous people through the slave trade and colonialism – but these projects often appear to take on an autonomous and uncontrollable form of their own. Modernity, in this respect, involves an inevitable dialectic between "free" and "determined" action, a play of limits and possibilities, replete with unintended consequences of a Faustian character. Although Marx does not develop the point himself, modernity also surely requires an understanding of this dialectic in spatial, and, indeed, racial and gendered terms, in addition to those of time and social class.

Marx's emphasis on the relentless pursuit of *"freedom" of trade* by the emerging bourgeois classes within the world's militarily and technologically powerful nations can be conceived of as having two variants. The first, in the "rosy dawn" of capitalism, refers to the imagined right of *"free"* access to resources in other lands. The quest for free trade, in this sense, was an important factor in the desire of European nations to acquire and expand their colonial territories, appropriate and exploit human and other resources, and compete for innovations in communication, transportation, production and military capability. As David Harvey has argued, drawing on Marx, the pursuit of colonial trade and the need to regulate colonial space at a distance strongly influenced the development and deployment of technologies that could "annihilate" space through the reduction of time, such as the compass, maps, steamships, and the telegraph.[28]

A second variant of the importance of "freedom" of trade arguably developed in, through, and as a result of the struggles noted above. In the transition from a purely mercantile free-booting mode of colonial exploitation to the growth of industrialization in Europe and its colonies, the idea of "free" exchange gradually extended to include human labor power. Without getting into the labyrinthian debates in western social thought about how, why, or precisely when capitalism developed in the way it did, it is important to acknowledge only that the widespread commodification of human labor power in European societies depended upon "freedom" from the constraints of feudalism.[29] A capacity for labor is commodified in the exchange value assigned to the bodies of slaves, but slaves themselves play no part in this negotiation. Marx sees the moment when labor power becomes "freely" exchanged through labor contracts as a decisive juncture in the history of capitalism.[30] However, he argues that what looks on the surface like the "freedom" to negotiate the contracted price of labor in capitalist societies is much less free than it seems. The rise of

101

"modern" bourgeois individualism, with its accompanying emphasis on reason and individual rights, is constrained by the bourgeoisie's systemic ability *as a class* to suppress the value of labor power beyond the value of the commodities that it produces.

Free trade, I shall argue in a moment, provides an important metaphorical framework for emerging understandings of internationalism in nineteenth-century modernity. The quest for free international trade by colonizing nations has also been closely connected to a number of "creatively destructive" effects associated with *capital accumulation through dispossession*. The forced migration of millions of dispossessed residents from Africa to western colonies through the slave trade was an early example of accumulation by dispossession, a practice that divided and sometimes destroyed whole African communities and created new hybridized diasporas throughout Europe and its colonies. At the same time, the growth of industrialization in Europe and North America featured creative destruction and accumulation by dispossession through the initially forced migrations of rural residents to cities, creating new factory labor forces in industrializing societies, as well as new social class, racial, ethnic, and gender polarizations.

The successful pursuit of "free trade" by colonizing nations resulted in significant infusions of money into European metropolitan centers from the sixteenth through the early twentieth centuries, which accelerated the ascendancy of western finance capital and technological innovation, with unevenly felt consequences in many parts of the world. Major European and colonial capitals also became important sites in new networks of capitalist exchange and accumulation, albeit in uneven and unequal ways. The competitive dynamics of international circuits of exchange with the major centers of wealth and power in the "modern" West had a particularly profound effect on the organization, value, and representation of urban space in Europe and North America, and on the meanings, struggles, and inequities that developed accordingly.[31]

Colonialism, capitalist technical innovation, and commodification were intertwined with the continued strengthening in European societies of the values of *reason and progress* during the eighteenth and nineteenth centuries. Confidence in these values led to the creation of new technical schemes for "rationally" organizing space and time, consolidating new ways of understanding the world, new urban and national spaces, new forms of social association, and new initiatives for educating and governing populations. This confidence arguably found its greatest expression in the universal histories of eighteenth-century French philosophers, such as Turgot and Condorcet, who advocated strongly for the accumulation of knowledge and the "continuous progress" that resulted.[32] In the early years of the nineteenth century, the doctrine of universal progress became closely linked to industrial development in the influential work of Henri Saint-Simon, who saw rationally administered systems, in alliance with "the industrial class," as the engine of progress, and imagined moral progress as an extension of industrial organization, refinement, and development.

Saint-Simon's most ardent enthusiasts elevated his views to a theological position in early nineteenth-century France.[33] At a similar time, his former secretary, Auguste Comte, "invented" the idea (and the word) of sociology as a "true science of social development," a positive science that resynthesized Saint-Simonian ideas, linking them to Adam Smith's discussion of refinements in the division of labor in *The Wealth of Nations* (1776), and to early eighteenth-century German biological writing on concepts such as development, homogeneity, and heterogeneity.[34] Comte's "positive philosophy" advocated a view of universal human history as a series of stages, culminating in an *orderly* modern world of scientific explanation, based on observation, experiment, and comparison.

As a final aspect of the making of modern European and colonial modern worlds, I want to note the steady growth from the sixteenth through the twentieth centuries of what John Thompson calls the "mediazation of culture," with particular attention to interconnections between media technologies and institutions, spectacle, consumption, the commodification of leisure, and the rise of new forms of symbolic power.[35] Somewhat differently, but not completely unrelated, over a century ago, the French poet and essayist Charles Baudelaire identified the shift to a more spectacular world of imagery as a significant aspect of modernity in his discussion of "phantasmagoria." As Walter Benjamin remarks: "The world dominated by its phantasmagorias – this, to make use of Baudelaire's term, is 'modernity.'"[36] The word "phantasmagoria" refers to constantly shifting, ephemeral, fantastic, or dreamlike, images. But, in Baudelaire's and Benjamin's use of the term, the reference is broadened to include the ideas of consumption and spectacle that have the characteristic of fetishes. The modern world, in this view, is a world of sensuous spectacles whose pleasures and identities belie the powers, contradictions, and inequities associated with their production.

The emergence of large-scale industrial exhibitions and international expositions in Europe during the nineteenth century was influenced by these tendencies and conditions, and contributed to them. According to Mattelart, the key rationale for these new spectacles of modernity was to dramatize "the degree of civilization and progress" that "various nations have attained."[37] However, as I will argue in a moment, organizers of these events constructed a view of civilization and progress from the privileged vantage point of the European and American dominant classes.[38] Their visions of "universal association" were closely connected to a colonial "ideology of progress" through capital accumulation and technological innovation and to the power and wealth of the modern industrial nations.[39] The expositions also constituted an important new *medium* of spectacular display and symbolic power. In Mitchell's apt phrase, they presented "the world as exhibition."[40]

In more material terms, these spectacular events promoted and showcased technological innovations and practices in communication, such as photography (including chronophotography and panoramas), underwater cable, the telegraph, and the telephone, and pressed them into the service of modernity's grand narratives of reason, science, and progress, while simultaneously providing new sources of identification, entertainment, and pleasure for millions of people.[41] Nineteenth-century international exhibitions also brought together previously diverse social practices from markets, fairs, festivals, circuses, and salons and reorganized them into what Maurice Roche calls a "performance complex" that articulated new understandings of "imagined community," and promoted the formation of new international institutions, organizations, and corporations.[42] For Benjamin, these exhibitions were also part of the reimagining and reorganization of modern urban life around modern *spaces of spectacle* and the consumer and tourist activities and commodities associated with them. He saw them as unprecedented manifestations of accumulation, as well as providers of phantasmagoria, and purveyors of new forms of social and political distraction.[43] Late in the nineteenth century, the exhibitions also created notable sites for displays of new pedagogical approaches to exercise and new models for balancing nationalist and internationalist aspirations that influenced the emergence of the International Olympic Committee and the "modern" Olympic Games.

Capitalism, imperialism, national and international exhibitions

After the fifth century CE, many of the trade-oriented fairs and religious festivals that had long been popular throughout various parts of the Roman Empire were reconstituted under the sponsorship and protection of the Catholic Church and continued to provide regularly scheduled opportunities for communities to celebrate and traders and travelers to assemble.[44] Whereas medieval *markets* provided goods for local people, and *festivals* celebrated local community life while providing opportunities for religious observance, pageantry, and entertainment, *fairs* typically ran for more extended periods and attracted merchants from farther away with more exotic merchandise.[45] In the fragmented social and political environments of early medieval Europe, fairs soon grew to play a more significant role in local economies and cultures. For example, during the thirteenth and fourteenth centuries, major trade fairs in the Champagne and Brie districts of France, positioned at the meeting point of old Roman roads, emerged as key nodal points in a strengthening international circuit of northern and southern European commerce.[46] Fernand Braudel points to the significance of these fairs as an "obvious sign" of the merging of the burgeoning industrial development of northern Europe with the wealthier, trade-centered, world of southern Europe, and its strong connections to the "accelerating presence of Islam and Byzantium."[47] Local aristocratic and administrative authorities recognized the economic value of the fairs and authorized the construction of permanent warehouses and sales booths. They also guaranteed safe travel within their regions to and from the fairs and, in the spirit of promoting attendance, they allowed people from different places a degree of latitude over their behavior and relaxed local restrictions on popular amusements, such as card games and dice.[48]

Not unlike the situation a millennium and a half earlier with Greek *agones*, competition arose between communities in Europe over the staging of fairs, their frequency and duration because of the economic advantages and status they appeared to bring to sponsoring communities and their rulers. By the sixteenth century, large medieval fairs had developed in places as diverse as Paris, Antwerp, Bergen op Zoom, Frankfurt, Leipzig, Medina del Campo, Lyons, Besançon, Beaucaire, and Nijni-Novogorod.[49] In addition to being "festive crossroads of commerce," these fairs provided vital, if temporary, spaces for cross-cultural association and popular entertainment. Mattelart argues that the fairs operated as medieval "territories of exception." Not only did they provide momentary reductions in restrictions around cultural or recreational behavior, they provided sites for free trade at a time when commerce was dominated by "tolls, taxes and privileges."[50]

With the instabilities and violence of frequent warfare, and the emergence of more fixed and permanent circuits of exchange in northern Europe during the eighteenth century, the episodic economic encounters characteristic of the fairs were gradually replaced by "a continuous flow of trade."[51] During the seventeenth century, Amsterdam and London, in particular, were home to powerful imperial trading agencies such as the Dutch East India Company and the British East India Company. The two cities developed successful stock exchanges, money markets, and banking innovations, along with spectacular urban architecture and new urban shops. As trade fairs lost much of their former economic role in smaller communities, what remained was their provision of festival entertainments. European fairs often retained cultural elements of their atmospheres of "exception" insofar as they provided opportunities for expressions of the carnivalesque and for hedonistic excess that were often at odds with what I described in the last chapter as a growing "bourgeois will to refinement." These could include games of various sorts involving hopping or jumping, animal baiting, tests of strength, or other forms of physical prowess. Through the eighteenth century, local and regional fairs also became sites for circus-style entertainments, including the "exhibition" of "unusual" or so-called "exotic" animals and peoples.[52]

However, in major European cities, a new "industrial exhibition formula" was emerging as a key organizing principle for large-scale public events. Mattelart argues that the formula was first initiated in post-revolutionary France in the context of newly imagined campaigns to rid the Republic "of barriers of all kinds that stood in the way of trade under the Old Regime."[53] The first industrial exhibition in France occurred in 1798 when the French director of the Interior decreed "an annual public exposition of the products of French industry."[54] The exposition had the double goal of putting French industrial products on display, promoting innovation and bringing industry closer to society, and "to stimulate French entrepreneurs in the struggle against Monarchic England." Many features of this first industrial exhibition had the character of a "war campaign," accompanied by competitive agonistic sentiment. Military processions, trumpeters, drummers, heralds, orchestras, and artists surrounded a gallery of 68 arcades, with medals, citations, and honorable mentions awarded to participants in various categories, including a gold medal to be awarded to "the exhibitor 'who did the most harm to English industry.'"[55] Interestingly, even though the exhibition itself focused on industry, a number of athletic and "sporting" contests, including running, wrestling, and horse racing, also took part in the grounds of the exhibition.[56]

Despite the presence of these activities, new industrial exhibitions in France were not conceived primarily as events and spaces for face-to-face trade nor festive amusement; rather, they were conceived to promote the spectacles of *industrial technology* and capitalist *entrepreneurial agonism*. On the surface, their major function was display. However, the same director of the interior who initiated the industrial exhibition formula was also instrumental in the expansions of general statistics in France. Another government official, responsible for executing the statistical measurement of the French population, "gave the inaugural speech at the first national exposition."[57] Thus the display of national production occurred simultaneously with the rational expansion of new forms of measurement and the administration of populations. In this sense, Mattelart concludes, these early industrial exhibitions were as much "life-size laboratories" as spectacles of industrial technology. The complexity of the machines they displayed suggested, for some adherents, that the "'division of labor,' theorized by Adam Smith in 1776, was gaining in perfection."[58]

France sponsored more than ten national industrial exhibitions from the late eighteenth century through the Napoleonic period and into the 1840s, and similar industrial exhibitions sprung up in other parts of Europe during this time.[59] The last of the French industrial exhibitions, held in 1849, had more than 4,500 exhibitors and stayed open for six months. Cultural and political elites in England were inspired to organize a royal commission to stage their own large-scale exhibition in London in 1851.[60] With the staging of the Great Exhibition of the Works of Industry of All Nations at Crystal Palace, London, in 1851, the French *national* industrial exhibition formula was reconceptualized as an *international* celebration of capitalist industrial modernity and the forms of "universal association" it seemingly made possible.[61] Joseph Paxton, the architect of Crystal Palace, designed the building as a symbol of a new era of reason. The building, and the exhibition it housed, would be a "faithful witness and a living image of the stage humanity has reached along this great path toward unification."[62] The London exhibition was thus conceived to display advancements in human knowledge, linking these both to England's growing power and imperial confidence and to the romantic dream of peaceful human unification through industrial progress.

Dreams of progress and unification were linked to ideas of human perfectibility through science, rational planning, and industrial engineering. As "life-size laboratories," industrial and international exhibitions and expos were not only influenced by new initiatives of statistical classification and measurement, they were also shaped by new ideas about personal and social hygiene. At the request of the French government, the 1851 London Exhibition became host to the first international conference on sanitation.[63] Earlier in the century, Henri Saint-Simon had begun to use the metaphor of "hygiene" in the development of his administratively planned "social physiology." Each historical regime, Saint-Simon argued, produces a "sanitary regime" that corresponds to its needs. At the "adult" stage of development, in mature industrial societies, the "social body" maintains its "health" when at work. If an "adult" society retains the sanitary regime from its "age of childhood," the resulting tensions can lead to "a veritable and immense retrogression toward barbarism."[64]

There were notable hygienist movements in Europe through the early years of the nineteenth century to control the "odors of the poor" and, supposedly, those of different "races," and to broadly sanitize and deodorize public and private spaces.[65] Issues of public sanitation and hygiene, and a quest for universal standards, were debated at all of the major nineteenth-century expositions and, as Mattelart suggests, served as a background for later debates in Europe over the nature of crowds.[66] Hygiene was one of the rationales that led Louis-Napoléon Bonaparte (Napoleon III) to embark on a massive project of creative destruction in Paris after the dissolution of the French Republic in 1852 and his ascendancy to the position of emperor. There had been repeated plans to "modernize" the medieval portions of Paris during the 1830s and 1840s, to improve sanitation, commerce, and transportation within the city, with modest success.[67]

But there was no consensus on any broad scale to remake the city's organization and infrastructure. Consensus was challenged by the long traditions of Parisian radicalism, the ongoing popularity of both republican and socialist ideas, and lingering resentments remaining from the revolutionary conflict of 1848. Many of Paris's politically radical and avant-garde groups had deep roots in the dense and largely inaccessible labyrinth of the medieval city. Louis-Napoléon's status as emperor allowed him to bypass political opposition to initiate an extraordinary project of creative destruction that managed to combine a variety of social and political objectives: improvements in health and hygiene; improvement of "free circulation" and movement for commercial purposes and for military responses to radicalism; and the promotion of a grand spectacle of revitalization to help establish legitimacy and social integration for his new imperial regime.

Between the early 1850s and 1870, hundreds of buildings in the medieval remnants of the city were destroyed and replaced with more than 80 kilometers of rationally planned tree-lined boulevards, along with numerous parks and major building projects aimed at harmonizing architectural styles and colors.[68] The man responsible for executing this "modernization" of Paris, Baron Georges-Eugène Haussmann, designed a city aimed at the promotion of consumerism and leisure – a city, in Berman's words, "of enticing spectacle, a visual and sensual feast."[69] Included in Haussmann's massive program were Louis-Napoléon's plans to upstage the 1851 London exhibition with a Parisian International Exposition in 1855. The goal was to position Paris, and the new French imperial order, as the "capital of modernity," a contemporary incarnation of the role once played by imperial Rome. Yet the destructive side of the creation of "modern" Paris was undeniable: as T. J. Clark points out, by Haussmann's own reckoning, more than 350,000 Parisians were displaced over the 17 years of the project.[70]

This massive program of modernization was subject to intense criticism and prompted a wave of self-reflection among Parisian artists and authors about the changing nature of the city, its conquest by bourgeois forces and interests, and transformation into a city of phantasmagoria, of spectacle, consumption, and leisure. Critics argued that Haussmann had destroyed the "multiformity" of Paris and "killed the street and the *quartier*."[71] T. J. Clark claims that spectacle, in this sense, had become *the new form* in which capitalism in Paris was representing itself, disguising the continued existence of class relations behind the splendor of the boulevards and the pleasures of outdoor cafés, while at the same time announcing the controlling presence of capital in new public spaces. Yet there was some irony in the fact that the displacement of workers to the fringes of the city created new and comparatively homogeneous working-class communities, where workers' groups found it easier to meet and organize.[72] Moreover, in some quarters there was a degree of grudging recognition of Parisian modernity as a space and time of contradiction and ambivalence, where brutal exploitation was juxtaposed with new pleasures of bourgeois consumption and the meanderings of *flâneurs*.

The ambivalent attitude to Parisian modernity – acknowledging, as Baudelaire put it famously, "the ephemeral, the fugitive, the contingent" as one half of art and "the eternal and immutable" as the other – was characteristic of the spread of modernist culture in other places.[73] In a world of extraordinary change and disruption, late nineteenth-century modernisms were polyglot conceptions, cultural mazeways, open to a variety of interpretations and resyntheses dependent upon the geographical location of their expression in major capitals of the world, with shifting associations with class, gender, and colonialism, and the paradox of combining an ideal of heroic unfettered artistic achievement with a need to survive in a commercial marketplace. The emergence of modernist cultural practice in Europe and North America before World War I represented at once a self-conscious break from earlier styles, and a reflexive recycling, reconstitution, and sometimes resynthesis of romantic and realist themes and of these styles, with criticisms or celebrations of the new industrial civilization and new modes of representation and experimentation. In Harvey's words: "Modernism internalized its own maelstrom of ambiguities, contradictions, and pulsating aesthetic changes at the same time as it sought to affect the aesthetics of everyday life."[74]

As a monument to French imperial modernization, the 1855 Exposition Universelle reflected and articulated themes that fed such ambiguities and contradictions. On the one hand, it drew criticism from artists and socialist intellectuals as an extension of capitalist exploitation and destruction. On the other hand, it appeared to have successfully combined imperial ambition with the dream of Saint-Simon and his later followers – to achieve harmony, social, and moral progress through planning and industrial and economic development. Outside of political and avant-garde intellectual circles, the exposition was hugely popular. Indeed, extraordinary popularity was a defining characteristic of all of the major nineteenth-century European exhibitions. Visitors experienced new public urban spaces that were at once sanitized, safe, and thrilling, where the products and cultures of the "world" were on display in an accessible way, and where visitors could purchase novel and otherwise unavailable consumer items and souvenirs.[75]

Roche argues that while the expositions were organized by political, economic, and cultural elites, they created spaces that were comparatively democratized for the time, opening up new pleasures to working-class male populations. Women were mostly addressed in their domestic and familial roles, as well as through representations of their sexuality and relationships with men. But expositions also provided temporary degrees of freedom and intense experience through the anonymity of crowds, as well as meeting places for the creation of feminist organizations and the progressive discussions of women's rights in modern life. In Roche's opinion, nineteenth-century expositions also provided opportunities for encounters with visitors from other races and cultures and, within the limits of a typically colonial framing, opened up cosmopolitan and sometimes progressive discussions of race.[76] For example, Susan Brownell recounts how debates in response to racist displays of otherness at the St Louis World's Fair in 1904 helped move the field of anthropology in the United States to embrace a more culturally relativistic stance.[77]

An even more notable example is "the Exhibit of American Negroes," organized for the 1900 Paris international exhibition with the assistance of the sociologist W. E. B. Du Bois to commemorate the lives of African Americans and to demonstrate their pride and progress. Du Bois described it as "an honest, straightforward exhibit of a small nation of people, picturing their life and development without apology or gloss, and above all made by themselves."[78] The exhibit took up nearly a quarter of the exhibition space allocated to the United States and included a statue of the prominent nineteenth-century reformer and abolitionist Frederick Douglass; books of bound patents awarded to African Americans; displays of Du Bois's sociological studies in Atlanta; a bibliography of African-American writing organized by the Library of Congress; and hundreds of photographs of African Americans from all walks of life, staged to reveal their humanity in opposition both to popular prejudice and to the physiological reductionism of racial science.[79]

There were 17,000 exhibitors at the London Crystal Palace exhibition in 1851 and the fair attracted more than 6 million people over a period of 141 days. After the 1855 Exposition Universelle, there were four more major Parisian expositions, in 1867, 1878, 1889, and 1900. Thirty-two million people visited the Paris Exposition of 1889, and the Paris Exposition that closed the century ran for 205 days, attracting more than 48 million visitors and featuring 83,000 exhibitors.[80] There were also major expositions in London in 1862, Vienna in 1863, Philadelphia in 1876, Chicago in 1893, and St Louis in 1904, as well as a myriad of large trade fairs and "imperial" or "colonial" exhibitions staged in major cities in powerful European colonizing nations, including Berlin, Amsterdam, Brussels, Barcelona, and Edinburgh.[81] The popularity of exhibition spectacles also spread rapidly through European colonies, championed by colonial business elites and endorsed by many local supporters, as opportunities to stage "modernity" outside the West. Although formats for these exhibitions often differed, large-scale industrial exhibitions were hosted in cities such as Sydney, Calcutta, Buenos Aires, Rio de Janeiro, Bogota, Bombay, and São Paulo.[82] Even in East Asia, where there was an initial lack of interest in expositions, several major industrial fairs and exhibitions were staged in Tokyo, Hanoi, and Nanking between the late 1870s and 1910.

The initial understanding of "unification" in European international expositions simply meant "openness" to "all the products of human labour." According to Mattelart, this was the nineteenth-century modernist dream of internationalization: the recovery of an imagined "lost paradise of human community and communion" through open communication, and the unification and perfection of labor to end human misery, ignorance, and social division.[83] But this dream of internationalization was always in tension with industrial progress as an expression of national pride and intense interstate competition for "free trade," leading to often violent struggles over geopolitical space.[84] The extent to which large-scale industrial expositions should have a *national* versus *international* focus was debated intensely in different countries, although there can be little doubt that even international exhibitions were pursued for nationalist reasons, and played a role in strengthening nations as "imagined communities."[85] Yet the liberal reformist dream of reconciling social antagonisms through the free circulation of ideas, trade, capital, and planned technological innovation was as a major theme throughout the nineteenth-century expositions.[86] In Roche's view, such tensions contributed to the cultural ambiguity and "multidimensional" character of these spectacles of modernity. As communicative events, they dramatized a variety of apparent contradictions and distinctions: not just modern and non-modern, but also local and non-local, national and international.[87]

To these dualisms I would add tensions between the educative and commercial, and cosmopolitan and orientalist, characters of international expositions. In the first instance, as in Paris, nineteenth-century expositions almost immediately tied their vision of internationalism to the promotion of tourism and consumerism.[88] Unlike industrial exhibitions staged earlier in the century, late twentieth-century European and US expositions initiated a policy of charging people for admission and encouraged a proliferation of commercial entertainments as part of the main exhibits or in addition to them. This created a commodity value to attendance and encouraged commercial face-to-face exchanges at the expositions. Part of this was undoubtedly driven by economic necessity. Increasing "place-based" competition between cities to stage international exhibitions created an environment of civic and national one-upmanship, where local boosters and administrators tried to outdo previous expositions, with increasingly grand projects for display and escalating costs as a result. For example, the scale and cost of the World's Columbian Exposition in Chicago in 1893 was influenced by the organizing committee's desire to outdo the spectacle associated with the exposition in Paris in 1889, where the Eiffel Tower was first unveiled.

Under these circumstances, the production of modern spaces of urban spectacle accelerated their integration into the realms of consumption and popular commercial entertainment. Nineteenth- and early twentieth-century exhibitions were promoted as events that provided rich and varied *educative* experiences based on exposure to the world's technological wonders and cultural differences, as well as salon-style cultural displays and competitions. Yet, at the same time, opportunities to purchase goods and a push to find newer and more spectacular means to entertain visitors became more prominent aspects of the exposition experience. Walter Benjamin suggests that the expositions had become "places of pilgrimage to the commodity fetish" as early as 1855.[89] Tourism and consumer activity associated with these exhibitions was revealing new capacities for cities to act as mechanisms of accumulation in themselves. But, for some critics, whatever economic benefits might be associated with exhibitions as sites for consumption were offset by a negatively perceived "drift toward amusement."[90] By the end of the nineteenth century, international expositions had moved substantially away from ritualistic celebrations of pedagogy, universalism, and progress in favor of somewhat less ritualized spectacles of commerce and entertainment.

Even so, the exhibitions continued to provide important opportunities to create what Roche calls "a new level and form of public culture."[91] This national and international public culture had two significant dimensions. Its most concrete manifestations lay in the numerous international agreements in trade, patents, diffusion of technology, and regulation of communications that emerged from interstate discussions and negotiations that occurred during the various expositions. The self-conscious commitment to internationalism and the immense public visibility of the expositions created opportunities for new quasi-governmental organizations and new interstate agreements designed to facilitate international communication, regulate the uses of new communications technologies, suppress barriers to the exchange of goods, and provide new models of political cooperation. Early examples included the International Telegraph Office in 1865 (later renamed the International Telegraph Union, ITU), the Universal Postal Union of 1874, and the International Bureau of Weights and Measures of 1875.[92]

As a second dimension of public culture, nineteenth-century international expositions exposed millions of people to romantic visions of internationalism and "universal association" which enabled the formation of uniquely new *voluntary* international associations, some-times with varied political orientations, such as the International Red Cross, the International Workingmen's Association, the International Esperanto Movement, and, by the end of the century, the International Olympic Committee (IOC). At the same time, the ritualized and cer-emonial trappings of large-scale expositions – processions, speeches, flags, anthems, medals, and marches – articulated a vision of public culture strongly focused on the production of social order at a time of considerable social unrest in many parts of Europe.[93] Tony Bennett suggests, that the making of spectacle in these instances was depend-ent upon the production of orderly audiences and on the surveillance, self-monitoring, and self-regulation of bodies and behaviors – the modes of governmentality – necessary to allow such large and well-attended events to occur without disruption.[94]

In addition, under the guise of internationalism, major nineteenth-century expositions in Europe and its colonies *exported* Eurocentric conceptions of modern progress, often with powerful and long-lasting effects. In this regard, Mattelart argues that the expositions played an important role in promoting a great wave of "Europeanization" in countries such as Brazil, Mexico, and Argentina. For example, late nineteenth- and early twentieth-century Brazilian elites elevated the ideas of August Comte, and his "positive philosophy," to the status of a cult. Comteanism merged with liberalism in Brazil to create a hybrid ideological discourse that celebrated modern rationality as a path to progress on the one hand, yet provided philosophical legiti-mation for an iron commitment to social order on the other. Mexican General Porfirio Díaz also took up Comtean thinking between 1884 and 1911 under the influence of advisors who claimed positivist "sci-entific" guidance in their brutal suppression of indigenous people. In a somewhat different register, the spread of internationalist novelty in late nineteenth-century Argentina resulted in the embrace of Parisian high culture by Argentinian elites as the desirable model for "legiti-mate culture."[95]

Notwithstanding Du Bois's exhibit of American negroes, interna-tional exhibitions more often provided collective representations of "otherness" that were racist and layered with Orientalism. Mitchell notes, for example, that the Egyptian delegation en route to the Eighth International Congress of Orientalism in Stockholm in the summer of 1889 stopped for a visit to the Paris exhibition. They were disgusted by the Egyptian exhibit, built by the French to repre-sent a street of medieval Cairo, made deliberately chaotic and dirty, crowded with stalls of merchant hucksters selling perfumes, pastries, and donkey rides. Worst of all, the "mosque" in the Egyptian exhibit was little more than a facade made into a coffee house and featuring "Egyptian girls" performing dances, where "dervishes whirled."[96] According to Mitchell, this representation of otherness made the "object" world seem "real" by implication. Displays of "human zoos," of all kinds at the exhibitions – such as mock Egyptian towns, "negro," "Philippine," or "Indian" villages – represented the world "as a thing to be viewed" and implied the reality of the existing referent or object.

This racist display of "otherness" was frequently integrated into the privileged observational mode of western scholarly discourse and given the trappings of science. Through much of the nineteenth century – in the thrall of "racial science," anthropometric measurement, and social Darwinism – ethnologists, anthropologists, and many sociologists were highly focused on the classification and measurement of apparent biological, as well as cultural, differences between human "races."[97] Mitchell notes that it was not uncommon for nineteenth-century ethnologists and anthropologists to *display* living "examples" of members of so-called "primitive" or "savage" cultures during talks or symposia.[98] A prominent American anthropologist was also one of the organizers of the infamous "anthropology days" at the 1904 St Louis World's Fair, where North American indigenous peoples, Africans, Asians, and Filipinos involved in the Fair's cultural exhibits were invited to compete in western sporting activities and were closely studied.[99] According to Mitchell, one ideological result of such exhibitions of otherness was the tendency of westerners, including colonial administrators who had actually visited Africa or the Orient, to naturally adopt the role of "observer" and even to interpret their new surroundings through the frame of their exposure to prior orientalizing and racist representations.[100] Through such representations, international expositions revealed a powerful ideological tendency to stage modernity as *a spectacle of binary division*, of past versus present, primitive versus modern, the exotic versus rational, and uncivilized versus civilized.

From international expositions to "Olympic" sporting spectacles

Nineteenth-century international exhibitions were important precedents for the advent of the Olympics as an international sporting spectacle in the twentieth century, as well as harbingers of the contradictions and problems that the Olympics would later face. Among others, these included the ideas of universal association and unification, juxtaposed with awards given to victorious national "representatives"; a commitment to peace, matched with the appropriation of quasi-militaristic parades, anthems, and pageantry; an obsession with classification and the statistical measurement of success; a concern for both physical *and* social hygiene; tension between the pursuit of excellence as a form of pedagogy or ritualized action and the fear of de-ritualizing commerce and "useless" public distraction; and tension between the dream of unification and the (uneven) competition between cities and countries to stage large-scale international events.

Cultural fragments and memories of the ancient Greek games at Olympia are evident throughout the history of modern Europe and its colonies, and have been synthesized and resynthesized in differing ways and for differing purposes. John Horne and Garry Whannel note, for example, that Shakespeare and Milton both mentioned the Olympic Games in their work, as did Goethe, Rousseau, Byron, and Voltaire.[101] There was an "Olimpick Games" in the Cotswold district of England in the early seventeenth century, running on and off for the next two centuries and featuring competition in the games and contests typical of European fairs of the era, such as stick fighting, wrestling, sack jumping, and shin kicking. There are also references to "Olympic Games" in the *Encyclopedia* prepared in France by Denis Diderot and Jean le Rond d'Alembert in 1751–2. In post-revolutionary France in the 1790s, the excitement of creating a new society prompted discussions about the possibility of staging "French Olympiads," proposed to be *"similar to those of the Greeks"* (emphasis in original).[102] In addition, there were athletic events that designated themselves as "Olympics," organized on the Champ de Mars in Paris, open to all competitors and held in conjunction with a host of other festivals staged during the early years of the new Republic.[103]

Horne and Whannel document numerous other "multi-sport events" in Switzerland, Sweden, Germany, Canada, and Hungary that referenced "Olympics," from the mid-eighteenth through the late nineteenth centuries, as well as many references to "Olympics" in the names of a variety of facilities, circus events, and shows such as the Olympia Hall in London and the Cirque-Olympique in Paris.[104] Walter Borgers also reveals metaphorical references to Olympics in descriptions of several of the nineteenth-century international exhibitions. For example, in 1851, the English magazine *The Spectator* referenced entrepreneurial agonism by describing the Crystal Palace Exhibition as "This Olympic Game of industry, this tournament of commerce."[105] In 1878, a German commission report on the French Exhibition Universelle chose instead to reference the idea of universal association: "What the Olympic Games were to all the tribes of the Greeks, that are in the spirit of modern times the universal exhibitions to all tribes, all nations of the civilized world."[106]

None of the metaphors or agonistic and other performative practices associated with these events or venues had anything to do with the ancient Greek Olympics, despite references to the word and occasional uses of classical imagery.[107] Rather, they were variously connected to longstanding traditions of European festival, fair, or carnival amusements; early commercially oriented athletic contests and displays in Europe and North America; new, nationally distinctive, promotions of health, hygiene, and "scientific" physical education and training; romanticized conceptions of progress and unity through industry; or agonistic representations of capitalist competitiveness. To reiterate my argument from the last chapter, prior to the middle of the nineteenth century there was only an inchoate idea of an independent or unified object domain called "sport," few institutional mechanisms for organizing sport as a distinctive field of practice, and no consensus on the extent to which sport could or should articulate moral principles.

Institutionally and culturally like modernism more broadly, sport in Europe and North America was a jumble of diverse practices and discourses, riddled with cultural ambiguities and contradictions. These included tensions between promoters of sport for commerce and those who saw sport's value in respect to military training, rational recreation, or health. Tensions also existed between muscular Christian "evangelists for exercise" and critics who (again) variously saw sports as: useless and unproductive activities in an age of industriousness; as "distractions" from an Aristotelian *vita contemplativa*, emphasizing the "higher" cultural pursuits of the mind; or, as promoters of seemingly irrational, infantile, and potentially dangerous crowd behavior. Even metaphorically, references to athletics, or games, and especially the idea of "Olympic Games," had the character of "floating signifiers" whose meanings could be pushed in this or that direction by differing economic or political interests.

For example, the 1850 "Olympics," noted in the previous chapter, organized in Much Wenlock, England by Dr William Penny Brookes, drew on a combination of festival, health, and moral reform motifs. His "Olympic Games" were open to all competitors, combined

117

"fun" festival events with serious competitions, and offered cash prizes as incentives. Brookes noted how, in his view, "such meetings as these bring out free minds, free opinions, free enterprises, free competition for every man in every grade of life. The Olympic Games bring together different classes and make them social and neighborly."[108] An ardent supporter of physical education in schools to promote "manliness of character," "temperance," and "moral virtues," Brookes went on to co-found a British "National Olympian Association" in 1865.[109] A few years earlier, Liverpool gymnasiarch, John Hulley, working with John Melly – a local philanthropist, ex-Rugby School graduate, social and moral reformer – staged Olympic festivals in Liverpool in 1862 and 1863 that drew thousands of spectators. Horne and Whannel argue that Hulley and Melly proposed to "revive ideas of physical perfection, drawing on what they knew of the ancient Olympic Games, and claimed the Liverpool Olympic Festivals 'were organised on the lines of the ancient Greek ones.'"[110] Brookes and the National Olympic Association went on to organize several well-attended national Olympic Games in London, although the Games were faced with strong opposition from the conservative Amateur Athletic Cub, who favored a more exclusive vision of sport that would only be open to amateurs.[111]

Outside of England, the poet and editor Panagiotis Soutsos had been lobbying the Greek government for Olympic Games to celebrate Greek independence from the Ottoman Empire, only to be told that his energy might be better spent organizing an industrial exhibition.[112] Eventually, a wealthy Greek businessman, Evangelis Zappas, privately supported a "revival" of the Greek Olympic Games, resulting in an "Olympics" staged in Athens in 1859 in conjunction with a national industrial exhibition. Zappas subsequently paid to rebuild the Panathenaic Stadium, where a successful Olympic Games was held in 1870, during another large industrial exhibition. These early Greek Olympics featured cash prizes and subsidized travel for participants, paid for by the Zappas family and other donors. Two more Greek Olympics, in 1875 and 1889, were organized and run by a government administrator in charge of "public gymnasia" and were "reformed" to include competition only open to university student "amateurs."[113]

This is the context in which Baron Pierre de Coubertin decided to create an International Olympic Committee (IOC) and envisioned the organization and staging of *international*, rather than national, Olympic Games. The aristocratic young Coubertin grew up in the turbulent time of imperial France's military defeat at the hands of

Prussian forces in 1870, and the subsequent creation of the third French Republic, as well as the unrest of the short-lived Paris Commune in 1871 and its violent suppression. John MacAloon provides a detailed discussion of his formative years, including his early exposure to Hellenism, his feelings of shame at France's wartime losses to Prussia, and his attraction to the conservative and reformist ideas of the French engineer and sociologist Frederic Le Play, among other influences.[114] There is no need to go over this biographical material again here. Still, it is analytically useful, I think, to offer a brief review of the broader intellectual and political milieu surrounding Coubertin in the 1880s and 1890s.[115] It is worth highlighting Le Play here because he provides an important mediating presence between Coubertin's ideas about science and pedagogy, French international exhibitions, and his project of creating a modern international Olympic "movement."

Le Play had begun his career as an engineer who conducted detailed statistical studies of the lives of workers in the mining industry in Germany, followed by forensically detailed analyses of the family budgets of the "laboring poor."[116] He was a political conservative, but also saw himself as a social reformer who admired the technical skill of workers and was strongly critical of the gap between rich and poor. Unsettled by France's half-century of repeated political disturbances, Le Play became disillusioned with purely "rational" statistical measurement and gradually adopted a more narrative approach to research, based on personal observation. As Theodore Porter suggests, Le Play's views were shaped by a concern for lost solidarities of the past, rooted in rural family life and the traditional ties "of seigneurs and *patrons* to the laboring poor."[117] The "best observer," Le Play argued, "is a man with responsibility for the observed, as when a patron knows and looks out for his laborers or a landlord for his tenants."[118]

Napoleon III gave Le Play the task of organizing both the 1855 and 1867 Paris international expositions. Both exhibitions put Le Play's aptitude for organization, classification, and social analysis on display. The 1855 exhibition was centered on a new and spectacularly designed Palais de l'Industrie and featured an extensive model of classification of everything from wine to human variation, with many exhibits strongly influenced by Saint-Simonian themes.[119] For the 1867 Exhibition, Le Play designed an even more spectacular stadium-like venue, surrounded by seven rings of attractions, consisting of more than 200 national pavilions, colonial exhibits, restaurants, shops, and other forms of amusement, with a central display of "national measuring systems" of the world. Exhibitions of physical exercise and education had an official place in the program, too, including a simulated Saxonian gymnastics academy and displays of gymnastic apparatus.[120] There were also rowing races between teams representing different nations and a major exhibition of French bicycles, displayed both as wonders of modern technology and as vehicles for mass public recreation.[121]

Amidst other spectacles of the 1867 exhibition, Le Play's strongly paternalistic worldview was evident in his decision to make industrial workers objects of exhibition while he studied them. There have been many commentaries in recent years on the racist and imperialist character of exhibits at the nineteenth- and early twentieth-century international expositions, but far less attention has been paid to similar representations of workers. In Le Play's case, workers were displayed as objects of spectacle in a "zoo-like fashion" by a sociologist who saw himself in the paternalistic role of patron-reformer.[122] In subsequent years, in studies of small communities, Le Play went on to stress what he believed were the "advantages of communities held together by bonds of affection between owners and workers, the poor and the rich."[123] From this perspective, like virtually all nineteenth-century views of social reform, conservative or liberal, there was simply no acknowledgment that relations between workers and capitalists might be fundamentally exploitative, or that their interests might be structurally at odds with one another. The workers at the exhibition appear to have had a far better understanding of this than Le Play. As Jacques Rancière points out, their response was to discuss new ways of organizing labor to preserve dignity, lower costs, and improve products. This led to the creation of worker associations that became key sites of opposition to the French imperial order in the 1870s.[124]

Coubertin studied in university with the prominent historian Hippolyte Taine, where, in addition to Le Play, he was exposed to the writing of reform-minded cultural conservatives, such as Alexis de Tocqueville. Taine is widely known as a thinker who retained a belief in reason, but rejected the idea of progress through science and unfettered democracy. He was suspicious of what he took to be the potentially irrational aspects of mass political movements and, like Tocqueville, of the capacity for democracies to end up as "tyrannies" of the majority.[125] For these reasons, he saw the British parliamentary system, with its balance of appointed peers and elected parliamentarians, to be superior to the French republican system. The young Coubertin shared Taine's interest in British politics and culture. Historians have suggested that he read Thomas Hughes's 1857 novel,

Tom Brown's School Days, as a teenager and was enamored with its romanticized representation of athletics in British public school life.[126] Some writers have suggested that it was Taine who encouraged Coubertin in 1883 to visit England for the first time, where he toured Rugby School, English universities, and athletic facilities, and took enthusiastic notes on English physical education and sport.[127]

Through the 1880s, Coubertin appears to have been influenced by Le Play's interest in education and moral reform as well as his penchant for classification and methods of observation.[128] I think, to this, we can also add the influence of Le Play's paternalistic perspective on the achievement of harmony and social solidarity. Coubertin joined the academic and reform associations led by Le Play and published in their journals, including a report on English physical education and sport in 1883 and another essay in 1889. In turn, Le Play supported Coubertin's efforts to build physical education as part of a project to strengthen French youth and provide them with appropriate physical and moral training.[129]

In 1889, at Brookes's invitation, Coubertin visited Much Wenlock and was introduced to the idea of a national "Olympic Games." However, according to Borgers, the idea of creating "international" Olympics was more inspired by the 1889 international French exhibition, which combined a centenary celebration of French republicanism with powerful internationalist themes. In an essay published in 1890, Coubertin expressed the thrill of witnessing the opening ceremonies, assisting a friend prepare one of the exhibits, and viewing the Eiffel Tower, illuminated, at night, which seemed "an appearance of supernatural construction."[130] In this context, he went on to add: "the 'Marseillaise' had lost all its bellicose character, it was an anthem of joy, an ode of peace." The exhibition, he believed, created an atmosphere of "unanimous admiration ... a type of union, of brotherhood that nations only know on the day after a great victory or when an irresistible stream of enthusiasm seizes them."[131]

This is an astonishing statement for two reasons. First, beyond the confines of the exhibition, the Marseillaise continued to be as "bellicose" as ever. France ruled the second-largest colonial empire in the world in the late nineteenth century. Through a combination of diplomacy and military force, France made colonial incursions from the 1870s through the 1890s into Tunisia, Dahomey (now Benin), French Sudan (now Mali), the "French" Congo, Guinea, Taiwan, China, and Polynesia, to name just a few regions.[132] Second, there is a hugely ironic aspect to Coubertin's analogy between the collective national effervescence that nations show after a "great victory," and the joyful unity of the peaceful "brotherhood of nations," unless one takes the view that nations who are achieving such great victories are, through their empires, forcibly creating the foundation for this peaceful international "brotherhood."

If anything, exercise and athletic practices had taken a *more* bellicose turn in Europe through the nineteenth century. This was especially true in Britain after the 1860s through a strengthening connection between training for sport, British imperialism, and militaristic conceptions of masculinity.[133] In France, following the Franco-Prussian war, gymnastic exercise became more closely connected with national military mobilization and the defense of republican ideals: exercise was made compulsory in schools, and gymnastic festivals and fairs, including demonstrations at the international exhibitions, were replete with flags and other national symbols.[134] However, just as in England, there were also countering discourses and opinions. For example, at the very moment that regular physical exercise through gymnastics and games was incorporated into French school curricula, with a view to strengthening masculinity for service to the Republic, there were those who endorsed gymnastic exercise to promote a "catholicized version of the Christian order," in opposition to republicanism and other secular influences.[135] There was also widely felt suspicion that acrobatics of any type, and displays of individual strength or athletic virtuosity, were too closely tied historically to festive and often "disreputable" popular recreational and carnival traditions.

This latter concern was almost a reflex among conservative Catholics, but it had a more radical history too, expressed in France as early as 1574 in a widely read book by Étienne de La Boétie, *Le Discours sur la Servitude Volontaire* (Discourse of Voluntary Servitude). Echoing archaic criticisms of the distractions of "bread and circuses," de La Boétie saw games and pastimes as "drugs," having the effect of making "free men effeminate" through their pleasures "so as to make them more docile for the yolk." He added, "to entertain an entire people in idleness, amusement" and "satisfy its vices" had become over time "an aid to governments that only have the means to take care of the pleasures of the moneyed classes."[136] Mattelart comments that the de La Boétie text "was still a beacon in the nineteenth century" and inspired a great deal of critical commentary in France about the political and ideological implications of amusements for the reproduction of relations of power. However, few writers took up his key point about the "voluntary" nature of servitude, about *why*, when given the choice, individuals will fight for practices that enable their servitude rather than their salvation.[137]

Coubertin himself had strongly promoted a national program of physical education to strengthen the bodies and the "spirit" of French youth, suspecting that the popularity of the Turner gymnastics movement explained the physical superiority of German troops during the defeat of the imperial regime in 1870. But it also seems clear that he was wrestling throughout the 1890s with how to reconcile these nationalist sympathies with the romantic idea of removing sport from petty nationalist political ambitions. In this regard, Quanz argues that Coubertin's romantic vision of joyful internationalism was due to his growing contact with fin-de-siècle "liberal pacifism" and the peace movement.[138] Still, I would be extremely hesitant to push this argument about Coubertin's pacifism too far. Coubertin continued to express a commitment to French colonial policy and stated his strong admiration for Jules Ferry, colonial apologist extraordinaire and French premier for several years during the early 1880s.

Ferry had a dual view of colonialism: as capitalist realpolitik, and as an imagined international cultural obligation. In the first instance, he saw colonialism as an obvious strategy of survival in the highly competitive world of nineteenth-century international capitalism. As Raymond Betts points out, Ferry recognized "the workings of the capitalist industrial machine: keen economic competition, [and] growing national protectionism expressed in tariff regulations. He acclaimed oversees possessions as the outlets for necessary markets for French goods, and as places for the investment of capital."[139] Secondly, Ferry believed that French colonialism could be justified as a "civilizing" mission, where it was the right and duty of the "advanced" modern nations to "assist" the "primitive" and "underdeveloped" parts of the world to reach the historical stage of modernity.

This latter cultural legitimation for colonialism appealed greatly to Coubertin, who described himself in the 1890s as "an enthusiastic colonialist."[140] According to Otto Shantz, on a number of occasions Coubertin argued that it was the "duty" of the "civilized race" to "assist" the "retarded peoples of the world" to embrace a "progressive of Europeanization," even if they don't immediately understand the need for it.[141] Writing in the first decade of the twentieth century, he expressed this point clearly in the classic metaphorical language of colonial-modern paternalism: "the colonies are like children: it is relatively easy to make them, but it is difficult to provide them with a good education."[142]

The Olympics, in his view, could play a role in this civilizing educational mission, not just for France but on behalf of the entire "civilized" world. Sport could also show the world how to peacefully balance nationalist and internationalist agendas. An international multi-sport festival could also provide a degree of *invigoration* that might offset the fatigue, ennui, and apparent *anomie* that seemed to be growing within modern industrial civilization. In these ways, Coubertin had the dream of making the "modern" Olympic Games into something fundamentally new, with exhilarating potential for social renewal. To do this, he promoted a modern resynthesis of classical and modern images and ideas variously inflecting differing aspects in differing times and circumstances. For example, he resynthesized ideas from Greek classicism; conservative paternalism; a liberal emphasis on the importance of free individualism and "self-help"; public school and British "muscular Christian" athletics; individual and social hygienism; and an emerging fin-de-siècle dream of "civilized" and peaceful nationalism. He believed that this distinctively modern project, and the resynthesis of ideas that supported it, would require the creation of a new and fully independent international organization. As Patrick Clastres suggests, Coubertin's vision flatly rejected the international socialist dream of a world without wars in favor of the attempt to "elaborate an international code based on principles of arbitration between nations, to educate the peoples teaching them history which is not restricted to the dry enumeration of the names of battles but which accounts for the progress of mankind, and to favour cross-border economic and cultural exchanges."[143]

According to Borgers, Coubertin initially imagined an international organization to elaborate this code that would be organized roughly along the lines of Le Play's group of reformist intellectuals, Unions de la paix sociale.[144] Stating his idealist vision in an "Olympic manifesto" in 1894, Coubertin drew on references to world fairs and new communications technologies, as well as a liberal market metaphor to describe his ambitions for his imagined new project of modernity: "It is clear and obvious that the telegraph, the railway, the telephone, the passionate research in the field of science, congresses, world fairs did more for peace than all the treaties and all the diplomatic conventions. Well, I do hope that athletics will do even more."[145] International sport should become "the free trade of the future," based on the "export" of "rowers, fencers and runners." "The day it is introduced into the customs of old Europe," Coubertin argues, "the cause of peace will have received a new and powerful support."[146]

By "free trade," Coubertin did not mean the unimpeded bourgeois and western quest for colonial booty. However, I think the fact that he used this market metaphor at all is subtly indicative of how automatic the equation of "freedom" had become in nineteenth-century

European bourgeois cultures with the idea of "trade." Coubertin means the term in the modernist *cultural* sense of free expression, the free pursuit of intense experience, and the open communication of ideas that had emerged in modern liberal democracies and had seemed so evident in the international exhibitions. But, as John Hoberman has argued, many of the voluntary associations that formed during the nineteenth century to internationalize such visions of the "freedoms" of European civilization – such as the Young Men's Christian Association (YMCA), Universal Esperanto Association, or international scouting movements – were profoundly Eurocentric, with founders who were typically men from the European upper classes.[147] At their worst, these organizations expressed a powerful European, paternalistic sensibility and acted as ideological evangelists for the colonizing West. At their best, late nineteenth-century international voluntary organizations that originated in Europe or the United States reflected well-meaning, but nonetheless paternalistic, intentions to extend the "aid" and/or "teaching" of modern civilizations to more "primitive and less civilized" regions of the world.

Coubertin arranged a congress of physical educators at the Sorbonne in 1892, where he first mentioned the idea of establishing modern Olympic Games as an international project, and then, a year later, at a meeting of the French Union des Sociétés Françaises de Sports Athlétiques in 1892, he launched a proposal to stage a congress in Paris in 1894 to discuss the idea further. Faced with a lack of interest, and even considerable bemusement, he recast the major congress theme to be "amateurism."[148] Although his Olympic project was largely a sidebar issue at the 1894 Congress, Coubertin convinced the delegates to support the idea of creating an International Olympic Committee (IOC). After discussion and debate, the delegates voted to stage an Olympic Games in Athens in 1896.[149] The philosophical underpinnings of the Olympic Games were also sketched out in principle: competitors should (ideally) be amateurs, not professionals; they should compete in a way that demonstrates the highest standards of "sportsmanship"; and the Games should attempt to promote, as much as possible, the principles of international peace and fellowship.[150] On the organizational side, Horne and Whannel argue that the International Olympic Committee that was formed at the conference emerged more as an elite club, modeled on the lines of the Henley Royal Regatta in England, than a democratic, international organization.[151]

Moreover, despite Coubertin's rhetorical embrace of the idea of a "free trade" in athletics, women were excluded from the first IOC-sponsored Olympics in Athens in 1896, and the organizers expressed a preference for "amateur" competitors. The IOC's 1896 Olympic "revival" was a comparatively haphazard and small-scale affair, involving fewer than 280 athletes and approximately ten to fourteen European national associations. It also faced a myriad of financial challenges before securing sufficient resources from a Greek government willing to support the project to make a statement about Greece's commitment to modernity. Still, in the end, the 1896 Athens Olympics reportedly attracted approximately 60,000 spectators, prompting an initiative to propose Greece as a permanent site for the Olympics. However, Coubertin strongly resisted this initiative, fearing that the IOC would lose its autonomy and that the Games would be overcome by Greek nationalism.[152]

The next two Olympic Games organized by the IOC were held in conjunction with international expositions in France in 1900, where women competed in some events for the first time (despite Coubertin's objections), and St Louis in 1904. In both instances, the IOC was forced to cede control to other organizing committees, and the Games were overshadowed by the scale, popularity, and visual spectacle of the much larger expositions. Nonetheless, the IOC was beginning to receive bids from cities wanting to host stand-alone Olympics and an application was accepted from a Roman delegation to host the Olympics in 1908. When Rome withdrew due to financial costs incurred after the eruption of Mount Vesuvius in 1906, the IOC arranged a partnership with London organizers to allow the Olympics to be held in conjunction with the Franco-British Exhibition. In London, a specialized stadium was built for the Olympics for the first time, and the Games were considered to be a success. Nonetheless, the IOC decided to break from the cycle of international industrial exhibitions in order to achieve greater autonomy and promote future Olympic Games as independent events.

The 1912 Olympics were awarded to Stockholm, who organized the first Olympic Games that bore a resemblance to Olympic Games in the present day. Similarities included heavily ritualized opening ceremonies, with processions around the stadium, organized by nation, along with Olympic songs and hymns, although in Stockholm the competition was still open to any individual who showed up to compete. In later Olympics, national Olympic associations selected "national" teams. The Stockholm Olympics were also the first to hold an accompanying arts competition. More than 2,000 athletes from 28 nations competed in Stockholm, and the Olympics began to receive some international press coverage. More dramatically, some events were filmed for the first time and a number of the event winners, such as the Hawaiian swimmer "Duke" Kahanamoku and US track athlete Jim Thorpe, emerged after the Games as sporting celebrities, particularly in the United States. The IOC's later decision to rescind Thorpe's medals due to professionalism initiated a storm of news commentary that brought the Olympics even further into the public eye.

In addition, like industrial exhibitions, the Olympics gained legitimation through the early years of the twentieth century as a western "export" that inspired imitation in the colonies. For example, the director of the YMCA in Manila organized the first "Far Eastern Championship Games" in Manila in 1913 (also known as the "Oriental Olympics") to promote the "western civilizing mission" of muscular Christianity.[153] A second championship was held in Shanghai in 1915, with biennial competitions that ran until the early 1930s when conflict between Japan and China resulted in the breakup of the Far Eastern Athletic Association. Asian Games were held again, beginning in Delhi in 1950, but through the 1970s they were taken over by Asian National Olympic committees affiliated with the IOC. Caught between the push and pull of Soviet and capitalist western interests in the Cold War, a number of "emerging nations" staged their own Games during the 1960s.[154] The Soviet entry into the IOC in 1951, and subsequent IOC reforms, soon led to the incorporation of sporting aspirations among decolonizing nations into the now well-established IOC Olympic Movement.

Conclusion

World War I challenged the ideology of reason and progress associated with modernity, along with unreserved enthusiasm about its technological advances. Berman suggests that in the twentieth century the creative ambivalence that had been such a prominent feature of late nineteenth-century modernism tended to be replaced by "rigid polarities" and "flattened totalizations."[155] Understandings of modernity divided into two readily identifiable camps that celebrated modernity uncritically, on the one hand, or pessimistically condemned it on the other. This division significantly influenced modern discourse on sport, with some promoting sport as a celebration of modernity's promise or as a solution to its problems, and others viewing it as a symptom of modernity's malaise. Some of these themes are explored in greater detail in the discussion of German modernism and critical theory that follows in the next chapter.

In the area of political economy, the war initiated the beginnings of a significant reorganization of global economic and political relations as the locus of power in international financial networks began to shift in the direction of the United States and, to a lesser extent, toward the fast-developing industrial power of Japan. In addition, the war created conditions that led to the formation of the Soviet Union in 1922, the world's first openly communist state, as well as the collapse and fragmentation of the Ottoman Empire and the emergence of fascism in Europe. European economies struggled through the early 1920s, strapped by the repayment of war loans to the United States, the scale of reparations in Germany, and from a crisis in overproduction brought on by the challenge of recalibrating industrial plants geared for war to peacetime production.

In an atmosphere of fiscal and economic crisis, the postwar rearrangement of the European political map led to the reintroduction or strengthening of protective tariffs, slowing down the mobility of capital and the flow of goods both within Europe and between European metropoles and their colonial hinterlands. With these events, the nineteenth-century dream of a free movement of goods, people, and ideas around the world, made possible by the achievements of science and technology, seemed more distant than ever. This arguably put an even greater premium on the colonial free trade that existed between European metropolitan centers and their empires. The interwar years featured an intensification of European imperialism, rather than its diminution.

However, once again, heightened nationalism was juxtaposed with the idealistic dream of true internationalism, prompting an upsurge of interest in new organizations and regulatory bodies, such as the League of Nations. The two formulae for the public staging of modernity as a form of spectacle that were inherited from the nineteenth century – *the industrial exhibition formula* and *the international multi-sport Olympic formula* – were flexible enough ideologically and organizationally to accommodate both of these positions. For example, a new postwar wave of industrial and "imperial" exhibitions in Europe addressed issues of trade and became part of capitalist and colonial agendas to get money and goods moving freely again. There were also four major international expos staged in the United States during the interwar period, reflecting not only an international economic and political power shift, but also the growing industrial capacity in the United States and the resilience of technological optimism there.

Still, as Geppert and others have argued, by the end of the nineteenth century there was already a widespread sense of "exhibition fatigue" in Europe and, to a lesser extent, North America.[156] For one thing, inter-city competition that had led to continually escalating costs was seen by many critics to be increasingly problematic. According to Geppert, the international exhibition equivalent to the Olympic motto of *citius, altius, fortius* was "faster sequences, higher buildings and structures, and wider sites."[157] The race for the biggest and most spectacular exhibitions peaked in the years before World War I. World's Fairs would undergo something of a revival during the 1960s, but they would arguably no longer be the iconic celebrations of international technology, science, education, and social philosophy that they had been in the nineteenth century.

Additionally, critics remarked that industrial, imperial, and international exhibitions had grown so numerous that they had become almost routine, thereby losing some of the sense that they still provided "states of exception" in comparison to entertainment and cultural options available on a day-to-day basis.[158] One obvious reason for this lay in the substantial growth of new industries of entertainment and leisure as key features of modernity on their own terms. The early twentieth century was vastly more "mediated" than the nineteenth century, with an accompanying expansion of commercial entertainments of all types.[159] The thrill of attending exhibitions was rivaled by the intense experience, pleasure, and entertainment associated with mass circulation magazines and newspapers, movie theaters, commercial amusement parks, sports stadiums and arenas, professional sporting events, recorded music, and the interrelated spread of radio. Moreover, from the standpoint of *both* industry and educators, the exhibition format appeared to lose some of its luster as a promotional medium. As the exhibitions turned more to amusement then display, industrialists turned to specialized advertising companies who could market products to specialized audiences through mass-circulation magazines, newspapers, cinema, and radio advertising. Similarly, educators lamented the decline in the pedagogical exhibition function in the face of what they saw as a drift to "mere" amusement and consumption. Exhibitions could no longer be relied upon to "stage" modernity as a discourse of progress.

After World War I, the IOC-sponsored Olympic Games slowly began to challenge international exhibitions as the world's most notable spectacles of modernity. Strongly pushed by US interests and ambitions to achieve a presence in international sport, the Olympics grew steadily in stature through the 1920s and early 1930s, as more

countries recognized the symbolic and political benefits of par-
ticipating.[160] One thing that differentiated the Olympics from major
international expositions during the interwar years was the way they
benefited from new mass media. Growing public fascination with
competitions between athletes from different countries, with different
political systems and ambitions, accelerated with the popularization
of radio and film, both of which provided enhanced international
access to images and journalistic narratives of the events.

A large part of the irresistible appeal of international sport lay in
its capacity to dramatize cultural differences and political tensions in
an extraordinarily immediate and direct way, and not just metaphorically. It *really* was black versus white on the track, athletes from *this*
political system versus *that* political system in the stadium. At the
very moment that international exhibitions were losing some of their
novelty – as well as their previous functions as prominent media on
their own terms and abilities to dramatize nationalist ambition –
Olympic sporting spectacle grew to occupy some of these roles.

I see this as one of the delicious ironies of the IOC Olympics as
a twentieth-century spectacle of modernity. Despite the rhetoric
about peace and internationalism in the Olympic movement, it was
the capacity *to dramatize* and *measure* the agonistic successes of
competing nations while serving the economic and status ambitions
of competing cities that solidified the steady growth in size, scale,
and popular interest in the Olympic Games through much of the
twentieth century. Another key part of that success lay in the IOC's
growing capacity after World War II to achieve a monopoly position
as the provider of international multi-sport spectacles. This point is
discussed in greater detail in the final chapter of this book. From the
1920s through the 1960s, there were numerous, and very credible,
attempts to develop international sporting festivals outside of, and
sometimes in opposition to, the IOC – such as Workers' Olympiads,
women's Olympic Games, Spartakiads in the Soviet Union, and the
Games of "emerging" postcolonial nations. In the end, though, all of
these initiatives were short-lived, leaving the IOC-sponsored Olympic
Games as the late twentieth century's most prominent international
spectacle of modernity.

— 4 —

GERMAN MODERNISM, ANTI-MODERNISM, AND THE CRITICAL THEORY OF SPORT

The historian Richard D. Mandell has argued that systematic criticism of modern sport was first developed by Weimar and Nazi social critics, and especially by writers associated with the Frankfurt Institute for Social Research.[1] Mandell situates the importance of a German "critical theory" of sport largely in the countercultural moment of the 1960s. However, the roots of a modern critical theory of sport lie in the 1930s and 1940s in the early work of Frankfurt School members and associates, such as Siegfried Kracauer, Walter Benjamin, Franz Neumann, Max Horkheimer, and Theodor Adorno. This early work was then taken up and popularized by numerous German and non-German critics during the 1960s.

It is worth a reminder here that criticisms of various aspects of athletics, body cultures, and spectacles were widely evident in Greco-Roman antiquity and continued through the advent of modern industrial capitalist societies. By the early years of the twentieth century, a growing number of intellectuals, journalists, and activists saw sport as a useless distraction or, worse, as a malaise of modernity: "bread and circuses" for the industrial age. Others saw sports training as a reduction of the body to the new logic of the machine age and as a popularization of uncivilized mass culture, to name just a few objections.[2]

As one might imagine, sports enthusiasts and promoters typically bristled at such criticisms, suggesting that they are exaggerated, that they threaten to politicize or intrude on the imagined autonomy of sport, or that they undermine playful sport, either by neglecting its inherent beauty or by taking all the fun out of it.[3] Roughly similar concerns were sometimes raised in response to early modern art criticism, suggesting that the act of criticism destroys or ruins the "object"

131

of art that should be experienced and appreciated *affectively,* rather than analyzed critically. In comparison to the skilled performance of art or sport, criticism can seem like a very weak substitute for the lived experience of the real thing – in Dave Hickey's striking metaphor, the intellectual equivalent of "air guitar."[4]

However, there are important performative dimensions and purposes of criticism too. As Marx noted in 1843, "criticism is no passion of the head, it is the head of passion."[5] He means thoughtful criticism that stems from *a socially produced need* to look behind the institutional and discursive facades of social structure and ideology in order to decipher the operations of class and state power. Criticism is necessary to assess the making of hegemonic structures and ideologies and to unmask attempts to normalize or win consent for them. For example, in earlier chapters I have argued that the emergence of sport "as its own object" in the nineteenth century and the production of a relatively coherent field of sporting practice was disproportionately shaped by masculine, upper- and middle-class, white and western colonial views, and was accompanied by a preference for idealized "classical" imagery.

This did not happen because people at that time suddenly "discovered" that sport had a timeless formal essence, similar to the "discovery" of artifacts in an archeological dig in Greece. As Stuart Hall once noted about popular culture in general, it occurred through "the process by which some cultural forms and practices are driven out of the centre of popular life, actively marginalized. Rather than simply 'falling into disuse' through the Long March to modernisation, things are actively pushed aside, so that something else can take their place."[6] Understanding the process of preferring some ideas and practices while pushing "other" ideas and practices aside, or of resynthesizing fragmentary ideas from the past to promote new agendas became key ideas in the development of a systematic critical theory of sport in the twentieth century.[7] Early critical theorists of sport sought to draw attention to how such processes were often little more than expressions of competing social interests, ideology, and power.

In this chapter, I explore these themes in a discussion of the growth of modernist culture in Weimar Germany and the accompanying emergence of the "critical theory" of the so-called "Frankfurt School" of German Marxism. This requires a brief discussion of the Frankfurt Institute for Social Research and the "modern" promotion of *anti-modernism* by the Nazis, including early critical reactions to Nazi sporting spectacle by members and associates of the Frankfurt School. The chapter then goes on to examine the resurgence of interest in Frankfurt School "critical theory" in the postwar era, including its profound influence on "countercultural" and leftist criticism of sport during the 1960s and early 1970s. As part of this discussion, I try to explain why many people who were initially attracted to the application of Frankfurt School critical theory to sport felt the need to retreat from this position. Finally, I shall argue that something important was lost in this retreat and, despite its limitations, that critical theory can still provide useful insights into the analysis of contemporary sport.

Weimar modernism and early twentieth-century social criticism

According to John Hoberman, sport was extensively debated in Germany through the Weimar and early Nazi periods "as an index of, or as a curative for, an imagined European crisis of values."[8] However, the issues under discussion often went far beyond the realm of "values" alone. They included: *sociological* questions about increases in the level of technological mediation in social life; the rise of mass media, mass consumption, spectacle, and mass propaganda; as well as *political* questions about relations between individualism, representation, and nationalism; and *cultural* and *aesthetic* questions about relations between art, free expression, and popular culture.

In the late nineteenth century, sports were largely viewed by German elites as pointless and distracting imports from England and North America.[9] As Jon Hughes points out, the word "sport" was barely used in German society until the late Wilhelmine era and tended to be "reserved for competitive Anglo-Saxon disciplines," such as boxing, athletics, and team games that emphasized individual performance and quantifiable results. This was in contrast to *Leibesübungen*, a term that encompassed Turner expressive gymnastics and dance.[10] German physical culture had a long association with military drills and non-competitive bodily exercise and health practices rather than sporting competition. Examples included the Turner tradition of mass gymnastic exercise as well as organized hiking and outdoor trekking for both men and women.

The Turner movement was fiercely conservative and strongly influenced by the *völkisch* racial doctrine of its founder, Friedrich Ludwig Jahn. Hoberman argues that Jahn founded a gymnastic movement to express an imagined transcendental German cultural essence.[11] The precise political orientations of hiking and outdoor movements were more varied and included representation by members of workers' associations and clubs. Although the political perspective of these groups was sometimes self-consciously radical, they shared the Turner movement's desire to create sites of "resistance to modernity or, at the very least, a refuge from modern life's most harrying features." [12] Erik Jensen suggests that activities such as "nudism, hiking and gymnastics" continued to be prominent in early twentieth-century German life, but "clearly positioned themselves as antidotes to the hectic, atomized and high-pressured environment that so many culture critics had come to associate with postwar society."[13]

In addition to these earlier strands of German "body culture," there was an upsurge of interest in organized sport after the turn of the century, and particularly in the Weimar years of the 1920s. Older traditions were discarded or substantially modified after the war in an attempt to embrace what many younger Germans saw as the advances of twentieth-century modernity. The result was a new urban postwar modern culture of change, experimentation, and cosmopolitanism. In this culture, Jensen argues that "athletes provided the template" for a new understanding of modern human bodies "engineered for maximum performance." In addition, competitive sports seemed to exude "a modern spirit . . . unbound by the tethers of tradition and social convention," including "open pride" in "physical displays, all of which prewar Germany had discouraged, especially in women."[14]

Christiane Eisenberg's research demonstrates the rapid development of organized sport as a cultural phenomenon in Weimar Germany: the number of Germans who joined sports clubs grew fivefold between 1913 and 1931. By 1929, nearly three and a half million Germans belonged to sports clubs and, if one counts gymnastics, hiking, and mountain-climbing clubs, the figure climbs to almost eight million members, although growth in membership appears to have fallen off after 1927.[15] The expansion in sport membership paralleled a degree of democratization in sporting experiences, as opportunities for participation opened up to a substantial segment of the German working classes.[16]

At the same time, a rapid growth of newspapers, popular magazines, advertising, and film in the Weimar era created new conditions for public visibility. According to Jensen, "between 1918 and 1933, forty new general sports magazines appeared on newsstands across the country."[17] The popular press included an emphasis on gossip, fashion, and personality profiles that helped to elevate sport to a higher place in a burgeoning consumer culture that included professional sports, such as boxing and soccer. In addition, Jensen argues that intensive media coverage of Olympic and professional sports made "household names" of athletes such as Finnish runner Paavo Nurmi, American boxer Jack Dempsey, and French tennis star Suzanne Lenglen, along with their homegrown counterparts Otto Peltzer, Max Schmeling, and Cilly Aussem.[18] Because sports revealed the results of hard work and dedication in the look and hardness of the body and in concrete measurable results, they dramatized, in Jensen's words, "the new republic's claims to emphasize talent and hard work over gender, ethnicity and birthright."[19] Athletics became an especially notable expression of the claims of "modern" German women to a new fusion of ideas about strength, beauty, and independence.

German interest in sport also appears to have been influenced by a view that the emphasis on competitive masculine athleticism in Edwardian England and the intensely competitive school and commercial sport in the United States had been factors in the successes of English and North American troops during the war. Sport was considered by some to have greater martial utility than mass gymnastics. In addition, competitive sport referenced an imported American "self-made" ethos similar to that championed by Henry Ford, whose autobiography had been translated into German in the 1920s and was a "runaway bestseller."[20] The idea of "Taylorism," the scientific management of work, was another US import, and German sports journals in the 1920s frequently published essays that "analogized affirmatively between athletic training and performance and the specialization of labor as it was exemplified by the principles of 'scientific management.'"[21] James Van Dyke suggests that "liberal intellectuals who affirmed industrial society" were attracted to sport as an "anti-metaphysical" objectification of the emerging modern age of science and technology.[22]

Sport was also sometimes seen in early twentieth-century German modernism as a potential compensation for aspects of human physicality that had been allegedly undermined or corrupted by mechanized industry and modern democracy. There were two distinctive variations of this compensation thesis, one closely related to German conservative, romantic, and nationalist traditions, and the other to liberal and capitalist conceptions. The first view tended to be profoundly Nietzschean in orientation. As noted earlier, Nietzsche celebrated the male body as a primary source of vitality and energy that expresses human will through a dominating instinct. Against the Platonic and Christian repression of the body in favor of the mind, Nietzsche believed that instinctive physicality "links the noble races" to the "beast of prey, the splendid blond beast prowling about avidly in search of spoil and victory."[23] He saw late nineteenth-century Germany as a society caught between constraining spiritual and contractual-legal principles and the backwardness and philistinism of traditional class cultures. In contrast, he proposed initiatives aimed at *self-creation* through joyous Dionysian excess, adventure, war, hunting, dancing, and games – all practices that celebrated vigorous, free, activity.[24]

The philosopher Max Scheler expressed somewhat similar themes in his assertion in 1928 that sport is a "self-conscious rechanneling of vital instinctive energy away from spiritual sublimation and into the development of the body and maximal physical performance."[25] But, according to Hoberman, Scheler was unwilling to push this call for a revolutionary reevaluation of the body too far. Despite his enthusiasm for bodily vitalism, he worried that modern sport had betrayed its promise and had instead become a "narcotizing overcompensation for feelings of exhaustion and spiritual emptiness."[26] Somewhat similarly, the Weimar critic Frank Theiss suggested that sport had been important as an emancipatory break from the authoritarianism of the Wilhelmine Empire, and suggested, in Nietzschean fashion, that sport carried the promise of a "new culture" that would emerge from giving priority to the body over the mind.[27] Weimar romantics and nationalists increasingly understood the purpose of sport as something that could link this new culture to established German ideas and traditions, thereby serving as an important mediator between "tradition" and "modernity."[28] Yet, among proponents of this view, as Theiss's writing suggests, there was also a concern that sport was becoming too professionalized, too tainted by the corrupting forces of money and greed.[29]

The liberal and capitalist variant of the "compensation thesis" focused more on the apparent problems of indolence, imbalances of energy, and fatigue in modern life. Western industrial capitalist societies had embraced the metaphor of the "human motor" in the late nineteenth century, raising serious questions about human performance for work-related tasks and about the limited energy of human bodies.[30] As early as the 1890s, the Italian physiologist Angelo Mosso had developed a theory that weighed human decadence against the economic successes of industrial civilization. The human body was an accumulator of energy that must be discharged to avoid torpor and illness. Increases in leisure threatened a build-up of destructive energy. In a manner roughly similar to hygienist thinking elsewhere in Europe, Mosso believed that modern physiology, science, and measurement, in combination with sport for the bourgeois classes and physical education for the masses, created opportunities not only to compensate for human physical decline but also to dissipate pent-up energies in ways that contributed to the overall "health" of modern societies.[31]

At the same time, sport could also be seen to provide a modern laboratory to test the human capacity for physical performance and the values necessary to achieve it. As individuals embraced the competitive ethos of modern sport, they willingly subjected themselves to the same kind of "scientific scrutiny" that workers were undergoing by physiologists and industrial engineers aiming to extend their productive capacities. In the quest for achievement, athletes were honed by the discipline provided by coaches and physiologists who determined diet, training programs, and competition schedules.[32] In an ironic attempt to escape from the constraints of the machine age, some critics were beginning to suggest that athletes were submitting to materialist logic in ways that overly privileged "modern" material life over consciousness and spirit.[33] For example, writing in 1935, Martin Heidegger saw sport as indicative of a broad "spiritual decline of the earth." In an age "when a boxer [presumably Max Schmeling] is regarded as a nation's great man," Heidegger argued, we can truly say, "sport is a plunge into idiocy."[34]

This brief overview of Weimar sport suggests how some of the rudiments of a later critical theory of sport were well in place in Germany in the 1920s and early 1930s. A unique conjuncture of circumstances and events led to significant philosophical reflexivity about the place of sport in modern German society, culture, and politics. The result can be measured not only in numerous discussions and debates in newspapers, magazines, and specialist journals, but also in a spate of books on the social and philosophical analysis of sport as its own object, including: Robert Hesse's book *Der Sport*, in 1908, in a series edited by the philosopher Martin Buber; Heinz Risse's book in 1921, *Soziologie des Sports*, the first self-designated attempt to understand sport from the standpoint of modern sociology; and Alfred Peters's book, *Psychologie des Sports*, in 1927, with a preface by Max Scheler. Of these, Hoberman argues that Peters's book was the most self-consciously "socialist analysis." But it is Risse who is frequently noted as the writer most closely associated with critical theory, largely because he is often said to have been a student of Theodor Adorno.[35] However, I find that highly unlikely, given that Adorno was only 18 years old when Risse's book was first published. Nonetheless, Risse sought to show the legitimacy of the analysis of

137

sport and related forms of body culture for sociology and argued that "mechanized man has only one form in which he can express [his] will in everyday life: the domain of physical culture."[36]

The "Frankfurt School," Nazi aesthetics, and the incipient "critical theory" of sport

Interestingly, despite the public and scholarly attention given to sport in the early Weimar era, the topic seemed to be of little interest to members of the Frankfurt Institute for Social Research. Felix Weil, a student of the unorthodox Marxist philosopher Karl Korsch, founded the Institute privately in 1923–4 to support and encourage independent Marxist criticism. At varying times, the Institute provided support and opportunities to exchange ideas for a diverse group of socialist, communist, and avant-garde writers of the time, including Karl Mannheim, Friedrich Pollock, Herbert Marcuse, Walter Benjamin, Henryk Grossman, Erich Fromm, and Franz Neumann, among others.[37] It is difficult to know exactly why sport seemed not to interest members and associates of the Institute through the 1920s. Given the strong emphasis on Marxian political economy in the early years of the Institute, this lack of interest may have had something to do with the idea that sport is merely a part of the "superstructure" of capitalist social relations, and therefore of secondary importance to the analysis of capitalist forces and relations of production. Or, more simply, perhaps researchers at the Institute tacitly agreed with Heidegger's equation of sport with idiocy. The Institute was also troubled after 1930 by the ascendance of Nazism in Germany and was forced into a series of moves that hampered the development of a systematic critique of German culture. The Institute's new director, Max Horkheimer, moved operating funds to the Netherlands in 1931 and day-to-day operations to Geneva in 1933, with branch offices in Paris and London. Horkheimer later moved the Institute to New York in 1935, where it became loosely affiliated with Columbia University. The Institute also developed a satellite émigré group in California in the 1940s, before relocating back to Frankfurt in 1951.

It was Horkheimer who first coined the phrase "critical theory" in an essay in 1937.[38] In that essay, he sought to differentiate "critical theory" from "traditional theory" in the social sciences. Horkheimer argued that the purpose of critical theory is to analyze forms of domination and oppression in social life *with the specific goal of human emancipation*. Critical theory does not pretend in the manner of traditional empirical science to merely describe or explain social situations. Rather, the goal of "critical theory" is to mobilize argument and diverse forms of evidence to act as a source of potential "liberation" – to provide a means for people to imagine and work toward a world that satisfies the "needs and powers" of all human beings, rather than a world that satisfies the needs and powers of dominant groups or, more abstractly, the needs and powers of scientific, technical, or bureaucratic administration.

Both in Horkheimer's early work, and in a later collaboration with his colleague Theodor Adorno, critical theory set itself the task of "negating" the powerful reifying tendencies that ran through human life in western societies. In their view, the negation of reification is "intellect's true concern."[39] These reifying tendencies refigured human social *relations* into the seemingly independent worlds of objects and things.[40] Horkheimer and Adorno were influenced by Kantian philosophy and German phenomenology, but it was a fusion of Hegelian and Marxist ideas, influenced by the work of the Hungarian Marxist theoretician György Lukács, that gave critical theory much of its polemical edge. The young Horkheimer viewed himself as a communist until the late 1930s, but many of his views differed considerably from the major tenets of Soviet Marxism.[41]

In the early 1920s, Lukács had argued that the combined forces of capitalist commodity fetishism, class relations, and instrumentally rational bureaucratic organization had broadened and intensified processes of reification in human life.[42] The commodity was the most obvious manifestation of the condition of reification, where something that is humanly created appears to exist, almost magically, as part of the world of things that come to dominate human existence. But Lukács extended this line of reasoning into a discussion of what he viewed as the broader forces of fragmentation of the "whole" of human life. The capitalist division of labor, the increasing specialization of tasks and skills, and the logic of bureaucratic administration conjured a world of seemingly independent object domains. This process even extended to social thought, as evidenced by the growth of specialized academic disciplines so highly focused on their own objects of analysis (e.g. history, the economy, society), that they tended to ignore everything surrounding them.[43] For Lukács, Marxian historical materialism was the only method that had effectively united these falsely separated objects into an analysis of the *totality* of social relations.

Lukács added to this by claiming that the worldviews of the bourgeoisie and proletariat were both distorted by reification, preventing either class from developing a meaningful analysis of the social whole. In his view, one of the central dynamics of capitalist ideology lay in a chronic confusion in social life of the part with the whole.[44] The bourgeoisie not only believed, falsely, that the narrow categories of bourgeois science could provide sufficient insight into history, economies, and societies; they inevitably misunderstood their own class interest as synonymous with the imagined universal interests of human beings. The western industrial proletariat was trapped in a somewhat different way because their immersion in reification prevented them from seeing how the objectification of their own labor power into the wage form was a constitutive feature of the oppressive world that confronted them. By attacking the influence of reification on the "consciousness of the proletariat," Lukács saw the development of a Marxian critique of culture as a necessary part of revolutionary practice.

Within orthodox Marxism, Lukács was labeled a renegade idealist philosopher who was forced by the Communist Party leadership to recant many of his early ideas. His sanctioning by the Party raised warnings among Weimar era German Marxists about the possibility of independent criticism within orthodox Marxism, and it appears to have played an important role in Horkheimer's suggestion that critical theory should devote itself to the critique of domination *without* submitting the adjudication of truth claims to the program of any political organization. As David Held argues, despite the debt that critical theory owes to a Marxian materialist "philosophy of praxis," the Frankfurt School theorists typically "defended the possibility of an independent moment of criticism."[45]

They also attempted to "justify critical theory on a non-objectivistic and materialistic foundation."[46] Critical theory thus involves the attempt to combine objective analysis with interpretive understanding, positivity with negativity, structure with agency, and empirical understanding with normativity. From the outset, critical theory was meant to be necessarily and thoroughly *dialectical*. In the later work of Horkheimer and Adorno, in particular, there are repeated attempts to consider how every affirmative modern historical condition tends to contain its own negation: for example, how progress can develop as regression, freedom as constraint, civilization as barbarism, enlightenment as despair.

Despite the initial lack of interest in sport at the Institute, there are some early examples in the 1920s and 1930s of themes that would be picked up in later critical theory. For example, one of Adorno's mentors, Siegfried Kracauer, wrote several essays in the newspaper

Frankfurter Zeitung in the late 1920s that discussed sport as part of a broader critical analysis of German mass media, mass consumption, and mass culture. For example, in a 1927 essay, "The Mass Ornament," Kracauer comments on similarities between the choreographed precision of the Tiller Girl troupe of dancers and crowds in sports stadiums, linking the latter to Roman circus games:

> Physical training expropriates people's energy, while the production and mindless consumption of the ornamental patterns divert them from the imperative to change the reigning order. Reason can gain entrance only with difficulty when the masses it ought to pervade yield to sensations afforded by the godless mythological cult. The latter's social meaning is equivalent to that of the Roman *circus games,* which were sponsored by those in power.[47]

Kracauer's concerns were partially inspired by his studies with Georg Simmel and tapped into a critique of modernity that was not necessarily shared by other leftist critics at the time. For example, some communist writers believed that sport contained the potential to *subvert* the authoritarian and repressive character of German bourgeois elite culture by replacing its fusion of lingering aristocratic and bourgeois notions with a meritocratic and democratic emphasis on performance and engagement. The apparent democratic populism of sport had a particular cachet in leftist avant-garde circles in Berlin and Frankfurt, where artists and literary figures, such as Bertolt Brecht and George Grosz, were frequent sports spectators.[48] The young Brecht was a boxing enthusiast, and, while boxing itself was not as popular in Germany as soccer, Brecht was struck by its combination of force and beauty. He was also impressed with the broader interest in boxing shown by the German working classes.[49]

In a short essay written in 1926, Brecht suggested that German artists should "pin our hopes to the sporting public" in opposition to the excessive sentimentality, elitist aestheticism, and an overly contemplative attitude in German theater.[50] In Brecht's view, the energy and vitality of sport echoed the energy and vitality of a new modern age, thereby forging an implicit connection with a democratic and revolutionary spirit. If exercise regimes in the interest of the state had a reactionary history, Brecht imagined the appropriation and reformulation of past practices in promoting a new democratic and communist future.[51] However, Brecht began to qualify this view in the 1930s as other avant-garde writers on the left began to ask harder questions about the balance of liberating versus repressive forces in German sport.

There was no clear or coherent Frankfurt School critical theory of sport during the 1920s, other than what can be gleaned through very occasional sidebar comments in the work of writers loosely associated with the Institute. But the fall of the Weimar Republic and advent of the Nazi state in the 1930s substantially raised the significance of sport for critical theory. Equally important was the political exile of many German leftists to the United States, including many of the Institute's most prominent members and their friends. It was only in the United States during the 1940s that the Frankfurt School's position on sport developed in any significant way and began to inspire more contemporary critical research.

Commenting on the seductiveness of Nazi aesthetics, Susan Sontag once noted in a review of a book by filmmaker Leni Riefenstahl that "never before in history was the relation of masters and slaves realized with so consciously artistic a design."[52] Nazi propagandists set themselves the task of responding to what they saw as the decadence, fatigue, and cultural decline of modernity and promoted a project of radical social renewal in its place. But this renewal was not articulated as a *complete* break from the past. In Germany it combined the theme of renewal with mythic references to an imagined history combined with a discourse of racial and cultural purification. Hitler argued in his May Day speech of 1935: "This Age must be called, not the decline of the West, but the resurrection of the peoples of this West of ours! Only that which was old, decayed and evil perishes; and let it die! But new life will spring up. Faith can be found if the will is there."[53] Roger Griffin suggests that Nazism *resynthesized* the modern capitalist premise of *creative destruction* with a powerful anti-modern discourse. Modernity was what had become "old, decayed and evil" and in its place a new society would arise.[54]

The project of creating this new society of renewal and purification was dramatized and celebrated through heavily aestheticized spectacles. The staging of mass rallies, mass exercises, and mass military displays was meant to articulate contrasts between decadence and energy, the impure and the pure, the defiled and the incorruptible, the mental and the physical, the critical and the joyful.[55] As Steven Connor argues, fascist modernism was a "modernism of force" that valued "dynamism, speed, striving, record-breaking and Nietzschean overcoming" in opposition to a "modernism of form" that valued perception, sensitivity, refinement, and suppleness, in addition to reflexivity, reason, cultural experimentation, and debate.[56] For the Nazis, this latter modernism was viewed as effete, lifeless, vapid, and degenerate, including the "corrupting" work of Impressionist and Expressionist artists allegedly "promoted by Jewish art dealers."[57]

Hitler proposed to launch "a tornado against modernism": the Bauhaus was closed in 1933, "Oskar Schlemmer's murals whitewashed, films by Sergei Eistenstein and music by Igor Stravinsky banned."[58] In addition, the Nazis staged "exhibitions of shame," featuring allegedly "degenerate" modern art influenced by the so-called "viruses" of communism and Judaism. By contrast, Nazism's aesthetic reference points borrowed from classicism, futurism, and Soviet constructivism to create a reactionary new mode of modern "heroic realism."[59] Roger Griffin underlines the extent to which these reference points had a strongly somatic character: "Both the heroic postures of liberated peasants and the idealized bodies of 'Aryan' manhood (and womanhood) are tokens of a new age, acts of creation wilfully purged of 'decadent' experimentalism, self-expression, and a fanatical cult of innovation."[60]

After 1935, the Third Reich officially began to promote neoclassicism in art and architecture, leading to increasing numbers of "de-eroticized, athletic nudes that gaze beyond the onlooker to a distant horizon, repository of the 'eternal' values of the culture-creating 'Aryan.'"[61] Nazi sculptors, such as Arno Breker, crafted massive works in the new neoclassical style of Nazi realism (Figure 4.1).

4.1 Arno Breker, *Die Wehrmacht* (1939/40)

These followed hard on the heels in 1934 of the Third Reich's Law for the Prevention of Genetically Diseased Offspring, which led to the forced sterilization of more than 250,000 people "diagnosed with alcoholism, manic-depression, schizophrenia, hereditary epilepsy, blindness and deafness, congenital mental deficiency, hereditary disease and physical deformity."[62] Faye Brauer asserts that this was "the first step in a complex and systematic eugenic campaign ... culminating in the extermination of Jews, homosexuals, gypsies, political dissidents and others classified as physiologically or psychologically 'degenerate.'"[63] Nazi "eugenics" was articulated with already existing discourses of "hygienism" in Europe and North America, and attracted interest from eugenic movements in other countries. Eugenic hygiene was also connected to a parallel discourse of "free" body culture movements, a continuing passion for athleticism and spectator sport, the modern dance movement, youth movements, back-to-nature movements and "philosophical, literary, and scientistic forms of vitalism."[64]

The 1936 Summer Olympic Games in Berlin, with their accompanying art competitions, provided the Nazis with an extraordinary opportunity to showcase German confidence, unity, organizational capacity, and technological sophistication, while also working to promote and celebrate allegedly "'anti-degenerate' neoclassical discourses of cultural renewal, physicality, Aryan superiority and somatic purity."[65] The heavily ritualized character of the Olympic Games and the IOC's previous philhellenic propensities encouraged the Nazis to introduce *new* neoclassical initiatives to the Olympics, such as the modern torch relay. The dominant themes for the Olympic festival were to be heroism, bravery, spectacle, nationalism, Aryan somatic purity, and beauty, all of which found expression in neoclassical monumentalism and the heroic athletic realism of sculptors such as Breker, Josef Thorak, and the Nazi filmmaker Leni Riefenstahl (Figures 4.2 and 4.3).

Germany is reported to have spent more than 100 million marks on the 1936 Olympics, upping the scale of Olympic spectacle to unprecedented heights.[66] Despite a boycott movement in other parts of the world, the "Nazi Olympics" were staged to a huge German and international media fanfare and were reported as an overwhelming success. I think it is important to note here that the Berlin Olympics provided more than the opportunity to promote mythic national self-imagery and Nazi ideology, although the Games certainly did that. The Nazis also saw the 1936 Summer and Winter Olympics as part of a larger program of political legitimation and economic stimulation,

4.2 Josef Thorak, *Sculpture on the Berlin Reich Sports Field* (1937)

4.3 Leni Riefenstahl, *The Javelin Thrower* (1938)

designed to jump-start the German economy, provide employment, and offer positive proof of the Nazi capacity to deliver a uniquely non-liberal form of modernization.[67]

Interestingly, Nadine Rossol has argued that emphasis on mass spectacle, the cult of celebrity, and idealization of athletic bodies were *already* well-established aspects of sport in Germany before the

145

beginnings of the Nazi state.[68] Indeed, the city of Frankfurt had hosted a "workers' Olympics" in 1925 that was accompanied by a "mass play" staged "in Frankfurt's stadium before 50,000 people, with mass choirs and acting groups," as well as "Socialist youth organizations making up the cast."[69] The play's content developed a left-wing narrative about the "Struggle for the Earth," and the opening ceremonies featured the socialist anthem, "the International," played before 45,000 spectators, with athletes from several countries carrying red flags bearing the names of their countries. Speeches spoke to the themes of peace, solidarity, and workers' community and were followed by mass gymnastic exercises.[70] The point, Rossoll argues, is that many of the themes viewed as unique to the Nazi state have a more complex history, reminding us that sport and idealized body politics were deployed in the interwar era for a variety of political agendas. In addition, she argues, the Nazis actually cut down on the number of politicized public events, opting instead for fewer but much larger spectacles.[71]

Still, there is no denying that there were very distinctive elements in these later Nazi spectacles. For example, in his book *Behemoth* in 1941, Frankfurt Institute for Social Research member Franz Neumann argued that the interventions of the Nazi state into *all* areas of life, including leisure and entertainment, resulted in a reconfiguration and acceleration of nationalist sensibilities.[72] All forms of culture, including sport, were removed from the realm of civil society and integrated fully into the realm of state pageantry and theatricality. This state-sponsored mass theatricality also drew commentary from Walter Benjamin in the same year as the Berlin Olympics. In the epilogue to his essay on "The Work of Art in the Age of Mechanical Reproduction," Benjamin retains considerable Brechtian optimism about the political and culture-creating possibilities of new technologies of reproduction, but he makes a point of remarking critically on the Nazi's self-conscious "aestheticization of politics."[73]

According to Benjamin, Nazism responded to the proletarianization of German society and the emergence of state-sponsored mass culture by giving the masses "a chance to express themselves," but only as a *substitute* for power. The aestheticization of politics hinged on the spectacular display of a politically chosen aesthetic – a production of beauty, joy, and ritual values through the apparatuses of the state. Mass displays, songs, visually arresting sculptures and posters, torchlight rallies, striking photographs, film clips, and charismatically displayed athletes and political leaders gave the German "masses" entertainment and reinforced a sense of German identity, but never changed the alienating structure of property relations. In Benjamin's prophetic view, such highly aestheticized politics can lead to only one conclusion: war. In this argument, which Benjamin developed only in passing, we see older ideas about the politics of "bread and circuses" resynthesized in a distinctively modern form of social criticism.

Neither Neumann nor Benjamin discussed sport, per se, in any detail. However, in the 1940s, references to sport began to surface in critical theory with greater frequency. One important early influence here was Horkheimer's belief that in order to understand the changing sociology and psychology of modern life in the mid-twentieth century, it was necessary for critical theory to engage with the work of the American sociologist Thorstein Veblen. In Horkheimer's words: "It became clear to us that thorough study and earnest analysis of Veblen, America's great sociological critic of culture, could help us understand the catastrophic change in human nature."[74] Sports figure prominently in Veblen's 1899 book, *The Theory of the Leisure Class*, and Adorno wrote a long review essay on Veblen in which he crucially analyzed what he took to be the strengths and weaknesses of Veblen's analysis of culture.

While disagreeing with several parts of Veblen's analysis of sports as expressions of an archaic "predatory temperament" and as sites for "emulative ferocity," Adorno finds resources in Veblen to build a more contemporary critique of sport in modernity. For example, Adorno argues:

> According to Veblen, the passion for sports is of a regressive nature: 'The ground of an addiction to sports is an archaic spiritual constitution.' But nothing is more modern than this archaism; athletic events were the models for totalitarian mass rallies. As tolerated excesses, they combine cruelty and aggression with an authoritarian moment, the disciplined observance of the rules – legality, as in the pogroms of Nazi Germany and the people's republics.[75]

However, for Adorno, sports are not so much "a relic of a previous form of society," as Veblen saw them, as an "adjustment to society's new form." He also accuses Veblen of failing to see the "masochistic" side of sports training and competition. Adorno does recognize some of the dialectical possibilities of sport, which I shall discuss in a moment, but overall he agrees with the spirit of negation in Veblen's analysis. According to Adorno: "Modern sports seek to restore to the body some of the functions of which the machine has deprived it. But they do so in order to train men all the more inexorably to serve the machine. Hence, sports belong to the realm of unfreedom, no matter where they are organized."[76]

Horkheimer and Adorno took these ideas further a few years later in their book, *Dialectic of Enlightenment*, which contains a detailed critical analysis of the mass culture industries. Here you see their dialectical minds turning to examine how the very things that human beings pursue for aesthetic, erotic, or non-instrumental/fun purposes have unintended consequence in postwar capitalist modernity of turning into their opposites: "free" leisure becomes the realm of unfree consumption, the pursuit of all that is useless and enjoyable is turned into what is instrumentally useful and subtly yoked to the reproduction of accumulation and domination on a broad scale. In a view reminiscent of Benjamin's remarks on the aestheticization of politics, Horkheimer and Adorno claim that people pursue short-term happiness in the realm of industrialized culture and confuse that for the more important goal of liberation.[77] Their summary position on sport is stated in the 1944 Preface to *Dialectic of Enlightenment*, where they compare "Volkswagen and the sports palace" as part of the "hygienic factory and everything pertaining to it." These things, they argue, "are themselves becoming metaphysics, an ideological curtain, within the social whole" and behind which "real doom is gathering."[78]

Herbert Marcuse would later refine and develop similar ideas in his books *Eros and Civilization* and *One-Dimensional Man*.[79] In a reference to Freud's discussion of the "reality principle," based on the repression of libidinal impulses that are necessary for civilization, Marcuse argues that modern capitalist societies, with their focus on competition, acquisition, accumulation, measurement, and administration, as well as the "mass manipulation of the entertainment industry," have substituted a "performance principle." Psychoanalysts have traditionally seen recreational sporting activities and entertainment as ways of desublimating repressed impulses. However, in capitalist modernity even these formerly desublimating activities have become repressive. Marcuse echoes Horkheimer and Adorno's suggestion of the homogenizing power of the culture industry by describing capitalist modernity as flattened and made one-dimensional by the dictates of capitalist accumulation, administration, and the performance principle.

Life in this one-dimensional reified world is dominated by a quest for "happy consciousness" rather than for meaningful social transformation. For Marcuse, like Horkheimer and Adorno, the traditional Marxist conception of the proletariat as the revolutionary agent in history is little more than a nostalgic fantasy. However, Marcuse offers a more optimistic view of this than Horkheimer and Adorno by suggesting the potentially autonomous and emancipatory character of "the aesthetic dimension" and noting that certain ethic and racial groups, or student activists, are often sufficiently insulated from the dictates of the culture industry and the bureaucratic state to provide sources of social opposition. Unlike orthodox Marxist analysis, Marcuse looks to the cultural, non-work sphere of society, and to the anti-racist civil rights movement or the student movements of the 1960s as sources of liberation.

Countercultural criticism and the retreat from critical theory in sports studies

In the heady days of student activism and "new left criticism" of the 1960s and early 1970s, many of these ideas drawn from Frankfurt School critical theory were taken up and integrated with ideas from other places, including French postwar social theory and early post-colonial thinking. This occurred in a spate of polemical "countercultural" critiques of sport published at the time, including works such as Gerhard Vinnai's book, *Football Mania*; Bero Rigauer's *Sport and Work* (written under Adorno's direction); Paul Hoch's *Rip Off the Big Game*; and Jean-Marie Brohm's set of essays in *Sport: A Prison of Measured Time*.[80] The uses of insights taken from Frankfurt School critical theory were not consistent in these books. For example, Jean-Marie Brohm draws from critical sources as diverse as Marcuse and the French philosopher, Louis Althusser, and Paul Hoch claims a debt to Antonio Gramsci. The most consistent uses of critical theory can be found in Rigauer's work and, arguably, in parts of Vinnai's attempt to merge psychoanalysis with sociological criticism of fan behavior. But all of the books express a countercultural critique of domination that owes a significant debt to critical theory.

Countercultural sports criticism of the 1960s and 1970s deserves a fuller discussion than I can give here, partly because in many instances the arguments and emphases expressed by different authors in this tradition vary. For example, Rigauer develops an analysis of the capitalist labor process using Marxian categories, whereas Paul Hoch's book is a more polemical and journalistic identification of examples where sport can be seen to serve the interests of monopoly capital, militarism, racism, and sexism. Still, at the risk of great simplification, I think the major themes and arguments outlined in the most notable "critical" discussions of sport in the late 1960s and early 1970s can be outlined in ten summary points, many of which draw strongly from earlier insights of Frankfurt School critical theory. I've listed these below in no particular order of importance:

1 Modern sports are the social form of play in an alienated society. In this sense, they can be seen as the alienated expression of the human play impulse.

2 Sports, like modern societies more generally, are shaped by modernity's drive to dominate nature, while simultaneously acting as a reflection of capitalist exchange relations, work, and the forces of administrative/technical rationality. Sports are now simply extensions of the capitalist exchange process, and "workers" in sport are subject to intense forms of labor discipline.

3 Sports promote aggression and brutality due to their capacity to symbolically represent, and inevitably fail to control, competing social interests and identities.

4 The intensity of training in high-level sport enables sadistic bodily regimes and their sadomasochistic acceptance. Here in the form of hyper-asceticism and mutilation, consciousness is reflected back on the body in an unfree form.

5 As archaic models for mass rallies, and in their rigid hierarchies of organization and production, sports contain anti-democratic and authoritarian principles and promote blind obedience to authority.

6 Sports promote hyper-masculinism and patriarchy through the celebration of force and the domination of opponents in pursuit of an instrumental goal, in addition to outright sexist discrimination.

7 Sports provide widespread distractions that are the modern equivalent of the political manipulation and barbarism associated with the "bread and circuses" of ancient Rome. But, additionally, through their agonistic and ostensibly meritocratic form, they are sites for the reproduction of the capitalist ideologies of hard work and bourgeois individualism.

8 Modern sports were founded through imperialist and colonial networks and carry the indelible stamp of this racist history. Race continues to be a major filter through which sport is understood.

9 Sports seem to offer opportunities for fun (Freudian), desublimation, and self-fulfillment, but in the end they provide the opposite of these positive social experiences.

10 Sports can offer glimpses of utopia, in addition to their negativity, through their idealized endorsement of the useless and the

gratuitous, as well as the socially positive idea of "fair play." But these utopian visions are false. More significantly, the fact that so many people believe in them allows sport to operate comparatively unimpeded as a site for the production of ideology.

The key themes that run through these summary points are the twin concerns for domination and ideology. The most significant contribution made by critical theory to the countercultural social analysis of sport in the 1960s and 1970s was its exposure of the problem of domination, hidden or disguised by the rhetorics of play, fairness, or meaningful leisure, based on the pursuit of non-instrumental activities. For anyone who was influenced by this literature in the 1970s it was simply not possible any more to view sport as an inherently disinterested, civilizing, or socially enabling aspect of modern culture, as was often suggested by "national" sports administrators, apologists for school physical education and sport, or proponents of modern "Olympism." Through the early 1970s, a discourse of *negation* and an accompanying tendency for radical pessimism emerged as the most significant markers of the application of critical theory to sport.

It is important to understand that critical theory's focus on negation emerged against the background of the totalizing character of domination evident in Nazi spectacles and Nazi aesthetics. Still, at the same time, for all its emphasis on negation, critical theory also implied that domination and ideology are not guaranteed. For example, there are numerous examples in the tradition of critical theory where it is suggested that sport's capacity to offer glimpses of utopian social relations are not *always* compromised. Adorno, in particular, was quick to condemn sport for its unfreedom, distractedness, and infantile character, but he insisted on maintaining a more dialectical viewpoint. Thus, in his critique of Thorstein Veblen's allegedly "gloomy" discussion of culture, he emphasized the all-important contrast between *what is* as opposed to cultural imaginings of *what might be*. This extends to an understanding of fetishism: "commodity fetishes are not merely a projection of opaque human relationships onto the world of things. They are also chimerical deities which originate in the exchange process but nevertheless represent something not absorbed by it."[81]

By analogy, even in its dominant reified forms, sport can also promote "a view of fairness and human dignity that is otherwise concealed and removed from the consciousness of the people."[82] Adorno makes the point more directly in a radio talk in 1966 on "Education after Auschwitz":

> Sport is ambiguous. On the one hand it can have an anti-barbaric and anti-sadistic effect by means of *fair play*, a spirit of chivalry, and consideration for the weak. On the other hand, in many of its varieties and practices it can promote aggression, brutality, and sadism, above all in people who do not expose themselves to the exertion and discipline required by sports but instead merely watch: that is, those who regularly shout from the sidelines. Such an ambiguity should be analyzed systematically.[83]

However, other than a number of references to fair play, Adorno did not set himself the task of exploring this dialectic in sport in any detail, and he consistently showed a tendency to focus more on negation: the critical unmasking of sport's dominant and repressive tendencies.[84]

I have argued elsewhere that the imagined juxtaposition of free play and constrained sport implicit in this dialectic is insufficiently materialist in its critical impulse.[85] At its best, the discourse of freedom versus constraint in sport tends to collapse into romantic wishful thinking about the need to recover or mobilize the spirit of free play or fairness, and fails to acknowledge the social constitution of structuring principles invoked to insure this possibility. At its worst, the free play versus constrained sport dialectic reproduces rigid conceptual dichotomies that have a troubled history in western societies. In this respect, Adorno's politics, which located sources of liberation in autonomous art and free critical self-reflection, never struck me as satisfactory. There is arguably more sociological merit in Marcuse's search for actually existing social sources of opposition to oppression by groups such as civil rights activists and students who tended to be on the margins of one-dimensional societies.

Still, even in Marcuse, the emphasis on negation often seems overwhelming. In his later writing, Lukács criticizes the trend among critical theorists to take up residence in the "grand hotel abyss."[86] A truly radical approach to critical theory, as Raymond Williams once put it, would surely strive to "make hope practical rather than despair convincing."[87] In addition, more traditional Marxists were troubled by critical theory's emphasis on reification and the "superstructure" at the expense of analyzing the workings of domination *within* the capitalist labor process.[88] Some writers saw Frankfurt School critical theory as just one more variation of a tradition of twentieth-century mass culture criticism that is arguably more conservative than radical.[89] Others argued that Frankfurt School critical theory carries the whiff of a troubling radical paternalism, implying, for example, that somehow the western working class has failed in what Lukács called its "world historical mission" by trading the pursuit of happiness for liberation.[90]

There was also widespread rejection of the unintelligibility and perceived cultural snobbery found in much of Frankfurt School critical theory. In her introduction to Benjamin's essays, Hannah Arendt reveals her admiration for Benjamin's insight as an analyst and commentator but she is also critical of Benjamin on many issues and admits "there are many pages in Benjamin that I do not understand."[91] Adorno's work is so theoretically complex, and obsessed with dialectics and rarified philosophical discussion, that it is often less accessible than Benjamin's work. Moreover, unlike Benjamin, who saw himself as an intellectual *flâneur*, Adorno tends more to adopt the philosophical pose of a high cultural mandarin.

Part of this undoubtedly stems from Adorno's own biography. He was trained as a classical pianist and composer and was a child musical prodigy, playing Beethoven competently at an early age. He went on to study with the German composer Alban Berg, and later became a devoted aficionado of the avant-garde music of Schoenberg. Adorno's personal high-cultural sensibilities are frequently on display when he sets out to analyze prevailing forms of mass culture, such as television, popular music, and astrology and sometimes demonstrate insensitivity to audience agency and the historical subtleties of the popular cultural traditions that he criticizes. An example is his misunderstanding of the meaning of popular dance crazes and popular music, evident when he ponders how to turn "jitterbugging insects" into thinking men and women.[92] There is arguably similar insensitivity to his understanding of the diversity of social meanings in sport.

Backlash against such popular-cultural myopia grew significantly throughout the 1970s, especially in work being undertaken in British cultural studies. Part of that backlash was not just about the recovery of a more populist understanding of cultural forms and practices. It also had to do with the blindness to race and gender that ran through much prewar and early postwar critical theory. An emerging view, to adapt a phrase used by feminist art critics, the Guerrilla Girls, was that critical theory was just "too male, too pale, and too stale."[93] For example, in hindsight, Adorno's earliest work on jazz is largely insensitive to the history and cultural dynamics of African-American culture. I think a similar point can be extended to Adorno's understanding of sport. Similarly, while sensitive to the horrors of the Nazi ideologies of authoritarianism and racial purity, some of Horkheimer's early ideas about the changing nature of the family in modern western societies seem no less antiquated from the standpoint of contemporary feminism.[94]

So, for many people when it came to critical theory, the late 1970s and early 1980s were times to move on to other modes of analysis. That trend is certainly evident in writing on sport – perhaps even more so than in social theory more broadly. From the 1970s to the present, the critical focus of research in sports studies moved in the directions of Antonio Gramsci, Michel Foucault, Jacques Derrida, Pierre Bourdieu, or Stuart Hall; the writing of prominent feminist theorists such as Donna Haraway and Judith Butler; the postmodern criticisms of writers such as Lyotard and Baudrillard; the critical spatial political economy developed by writers such as David Harvey and Neal Smith; and the postcolonial and critical theories explored by writers such as Frantz Fanon, Edward Said, and Gayatri Spivak.

Why critical theory still matters

These diverse theoretical influences provided extremely important resources for the development of sophisticated social criticism in sports studies. Nonetheless, despite critical theory's weaknesses, some important ideas and insights were lost in the retreat from it that occurred in sports studies in the late twentieth century. For one thing, it is important to understand that critical theory has not stood still. Notably, academic journals such as *Telos* and *New German Critique* played a major role in refining and developing critical theory in the late twentieth century. Today, the Frankfurt School tradition extends to include the work of a wide range of more contemporary writers such as Claus Offe, Albrecht Wellmer, Oskar Negt, Alexander Kluge, Axel Honneth, Jürgen Habermas, and Seyla Benhabib.[95] The range of ideas in this expanded tradition has taken critical theory far beyond Horkheimer and Adorno's analysis of the culture industry. For example, during the 1980s, at a time when I had little interest in Horkheimer and Adorno, I found Offe's work on the contradictions of the capitalist state to be very helpful in conceptualizing a shift in the provision of community recreation in Canada from an emphasis on equal opportunity and citizenship to an emphasis on economic growth and revenue generation.[96]

More importantly, as global warming and ecological destruction have become more pressing topics, the Frankfurt School tradition continues to be relevant because it positions human interaction with nature as a core idea in understanding the forms of domination that have emerged in the West over the last three or four hundred years. This is an important theme in Horkheimer and Adorno's analysis of Francis Bacon in *Dialectic of Enlightenment,* as well as in Marcuse's critical analysis of technology. The domination of nature through science and technology remains an underdeveloped theme in critical analyses of sport. Much of the writing on "doping" in sport, for example, seems overly focused on the moral question of "cheating," and not on doping as a "technology" of human performance that resonates with nineteenth-century conceptions of human improvement through scientific intervention. A concern with the domination of nature, say, through the environmental consequences of producing large-scale international sporting events, can also lead to discussions of "risk" in sport which might conceivably connect with the work of Ulrich Beck, whose ideas on risk and "new modernity," in my view, have not had the influence on sports studies that they should have had.[97]

There is also a basis in critical theory for a deep and wide-ranging challenge to the forces of rationalization and the technical operations of both capitalist and administrative power in modern life, not only in respect to a critique of training regimes and sport science in "elite" sport, but also in the way that sport at all levels reproduces and normalizes new kinds of "government" of the body. In an era of wearable fitness technology, the omnipresence of measurement of the body, "big data," and increased digital surveillance, this seems a more pressing need than ever.[98] There are important connections here between critical theory and Foucault's writing on the self, governmentality, and biopolitics, yet Frankfurt School critical theory is too rarely integrated into such analyses. It is surprising because Foucault commented on his admiration of *Dialectic of Enlightenment* and praised German critical theory on several occasions. He once remarked in an interview: "If I had been familiar with the Frankfurt School, I would not have said a number of stupid things that I did say and I would have avoided many of the detours which I made while trying to pursue my own humble path."[99] The shared influence of Nietzsche is especially notable on both Foucault and the Frankfurt School. This is not to say that a theoretical synthesis of the dialectical reasoning of critical theory and Foucault's genealogical reasoning is always methodologically feasible. My point is only, when it comes to the study of administrative technique, power, and domination, there are insights in an application of critical theory to sport that can augment, or even rival, a Foucauldian perspective.

There are also vital starting points in critical theory to develop more thorough and sophisticated analyses of ideology in contemporary sport. Ideology fell out of favor as a concept in social theory during the 1980s and early 1990s, based largely on the argument that the critique of ideology requires a contrast with some idea of truth, or real consciousness, versus the allegedly false or distorted character of ideology. For many people, especially those influenced by Foucault, critical analysis is better served by concepts such as discourse, knowledge, and power. I have never been fully persuaded by such arguments. For example, at the very moment that many people were rejecting the relevance of the concept of ideology in western social thought, neoliberal ideology was remaking economies around the world, an issue I turn to in the next chapter. By the end of the 1990s, ideology critique was making a comeback in social theory in the work of writers such as John Thompson, David Hawkes, David Harvey, and Slavoj Žižek.[100]

Critical theory has provided the study of ideology with some of its most important insights, for example by showing how ideology could be "productive" on its own terms rather than existing merely as something dependent on a materialist productive base. Critical theory has also had useful things to say about distraction, about the internalization of bourgeois ideals, and the effects of more anonymous ideologies of technique and administrative organization. Most importantly, ideology came to be seen in critical theory as an important form of mediation between subject and object, base and superstructure, in modern life. Following Lukács, this required an understanding of reification and especially of how ideologies often make their claims by confusing the part with the whole. We might well explore the operations of ideology in sport, for example, by noting how things become ideological, not because they are completely false but because they are only partially true. The ideological moment occurs when partial truth substitutes for a full and complete understanding of the social situation. Critical theory asserts that the study of symbolic forms of any type should be analyzed with respect to how they might be seen to serve the material interests of dominant groups, of certain worldviews, or of particular sets of sedimented practices. In my view, studies of ideology in sport are nowhere near as well developed theoretically as they should be. Critical theory can help in this task, even if it shouldn't be relied on to provide final answers.

Critical theory's dialectical rejection of any reified understanding of history or society also contains an important counterpoint to empiricist and positivist thinking. Critical theory urges us, time and again, not to confuse our own analytical constructions with an unmediated, objective "reality." Adorno, in particular, wanted to retain a dialectical focus on "relations" more than "things," and on the process of "becoming" more than on falsely conceptualized static objects. But he correctly severed these ideas from Hegelian-Marxist teleological thinking that ascribed a purpose to history. I believe that a non-teleological yet dialectical critique of reification, especially as noted in Walter Benjamin's approach to history, holds promise as a way of reconceptualizing historical understandings of sport. Instead of approaching the emergence of modern sport only in institutional terms – for example, as an expression of such things as social trends toward rationalization, bureaucratization, secularism, or commodification – critical theory invites us to understand the very invention of modern sport as an exercise in reification.

The germ of my discussion in this book of the emergence of sport as "its own object," with its own essence and imagined properties, came initially from rethinking Lukács's discussion of reification a few years ago, followed by the idea of linking this to Habermas's conception of modernity as a "project." This led me to understand the construction of philosophical concepts such as the "autonomy" of sport as historically constituted objectified abstractions. My starting point for mapping the emergence of the idea of sport as its own object also took inspiration from Pierre Bourdieu, but it was only by rethinking ideas found in critical theory that I have been able to develop the argument in the way that it has unfolded. Moreover, it was the Frankfurt School, and its constant negotiation with aesthetic theory, that led me to an emphasis on representation and discourse in sport and drew me into literature on art, aesthetics, and cultural history.

In addition, critical theory continues to be relevant today because it is one of the only critical traditions devoted to *combining* a critique of modern society and culture with a critique of capitalist social relations. Critical theory has always sought to *unify* the often disparate strands of western cultural criticism and radical political economy. In a world increasingly influenced by internet memes, "fake news," and powerful cultures of celebrity, critical theory's emphasis on the fusion of authoritarianism, economic inequality, and popular cultural distraction seems more relevant than ever. There are some haunting similarities between right-wing neo-populist, racist narratives and authoritarian politics in North America and Europe today, and roughly similar conditions in the 1930s. In this context, Horkheimer, Adorno, and Marcuse arguably begin to look less like artifacts of the early postwar era than visionaries of the future.

Finally, the critical theory tradition directs us to conduct research first and foremost for emancipatory purposes through the critique of various forms of oppression and domination.[101] It does this against the postmodern emphasis on difference and fragmentation that was so prominent in the 1990s by retaining a commitment to understand the "totality" of social relations, as much as this is possible. Moreover, in critical theory, imagined divisions between "normative" and "non-normative" sociology and social theory are viewed as expressions of ideology. In contrast, critical theory continually sets itself the task of exploring relationships between knowledge and human interests. Building on a critique of reification, critical theory insists on erasing the lines between philosophy, history, and the social sciences. In the same way that the world is not divided up into disciplines the way that universities are, critical theory aims to produce broad-ranging, trans-disciplinary, and self-reflective knowledge.

Conclusion

The visibility and popularity of sport in Weimar Germany was a constitutive feature in the development of both German modernism and anti-modernism and fueled the growth of systematic social criticism. The early outlines of a German leftist critical theory of sport were drawn as part of a broader critique of Nazi aesthetics and spectacle during the 1930s. This work developed further from the 1940s through the 1960s and drew more strongly from the example of US culture. In this way, it became strongly shaped by the broader critique of the capitalist culture industries developed by writers such as Horkheimer, Adorno, and Marcuse. These works inspired a much broader range of critical analyses of sport undertaken during the 1960s and 1970s. While much of this work raised important issues, it also suffered from severe limitations, partially through its heavy dependence on the tradition of negation that was such a prominent aspect of Frankfurt School critical theory. Perhaps most notably, sport's ability to inspire activism and alternative understandings of history and society was left as an undeveloped theme during the 1960s. Still, despite these limitations, I have tried to show that there continues to be utility in a critical theory perspective.

Above all, the Frankfurt School tradition demands that social criticism should explore the contradictions between what modern societies potentially make possible and what they actually deliver. We live in a world with the greatest combination of wealth and technological innovations in human history. Yet it is a world where the dissemination of information is often indistinguishable from fiction and ideology and, to use Adorno's words, where "great stretches of human populations live in misery."[102] In this world, humanity's progress, hopes, and dreams often turn into their opposites. What seems like progress in one moment can seem like regression in another.

For example, in the next chapter I argue that large-scale sporting spectacles – often heralded during the 1990s as indices of modernity through "globalization"– have increasingly become sites for social exclusion, corruption, and widespread social unrest. Organizations, such as the IOC and the Fédération Internationale de Football Association (FIFA), which often claim to endorse progressive social missions of poverty reduction and the reduction of racism, ironically act in ways that reinforce poverty and racism. It is precisely by examining such apparent contradictions that a renewed critical theory can contribute to a better understanding of sport and global modernity.

— 5 —

A SAVAGE SORTING OF "WINNERS" AND "LOSERS": MODERNIZATION, DEVELOPMENT, SPORT, AND THE CHALLENGE OF SLUMS

In the opening passages of his book *Planet of Slums*, Mike Davis notes that there were eighty-six cities in the world in 1950 with a population of more than a million people.[1] In 2015, there were more than five hundred cities with populations in excess of a million.[2] China, in particular, has been urbanizing at a rate that is unprecedented in human history. Between 1978 and 2007, the number of official cities in China jumped from 193 to 640, and as of 2015 China had 224 cities with a population in excess of half a million.[3] In Africa, urban population growth since the 1950s has followed a similar pattern. Dhaka, Kinshasa, and Lagos have evolved into sprawling megacities. By the early 2000s, they were already nearly forty times the size they were in 1950.[4] According to a 2016 compendium of built-up areas, of the fifty largest cities in the world, forty-five can be found in the global South – cities such as Jakarta, Mexico City, Seoul-Incheon, São Paulo, Mumbai, Karachi, and Manila.[5]

In southern nations – the so-called developing world – this extraordinary urban growth has been driven by a complex set of global forces that have either pushed people out of rural areas against their will or drawn them to the city with promises of a better life. Across Africa, South Asia, Latin America, and South America, the mechanization of agriculture, the consolidation of small holdings into larger ones, and the competition from international agribusiness have challenged the ability of subsistence farmers to generate enough money for water, clothing, or school books.[6] In many parts of Africa, these pressures have been exacerbated by recurring drought and civil war. In China, migration from the countryside has been driven by an erosion of the social guarantees that once protected rural living standards, matched with the promise of steady factory wages in the

160

city and more cosmopolitan lifestyles. Some estimates suggest that by 2020 a staggering 300–500 million people in China will have moved from the countryside to urban areas.[7]

All of this has led to unrelenting economic and social pressures in cities across the global South. People continue to stream into the largest urban areas despite ongoing economic weaknesses in many cities and the cities' inability to provide adequate housing, public services, or sanitation. Accordingly, one of the most visible features of urban development since the mid-twentieth century has been the dramatic spread of squatter cities, shantytowns, and tenement districts. These slum districts now absorb the majority of population growth in many of the world's poorest countries. By the early twenty-first century, the number of squatters, people living illegally on land they do not own, was already well over a billion worldwide, approximately one out of every six human beings on the planet.[8] The situation is worst in cities with the highest population densities and, in addition to population size, the fifty densest cities in the world in 2015 were all found in the global South.[9] Even in North America and Europe, while the trends are far less dramatic, research has shown a pattern of increasing homelessness and squatting and the displacement of former slum populations into peripheral pockets of suburban poverty.[10]

In this concluding chapter, I argue that the challenges of urban creative destruction and the dispossession of poor urban populations to prepare for international sporting mega-events are significant issues of twenty-first-century modernity and should therefore figure prominently in any critical theory of sport. There is some encouraging work that has taken up aspects of these issues in areas such as sport and globalization, sport and social movements, and sport and subaltern studies.[11] There has also been considerable discussion in recent years of the uses of sport for development and the promotion of peace, and the literature in this area is growing rapidly.[12] Furthermore, a number of studies undertaken since the early 2000s have focused on relations between development, international sport, dispossession, and poverty.[13] Still, I think there is insufficient research on the political and economic interests and ideological assumptions associated with sport and development initiatives of various types, particularly those that claim to include poverty reduction as an objective.

With these concerns in mind, the analysis that follows situates the enthusiasm for sport as an aspect of development policy in its historical and political economic context, beginning with a consideration of mid-century Keynesianism and "modernization theory." This leads to a discussion of the rise of non-governmental organizations (NGOs) as promoters of sport as a tool for "development" in the early twenty-first century, including an evaluation of several foundational policy documents and discussions of inequality found within them. Following this, I turn to an evaluation of whether recent attempts to achieve modernity through hosting large-scale sporting spectacles, especially in cities located in the global South, have provided effective responses to the challenge of slums.

From state investments to civil society: modernization theory, development, and the rise of NGO "partnerships"

For most people, the word "slum" refers to large-scale zones of urban habitation that are economically impoverished, overcrowded, and lacking an adequate health and services infrastructure. Yet it is an imprecise term that blurs the vast distinctions between the environments inhabited by the world's dispossessed. The word "slum" also often carries with it an implicit sense of judgment.[14] On this point, Robert Neuwirth notes that slums are everything that people who do not live in them tend to fear: dirt, decay, disease, despair, degradation, horror, abuse, crime, uncertainty, and danger. To use the word "slum" risks conjuring an implicit morality. "Slum" means something bad and, indeed for outsiders who often have the best of intentions, something to be "improved" or "developed."[15]

Still, in contrast to this depiction and for all their problems, slums are also neighborhoods and communities – sometimes in the best sense of these terms. While slum neighborhoods may be economically depressed, they can be alive with an anarchic blend of mutualism matched with high levels of individual freedom and creative energy. It is important not to romanticize these communities, where people often lead very desperate lives, but slum communities should be neither demonized nor patronized. Too often, programs to eradicate slums seem merely intent on relocating "the problem" elsewhere or to seek paternalistic solutions from outside the community. Alternatively, many slum development programs tend to be temporary and ameliorative, unable to respond to the structural dynamics that are creating the problem of slums in the first place. Others, such as the favela "pacification" programs launched in Rio de Janeiro prior to the 2013 Confederation Cup and the 2014 men's football World Cup, are more coercive in character and linked to initiatives associated with crime prevention and gentrification. Neuwirth suggests that the only practical solution to the problem of slums is not to try to eliminate slum conditions; rather, the solution lies in *not* treating poor urban communities as slums – that is, as "horrific, scary and criminal – and start treating them as neighborhoods that can be improved."[16]

Nonetheless, the phrase *poor neighborhoods* lacks the evocative power of the word "slum," and it is the latter word that has figured centrally in key programmatic discussions of global urban poverty since the beginning of the twenty-first century. For example, in 2003, UN-Habitat released a landmark report, *The Challenge of Slums*, that urged donors and governments to improve the lives of five to ten million slum dwellers by 2005, and one hundred million by 2020, in line with the broader Millennium Goals (UNMGs) announced in the United Nations' *Millennium Declaration* in 2000.[17] In its declaration, the United Nations announced a commitment to work toward the eradication of extreme global poverty and hunger by 2015 (an impossible target that has since been pushed back to 2030).[18] Other UNMGs included the achievement of universal primary education; promotion of gender equality and women's empowerment; reduction of child mortality; improvement in maternal health; the combating of HIV/AIDS, malaria, and other diseases; environmental sustainability; and the pursuit of global partnerships for development. *The Challenge of Slums* embraced a similarly broad set of objectives, including "leading a worldwide effort to move from pilot projects to city-wide and nation-wide upgrading, and to generate the required resources to do so; and investing in global knowledge, learning and capacity in slum upgrading, and reducing the growth of new slums."[19] The report suggested that such broad-ranging objectives would only be achieved by increasing investments aimed at providing basic services to the world's urban poor.

In the immediate aftermath of World War II, it was widely assumed that governments would be the most likely source of such investments. A postwar economic boom in western societies was strongly shaped by a rejection of the laissez-faire policies seen to have caused the Great Depression. The influential British economist, John Maynard Keynes, criticized the free-market fundamentalism of neoclassical capitalist economics, arguing that building and maintaining aggregate demand in modern societies and eliminating financial instability were keys to economic prosperity.[20] Influenced by Keynesian thinking, western capitalist industrial states borrowed for infrastructure investments and enacted capital controls, corporate tax rates rose, government regulations proliferated, and fiscal and monetary policies were employed to "dampen business cycles and . . . ensure reasonably full employment."[21] Governments worked hard to keep economies stable, "using new techniques of Keynesian pump priming through the public sector."[22] The postwar boom was also influenced by "the state-sponsored reconstruction of war-torn economies, suburbanization, particularly in the United States, urban renewal, geographical expansion of transport and communications systems and infrastructural development" and by an expanding consumer market driven by the entertainment industries associated with film, television, recorded music, and sports.[23] The capital for such growth was coordinated through a range of national *public* institutions in individual industrial societies, as well as through a web of interlinked financial centers, with the United States, especially New York, leading the way.[24]

According to David Harvey, postwar stability was further underpinned by wealth redistribution through the institutionalization of collective bargaining, and state provision of a social wage, while "working class institutions such as labor unions and political parties of the left" gained influence.[25] Under pressure from communist countries, and social democratic and socialist movements at home, capitalist regimes expanded public expenditures in areas such as health care, social security, and education. An uneasy compromise between labor and capital underpinned this stability, with capital "grudgingly tolerating" Keynesian intervention in return for high growth rates and diminished working-class militancy.[26]

If Keynesian thinking boosted confidence in state solutions to domestic social problems after World War II, it also underpinned a renewed US confidence in the role of governments in ameliorating perceived "backwardness" and poverty elsewhere in the world. In a postwar environment of Cold War politics, when many nations in the global South were breaking from colonial rule, models of development were influenced by capitalist and socialist competition for geopolitical leadership. Fear of the spread of communist influences in the industrialized West coincided with an upsurge of confidence in liberal democracy and pluralism in the United States during the late 1950s. After the war, US intellectuals had debated alleged threats to modern "mass societies" suggested by early twentieth-century critics of modernity – such as urban loneliness, normlessness or "anomie," and the susceptibility of modern masses to political manipulation. However, there was a growing belief that such threats had passed.[27] To cite one well-known example, the Harvard sociologist Daniel Bell argued forcefully that the postwar United States should not be characterized as a modern "mass society."[28] Rather, it was a pluralist democracy with high levels of individual freedom, civic participation, citizen satisfaction, and agreement on core values, including "a rough consensus among intellectuals on political issues; the acceptance of a welfare state; the desirability of decentralized power; a system of mixed economy and of political pluralism." In the postwar United States, Bell concluded, "the ideological age has ended."[29]

These circumstances and ideas both contributed to, and reflected, an emergent *theory* of "modernization" that swept through US social science, think tanks, and government agencies during the 1950s and 1960s.[30] A rough genealogy of the theory would include several of the ideas discussed in earlier chapters of this book: that knowledge is cumulative and contributes to a human ability to understand and dominate nature through science and technological innovation and that increasing complexity in the division of labor through industrialism contributes to social "development." As Armand Mattelart points out, the earliest conceptions of "western development" in European thought also embraced an evolutionary organicism that saw *progress* as natural and inevitable: "a phase of nature, 'like the development of the embryo and the opening of a flower.'"[31]

Selective threads of these ideas were evident in the work of early European social theorists such as Henri Saint-Simon and August Comte through an emphasis on the advancement of secular reason and industrial development. In a different way, these ideas were taken up and popularized in the mid-nineteenth century in the evolutionary "social Darwinism" proposed by the English sociologist Herbert Spencer. By the end of the century, the idea of progress through industrialism and increased social complexity took new form in the theories of sociologists such as Émile Durkheim and Max Weber, whose work contributed to an emerging "general theory" of industrial society, characterized most famously by transitions between differing forms of social organization, such as "organic" and "mechanical" solidarity and "traditional" and "modern" societies.[32]

The influence of this emerging general theory of industrial society – and especially of Weber's contrast between the ideal types of "traditional" and "modern" societies – was very strong in mid-twentieth century US social science. However, whereas both Durkheim and Weber had ambivalent views of modernity at best, many mid-twentieth-century US social scientists tended to see the transition from "traditional" to "modern" forms of authority and social organization as "a singular path of progressive change" driven by the "rationalization" of the West."[33] This view was also influenced by growing belief in the US ability *to lead* the "free world" against communism as well as by palpable fears that "western progress" would be undermined by the global expansion of communist, or even milder socialist, influences.

Promoters of modernization theory contrasted the virtues of capitalism, liberal democracy, and the Keynesian policy state with the pursuit of "development" through bureaucratically planned communist or socialist societies.[34] According to Nils Gilman, "by defining a single model of progressive change," the conception of modernization promoted by postwar US liberal-democrats "simplified the complicated world-historical problems of decolonization and industrialization, helping to guide American economic aid and military intervention in postcolonial regions."[35] Modernization was abstracted from its origins in European history and social theory – a more correct label might be "Euro-modernization" – and was conceptualized instead as a spatially and temporally *neutral* model of social development in general.

Yet there were familiar echoes here of earlier western imperialist assumptions. "Traditional societies" were said to be in their "infancy" compared to the modern industrial West. As such, they could be characterized as "undeveloped": inward-looking, passive toward nature, superstitious, fearful of change, economically and technologically simple, and politically autocratic, with a low emphasis on values of individual achievement.[36] Gilman argues that the *project* of postwar modernization theory was to achieve "modernity the world over" modeled on the lines of the western democracies, with the United States as the exemplar: "By learning from the history of industrialized countries, 'latecomers' could bypass the various historical cul-de-sacs that had slowed the growth of these first movers. Given proper technical guidance and financial help, as well as political education and institutions, poor countries ought to be able to catch up with the rich countries."[37] To many business and political leaders in "recovering" or "developing" postwar societies, the affluence, freedom, and stability of postwar western nations provided evidence for this promise. Modernization through state encouragement of capitalist investments was something that decolonizing societies should aspire to.

However, the politics of such aspirations in newly modernizing societies, and visions of the best path to achieve them, were extremely complicated and sometimes contradictory. Communists, socialists, and militant trade unionists of the era typically mounted an offensive against US-led approaches to modernization by emphasizing its exploitative history in peripheral nations and its longstanding association with western imperialism. In their view, the sting in the tail of the promise of liberal capitalist modernization was continued *dependency* – the assumption that "proper technical guidance and financial help, as well as political education and institutions" noted above would necessarily come from the imperialist West. Leftist militants suggested that socialism could deliver a standard of social, economic, and technical "development" that would rival that of the United States or northern Europe. In opposition, liberal modernization theorists portrayed the socialist path to modernity as "deviant" or "pathological."[38]

After more than three decades of struggle, with the exceptions of a handful of countries such as the Soviet Union, Maoist China, and Cuba, socialist models of modernization and development were pushed – often forcibly – to the international margins by variations of Euro-American modernization theory. At the same time, the world's leading socialist countries and decolonizing nations retreated from staging "alternative" international sporting competitions and opted to join more established international organizations, ostensibly to dramatize the political and economic successes of socialist and decolonizing nations on a larger stage. Yet the collapse of alternative models for international competitions effectively guaranteed that the pursuit of modernization through sport in peripheral nations would be linked in future to market-centered industrial growth and require coordination with the goals of international non-governmental organizations (INGOs), such as the IOC and FIFA. As Darnell and Millington point out, the case of Mexico provides an illustrative example.[39] Mexican officials turned to mass sport as early as the 1920s as means to promote discipline, achievement, vitality, and national unity. More notably, Mexico's bid for the 1968 Summer Olympics was strongly shaped by a discourse of modernization that embraced market principles. Supporters saw the Olympics as a showcase for "a modern Mexico that had broken away from its pre-modern past." The Olympics were also pursued as "a final push towards modernization; growth in tourism, foreign investment, elevated nationalist spirit, and international recognition brought about by hosting the Games would mark Mexico's transition from a 'developing' to a 'developed' state."[40]

Rather like the World's Fairs and Olympics earlier in the twentieth century, the use of sport to advance such ambitions became increasingly competitive after World War II. Aspiring postwar cities and nations tried to outdo each other to achieve international recognition and prestige, as well as promising INGOs, such as the IOC or FIFA, to build more and better facilities. For example, there were 4,900 athletes from 69 countries at the 1953 Helsinki Summer Olympics, but by the 1972 Munich Summer Olympics the size of the Games had grown to 7,000 athletes from 122 nations. Somewhat similarly, there were only fifteen teams involved in the 1950 football World Cup, playing in six venues, although Brazilian authorities invested heavily in a dramatically modernist stadium, Estádio de Maracanã, capable of seating nearly 200,000 spectators. By the time of the 1982 football World Cup in Spain, the number of teams had grown to thirty-five, playing in seventeen stadiums in fourteen host cities.

Growth in the size and complexity of such events was accompanied by increasing public investments, justified largely as Keynesian policies designed to meet postwar modernizing social planning objectives. For the 1952 Summer Olympics in Helsinki, the Finnish government built highways and railroads and laid new telephone cable between Finland and Sweden. Eight years later, Rome spent lavishly on sports facilities, highways, and beautification projects for the Summer Olympics. Tokyo continued this upward trend by spending an estimated US$2 billion for the 1964 Summer Olympics on administration, facility construction, transportation, and urban infrastructure. Expenditures for the Munich Summer Olympics in 1972 were no less dramatic, with more than DM 1,972 million (more than US$600 million) spent on construction of sports facilities, student dwellings, daycare centers, miles of road improvements, and a new subway system. Four years later, the total cost of the Montreal Summer Olympics was an estimated Canadian $1.4 billion, while estimates for the 1980 Summer Olympics in Moscow have been in excess of US$2 billion.[41]

A comparatively low level of investment from private-sector organizations in the early years after the war also influenced reliance on state investments. From the 1940s through the 1950s, there were limited media or sponsorship revenues available to organizers of international sporting spectacles. Cinema and radio had helped to build audiences for professional sports and international championships around the world through much of the first half of the twentieth century, but the electronic media systems in many nations were *public* rather than *private*, meaning that audiences were not treated as commodities that could be sold to advertisers. Even in the commercial US electronic media system, where radio audiences were well-established commodities, advertising budgets were initially suppressed by flattened consumer demand during the depression years and later wartime austerity. Television technology was in its infancy and the technical capacity for transmitting electronic media signals *internationally* was rudimentary and fragmented. In addition, the IOC and FIFA, the sponsoring organizations of what would become the largest international sporting spectacles in the postwar era, had yet to fully embrace or understand the logic of profit maximization. The IOC was philosophically committed to controlling the scale and non-commercial "amateur" status of Olympic competition. FIFA openly embraced "professionalism," but in step with the tenor of the times was slow to grasp the commercial potential of media revenues and the economic value of its "brand."

Much of this began to change in the 1980s with a widespread retreat from Keynesian economics in capitalist nations around the world, the collapse of state socialism in the Soviet Union and eastern Europe, and an accompanying rise of triumphalist neoliberal globalization. In this context, early postwar capitalist discourses on Euro-modernization were subtly reconfigured into "end of history" or "there is no alternative" endorsements of liberal capitalist globalization. In the case of international sport, the influences of these changes can be usefully mapped along three related lines of analysis: (1) the growth and institutionalization of "civil society" approaches to sport and development; (2) the systemic deepening and integration of capitalist relations in the postwar cultural industries, and their growing importance in the global economy; (3) new patterns of civic and national aspiration, associated with broad changes in economic and political global networks that intensified the perceived value of sporting mega-events in a new *global* competition for investment capital, international status, tourism, and geopolitical advantage.

Consider first the emergence of civil society approaches to development. In its simplest form, the phrase "civil society" refers to social organizations and associations that are independent of the state.[42] Enthusiasm for civil society organizations in international development in the 1980s and 1990s occurred in conjunction with a loss of faith across much of North America and Europe in the ability of state organizations to resolve major social problems. It also reflected a trend toward non-state approaches to development that were ascendant in large international economic organizations such as the International Monetary Fund and the World Bank.[43] Here the emphasis was less on state "policies and planning" than on free-market principles and the ideals of entrepreneurialism and individual initiatives.

In an environment permeated by distrust of state agencies' abilities to find solutions to contemporary social problems, a turn to civil society organizations, buttressed by donor partners in the corporate sector, came to be seen as an inevitable, and in some cases a

169

progressive, alternative. For progressively minded individuals and groups, the NGO path to development connected strongly to an emphasis on the role of autonomous organizations in civil society as agents of change, against the inequities and constraints of the state and the market. For postwar free-market evangelists, who tended to be suspicious of the state, the pathway to social progress was seen to lie with the private sector in combination with other "stakeholders" represented by civil society organizations. Each of these political perspectives embraced the importance of civil society organizations in social change and development, albeit for different reasons. Nonetheless, from the 1980s onward, the idea of NGO-led approaches to development was able to draw subtly on both traditions in making a claim to legitimacy, sometimes blurring their lines in new ways.

By the early 1990s, the idea of necessary partnerships between large multilateral organizations – such as the United Nations and its agencies, national governments, NGOs, and new national and multinational corporate supporters – was emerging as the cutting edge in international development circles. According to the World Bank, 12 percent of foreign aid to developing countries, amounting to a few billions of dollars, was already being channeled through NGOs in 1994. By 1996, the total amount was US$7 billion worldwide. In Africa alone, NGOs managed nearly US$3.5 billion in external aid in 1998, compared to under US$1 billion in 1990.[44] By 2004, it was estimated that NGOs contributed to US$23 billion of foreign aid money, or approximately a third of global overseas development aid.[45]

Making poverty history? Sport in the neoliberal discourse of rights, stakeholders, and partnerships

Despite the growth noted above, many NGOs were finding it difficult to raise enough money from memberships and private donations to take on the larger role that they were being invited to fill, and there was increasing competition for traditional sources of funds arising from the proliferation of new NGO competitors. The logical solution to such funding problems was to augment the traditional sources of donor revenue through new partnerships with governments and the private sector. An international framework for such partnerships was initiated in 1999 when the United Nations launched a new global compact (UNGC) program with more than three thousand companies willing to partner with NGOs, governments, and other international

170

agencies to work toward meeting United Nations development goals. In this global compact, public-minded corporations, and NGOs committed themselves to principles of sustainability, social justice, health, and economic development to build what the UNGC final report called "a better world for all."[46]

It is not surprising that sport would quickly be seen as a useful ground for forging development partnerships through the Global Compact. The idea of individual, social, and cultural development through sport has a long history, stretching back to nineteenth-century middle- and working-class movements for rational recreation and muscular Christianity. As Bruce Kidd notes, this tradition was taken up by professional physical educators, amateur sports organizations, and prominent international athletes, and soon forged connections with the philosophy of Olympism, with its emphasis on fair play and internationalism. A belief that sport can be a source of social improvement and development can also be found in sources as diverse as the playground movement of the early twentieth century and the workers' sports movements of the interwar period.[47]

However, Kidd suggests that a late twentieth- and early twenty-first-century view of sport as a vehicle for development is markedly different, even though it draws on some of the ideas and assumptions of earlier traditions. It is different "in the rapid explosion of the agencies and organizations that are involved, the tremendous appeal it has for youth volunteering, the financial support it enjoys from the powerful international sports federations and the extent to which it has been championed by the United Nations, its agencies and significant partners."[48] In addition, he notes that a movement for "sport for development and peace" was able to take root in the 1990s, given the collapse of the Cold War and its attendant complications for development programs. Just like the NGO sector more broadly, the neoliberalism of that decade enabled a "new focus on entrepreneurship as a strategy for social development, creating new openings for the creation of non-governmental organizations and private foundations."[49] At the same time, the movement also fed on a spirit of "humanitarian intervention" associated with the growing legitimation of international legislative bodies, such as the International Court of Justice, and the accompanying notion of the "right to protect" in the wake of the "genocides in Rwanda and the former Yugoslavia, the tremendous visibility of the worldwide appeals to combat famine and the pandemic of HIV/AIDs in Africa," as well as various campaigns to end global poverty.[50]

In this context, older connections between sports organizations and the United Nations solidified in new ways. United Nations agencies had used major sporting events and star athletes in the past in campaigns to promote immunization against childhood diseases, along with other public health measures, and to support human rights, especially the postwar fight against racism and apartheid. The right to play and to participate in sports regardless of race, ethnicity, or gender was solidified in UN policy through such events as the Convention on the Elimination of All Forms of Discrimination against Women in 1979 and the later ratification of the Convention on the Rights of the Child in 1990. Since the early 1990s, UN agencies such as UNESCO, UNICEF, and the UN Development Program (UNDP) have worked out cooperative agreements and programs with international sporting associations in the interests of promoting social responsibility and meeting the UNMGs. Major examples include the IOC, which continues to form alliances with a diversity of UN agencies and is a partner in a variety of innovative development projects, and FIFA, which established working relationships with the World Health Organization and UNICEF for campaigns against polio and for the rights of children.[51]

By the turn of the twenty-first century, it was impossible to ignore the seemingly insatiable desire for sport in countries around the world, the increasing size of global audiences for international sporting events, and the striking growth in the numbers of sports organizations and NGOs interested either in developing sport opportunities in disadvantaged communities and countries or in using sport as a platform for development programs in areas such as maternal health, gender equity, and HIV/AIDS promotion. In an attempt to promote and coordinate these developments better, in 2002 the United Nations created the Inter-Agency Task Force on Sport for Development and Peace. The task force released its initial report, *Sport for Development and Peace: Towards Achieving the Millennium Development Goals*,[52] in 2003, the same year that UN-Habitat released its report *The Challenge of Slums*.

The two reports are a study in contrasts. *The Challenge of Slums* was a culmination of years of research and analysis developed through a large UN agency, whereas the 2003 *Sport for Development and Peace* report was a preliminary statement from a small task force that was meant to pave the way for subsequent organizational coordination, research, and development. In contrast to the 310 pages of research and discussion in *The Challenge of Slums,* the UN inter-agency task force's report is a mere 36 pages, consisting mostly of programmatic statements drawn from other UN documents, a superficial and selective use of academic research, and some examples of existing programs. Although *The Challenge of Slums* is not without its limitations, it nonetheless makes an attempt at detailed social analysis, including discussions of the global ascendancy of neoliberalism and the comparative failure of market-oriented globalization strategies espoused through organizations such as the International Monetary Fund. At the other end of the spectrum, the UN task force's report on sport for development and peace is filled with platitudes and generalizations and contains little social analysis of any depth or consequence. Significantly, while much is made in the 2003 report on *Sport for Development and Peace* about using sport to achieve UNMGs, the vitally important millennium goal of eradicating extreme global poverty and hunger is ignored in favor of a few passing observations to suggest how sport can help with economic development.

It is important to acknowledge that the 2003 UN inter-agency task force report on sport for development and peace was meant only as a springboard for subsequent policy development, and on these terms it was successful. The report led to the creation of a Sport for Development and Peace International Working Group (SDP IWG) at the Athens Olympics in 2004 (affiliated with the prominent NGO Right to Play), in addition to a United Nations Office on Sport for Development and Peace (UNOSDP).[53] The 2003 UN inter-agency task force report also played a role in the United Nations' declaration in 2005 of the "International Year of Sport and Physical Education," with a strong emphasis on the ideals of social responsibility, development, and sustainability, and it provided a stimulus for a growing body of more developed work. Examples include the literature review prepared by Donnelly, Coakley, Darnell, and Wells in 2007 for the SDP IWG Secretariat in Toronto, as well as a 176-page SDP IWG preliminary report in 2006, a final report presented at the Beijing Olympics in 2008, and annual reports produced by UNOSDP in 2013 and 2014. The 2003 inter-agency task force report also provided a set of working principles that continue to guide multilateral agencies, NGOs, and corporations in their efforts to form more effective partnerships. Largely as a culmination of these initiatives, the IOC now has observer status at the United Nations, and in 2014 the UN General Assembly passed a formal resolution to support "sport as a means to promote education, health, development and peace."

A majority of the foundational SDP IWG documents and studies written in the middle of the first decade of the 2000s were more programmatic than analytical. They tended to map existing sport and development initiatives in various countries and made programmatic assertions, but they offered little in the way of detailed social analysis or critical reflection. More recent annual reports from the UNOSDP for 2013 and 2014 reproduce the marginal and inadequate consideration of global poverty evident in the initial 2003 inter-agency task force's report. Nowhere in any of these documents can one find a detailed analysis of how sport might be mobilized to meet the key UNMG target of substantially reducing global poverty, or how some approaches to meeting this goal might be more or less successful than others. When there is any discussion about how sport might advance goals of poverty reduction, the analytical position in early SDP IWG reports and in later UNOSDP annual reports typically defaults to the broader development goals and objectives of major players in the UN Global Compact, such as the World Bank and the International Monetary Fund.

Consider, in this regard, the brief discussion of how sport might be used to meet the UN anti-poverty targets outlined in the 2006 SDP IWG interim report, *From Practice to Policy*. After asserting that sport can play a role in meeting the UN Millennium Goal of poverty reduction, the report acknowledges "most countries will not be able to attain the eight goals by 2015."[54] The report then goes on to list the "common reasons for shortfalls in the attainment of the MDGs" in different countries, including "poor governance, poverty traps with local and national economies unable to make investments, unequal distribution of economic development within countries, areas with multiple complex challenges that defy solutions, and the simultaneous occurrence of all or some of these factors."[55] Despite these problems, the report concludes that "urgent action is needed" and that success will depend "on the international community's willingness to make significant economic investments and, in many cases, policy and institutional improvements to allow implementation of practical measures that have already been shown to work."[56]

Once more, a comparison with the UN-Habitat's 2003 report *The Challenge of Slums* is instructive. In contrast to a single sentence in the SDP IWG interim report that lists some possible reasons for the likely shortfall in meeting the UNMGs, the 2003 UN-Habitat report offers a much more sustained analysis, including discussion of histories of colonial underdevelopment and consideration of the failures of more recent market-centered policies such as the structural adjustment policies of the International Monetary Fund.[57] Yet there is not the slightest critical reflex in the SDP IWG interim report, let alone any suggestion of the need for a comparable sociohistorical analysis of sport or of sport development policies. Instead, the report suggests that developing countries *already have* the tools to meet anti-poverty goals through national "Poverty Reduction Strategy Papers" (PRSPs) prepared "through a participatory process involving civil society and development partners, such as the World Bank and the International Monetary Fund."[58]

The confidence expressed in this assertion about PRSPs is both striking and dubious, given competing assertions found in documents from other UN agencies as well as in the substantial literature in the field of international development studies.[59] At one moment, the SDP IWG 2006 report makes the claim that sport can play a role in meeting the UN Millennium Goal of poverty reduction, but at another moment it passes up the opportunity to develop the point and suggests that national governments should simply work harder to integrate sport into IMF-supported national poverty reduction strategies that have been widely criticized.[60] To be fair, the SPD IWG interim report does argue for investment in programs for poverty reduction; however, it is vague about what such investments might look like and what priorities should guide them. The 2006 report merely echoes the suggestions introduced in the earlier 2003 report, namely that sport can play a role in economic development and that economic growth has a positive effect on poverty reduction.

The superficial treatment of the problem of urban poverty, including the expansion of slums, in SDP IWG reports and in later annual reports from the UNOSDP exists in conjunction with a broad rights-oriented perspective that is pervasive in the mission statements of related UN agencies and NGOs. Despite frequent mention of the need to eradicate global poverty and hunger, most of the programs and policy statements from these groups focus on the expansion of individual rights associated with such things as the right to health, education, social inclusion, and, of course, play. Not surprisingly, the inadequate consideration of poverty found in the documents produced by sport and development groups are reproduced in their organizational structures. For example, in 2011, the SDP IWG had working subgroups listed on the website of the UN Office on Sport for Development and Peace in the areas of sport and health; sport, child, and youth development; sport and gender; sport and persons with disabilities; and sport and peace. But there was no SDP IWG subgroup listed in the area of sport and poverty. There is no evidence in the UNOSDP annual reports from 2013 or 2014 that this situation has changed.

Admittedly, it is asking a lot of development policies involving sport to contribute substantially to the resolution of such complex problems as global poverty and the expansion of slums. So it is perfectly understandable that contemporary supporters of civil society approaches to sport and development policies focus instead on expanding rights and opportunities for individuals and communities in more modest and immediately achievable ways. Examples include opening up opportunities for sports participation or coaching in disadvantaged communities or, more ambitiously, using sport for the advancement of broader agendas such as the promotion of anti-racism, the rights of the disabled, the empowerment of girls and women, HIV/AIDS prevention, and peace in war-torn societies.

If we accept Robert Neuwirth's view of slums as "neighborhoods to be improved," many recent NGO-led sport and development programs appear to be doing exactly that. For example, one of the most commonly noted success stories in the literature on sport and development is the Mathare Youth Sports Association (MYSA) located in a crowded and desperately poor slum community of Nairobi, Kenya.[61] The MYSA was started in 1987 by a Canadian UN diplomat, Bob Munro, as a self-help project to organize sports while involving local youth in environmental cleanups. Since then, the MYSA has grown to approximately twenty thousand members, with numerous football (soccer) teams, ranging from recreational to semi-professional, and several development initiatives in areas such as AIDS prevention, leadership training, and the empowerment of girls and women.

The MYSA shows the impact that NGO-led sport and development programs can have on an impoverished community. Providing opportunities to participate in sport undoubtedly creates new and positive experiences for young people in these communities. This may include a sense of confidence and personal fulfillment, as well as a sense of belonging and citizenship beyond the immediate needs of day-to-day economic survival. By the promotion of healthcare messages and the provision of new opportunities for individual empowerment, self-expression, and belonging, it is easy to see how sport can play a small role in the fight against various forms of impoverishment.

In other words, despite the seeming intractability of so many of the world's greatest problems, proponents of sport as an agency of development are not being unrealistic when they claim that sport can at least do *something* to help. Indeed, as John Sugden has suggested, for socially conscious individuals, "doing nothing may no longer be an option."[62] More and more people in recent years appear to feel this way. According to Kidd, as early as 2008 there were 166 organizations devoted to sport and development programs listed on the

International Platform on Sport and Development maintained by the Swiss Academy for Development, and this list appears to be far from exhaustive.[63] Over the past two decades, the idea of using sport to "build a better world" has achieved unprecedented social, political, and cultural momentum.

Unfortunately, when an idea develops such widespread social, political, and cultural momentum, the urge to *act* sometimes pushes critical reflection aside in favor of unreflective evangelism. In the area of sport and development, that evangelism is positive insofar as it provides the energy for NGOs and UN- and government-affiliated organizations to do good work. However, it also lends itself to silences and blind spots, some of which are evident in the priority given to civil society organizations in international development and in the tendency to downplay the systemic causes of poverty in favor of a focus on individual rights. This rights-based discourse has not emerged in the area of sport and development simply as a pragmatic response to the unmanageable nature of the world's greatest problems; it is also a corollary to a neoliberal policy logic that shifts responsibility for development away from national and regional governments and toward international partnerships of civil society organizations, agencies, and private corporations. A focus on improving human rights in development promises to open up *opportunities* for marginalized individuals but also risks deflecting attention from less immediately evident social and organizational features that reproduce broader inequalities in *condition*. When this latter situation occurs, rights-based approaches to development can echo the paternalism of mid-twentieth-century modernization theory while becoming disconnected from the structural changes that many community groups argue are necessary to improve the lives of the world's poorest citizens.

Commenting on this point in the case of Africa, the Tanzanian legal scholar Issa Shivji notes that NGO-led development policies originating in western (sometimes called "northern") nations since the 1990s have often been justified by arguments about the corruption of African governments, or a fear of African-based social movements struggling for autonomy and greater control of self-destiny. Rather than working with activist groups and governments in ways that respect their autonomy, the challenge of development has typically been passed on to northern-based multilateral organizations, NGOs, and their public and corporate partners.[64] The aid that comes to Africa is well intentioned, there is often consultation in local communities, and many of the programs provide real opportunities for certain individuals and communities but, consistent with the mid-twentieth-century discourse on modernization, the policy logic is almost always developed by educated elites in the West. It is then applied to "problems" viewed from afar and in a global political economic environment where northern ambitions and agendas shape international circuits of economic exchange and political power, typically to the detriment of former colonial societies.

The result is a widespread tendency to lose sight of the way that real people live their lives in favor of abstractions such as "the chronically poor," who then become the "subject matter of papers on strategies for poverty reduction authored by consultants and discussed at stakeholder workshops in which the poor are represented by NGOs."[65] Too often, Shivji claims, "the 'poor,' the diseased, the disabled, the AIDS-infected, the ignorant, the marginalized" are not seen as active agents themselves in the development process; rather, such groups tend to become objectified in a paternalistic equation – "the needy recipients of humanitarian aid given by well-meaning 'friends' in the North" and dispensed by non-partisan, non-political and presumably non-involved, non-governmental organizations. In these societies, "where stakeholders never tire of policy making on the poor, there isn't its twin opposite, the rich. These societies apparently do not have producers and appropriators of wealth; they only have the poor and the wealth creators."[66]

The last comment points to a half-hidden theory of society implicit in discourses of development centered on the idea of a global compact of partnerships between civil society NGOs and corporate "stakeholders." This theory posits a world that may be unequal and unjust but is composed of multi-party groups who have a shared will for change matched with broadly shared political, cultural, and economic interests. In this perspective, while various stakeholders may have conflicts or disagreements, there is no perception of a fundamental contradiction between their interests. The result is a chronic inability to analyze the way in which *some* stakeholders in development partnerships may be more powerful than others and able to pursue their own interests to the detriment of others. It is one thing to say that we should "make poverty history" (to use the phrase adopted by a prominent activist coalition), but this will only happen if we understand the history of poverty.[67] Wealth creation does not necessarily lead to poverty reduction in situations where certain groups in societies are able to appropriate more of the wealth for themselves than for others, especially when these groups are able to make the resulting forms of inequality seem natural, inevitable, or representative of the general public interest.

Even a cursory analysis of the history of poverty over the past two centuries underlines this point in dramatic fashion. While urban poverty and slums are as old as human cities themselves, the nature and character of global poverty in the late nineteenth and early twentieth centuries changed in conjunction with patterns of creative destruction and accumulation by dispossession associated with factory-based industrialism, burgeoning monopoly capitalism, the consolidation of the modern state system, and the formation of European and US colonial networks. Industrialization featured the first modern migrations of dispossessed rural residents to cities, where they became factory labor forces and working-class slum dwellers in industrialized nations. At the same time, colonization accelerated the international ascendancy of western industrialism and finance capital, often with disastrous consequences in many parts of the global South. For example, in 1800 China's per capita income was equal to or higher than Britain's per capita income and Asian countries produced 56 percent of the world's gross domestic product (GDP), compared to western Europe's 24 percent. Throughout the nineteenth century, there was a significant drop in Asian GDP relative to that of the western nations. By the end of the century, the colonial and industrial West had achieved a position of economic and political dominance over most of Asia.[68]

Western domination of the nineteenth- and early twentieth-century global economic and geopolitical order was simultaneously strengthened in the mid-twentieth century by Keynesian economic policies and postwar capitalist expansion and challenged by mid-century movements for decolonization. Following the Great Depression of the 1930s and World War II, a combination of affluence and the development of "the welfare state" in many nations eroded the extremes of earlier inequalities. At the same time, many of the countries in the global South won independence from colonial rule, creating a situation in which "dreams of industrialization and 'catching up' could be realistically entertained."[69] Over the period of postwar growth between 1950 and approximately 1972, inequality not only fell *within* countries but also lessened somewhat *between* countries in the industrial West and the "developing" South. In some parts of the world, this trend extended into the late 1970s, although it is important not to overstate the extent of postcolonial "catching up."[70] At the peak of the postwar boom in 1970, "the top 20 percent of the world's people in the richest countries had 32 times the income of the poorest 20 percent."[71]

Still, while the reduction of inequality between nations may have been modest in the early postwar period, there was at least a brief time during which the economic chasm between West/North and South seemed to be eroding. In contrast, from 1973 to the present, inequality has increased dramatically.[72] The gap between the top 20 percent of people in the richest countries and the bottom 20 percent in the poorest countries grew forty-five times in 1980, fifty-nine times in 1989, and about seventy-eight times in 2003.[73] The gap between rich and poor within countries also began to grow, against the tide of the comparative gains of the 1945–72 periods.[74]

International sporting spectacles, modernization, and the challenge of slums in late twentieth-century neoliberal globalization

It is more than coincidental that growing social inequality around the world from the early 1970s to the present day correlates with a dramatic growth in the economic scale and significance of the world's largest international sporting events. There is no direct causal relationship between these two circumstances, but I want to argue that international sporting events in the late twentieth and early twenty-first centuries have benefited from, and contributed to, economic and political policies around the world that have exacerbated global poverty. Four developments have contributed both to the growth of these policies and to the accelerating economic and political importance of sporting mega-events between the 1960s and the present day.

First, the global deflation of the mid-1970s demonstrated substantial limitations to the settlement of the international economic and political interests that had emerged at the end of World War II. A "stagflationary spiral of high inflation and low growth proved resistant to all conventional measures," initiating a debate about the apparent weaknesses of Keynesian economics.[75] This opened the door to a new coalition of political and economic actors in North America and Europe who were determined to liberalize what they saw as excessive regulation in both national and international economies. The mantra of this new coalition was focused on the need to reduce government regulation in the interests of promoting greater flexibility in production and easier mobility for capital.[76]

Second, in conjunction with this push for deregulation and flexibility, there was an aggressive campaign in many northern nations to reduce public expenditures while providing tax incentives to induce private investment and to reorient state policies toward activities that would be economically beneficial. The social-democratic movements of the earlier postwar period were weakened, and the "collapse of communism eliminated the external threat and freed capitalist interests to pursue unhindered objectives of global profit maximization – without much regard for social consequences."[77] In this context, campaigns for debt reduction by federal and regional state governments, matched with a growing political commitment to reduce taxes in general, meant a widespread offloading of public-sector responsibilities onto lower levels of government, such as municipalities and cities. This forced lower levels of government to become more focused than ever on the pursuit of economic and social development. In addition, the mid-twentieth-century positive evaluation of public investment to meet social needs shifted to accommodate a stronger emphasis on policies that promoted capital accumulation and economic growth, with a view to having the benefits "trickle down" through the community.[78]

Third, in an emerging digital age, new technologies became the mechanism for accomplishing a late twentieth-century neoliberal agenda and extending it to new global networks. Taking advantage of the vistas of managerial control opened by new technologies of communication, computerization, and robotics, firms moved aggressively toward automated decentralization. The drive to more "flexible" production and accumulation included "just-in-time" and small-batch production techniques, new forms of inventory control, as well as the hiving off and contracting out of many functions previously performed in-house. Reliance on standardized products did not die out, but the older form of mass production was increasingly augmented or challenged by market segmentation and the need for customization.[79] Digitization was part of a broader revolution in global communications technologies, including the proliferation of satellites, cable television, and the internet, that accelerated and intensified the commodification of culture by increasing the size of audiences that could be sold to advertisers.

Finally, the deregulation and privatization of the postwar welfare state opened up new areas of commodification as capital became more mobile and nomadic, taking advantage of geographical differentials in market opportunity and labor costs on a broader international scale than ever before. Faced with such changes, the old mid-twentieth-century industrial labor force in northern nations was fractured and remade to include a new breed of knowledge or cultural worker.[80] At the same time, international relations were reconfigured by the newly unfettered mobility of capital, accompanied by a sweeping deregulation of the international financial system in the 1970s, a neoliberalization of monetary policy in the world's major economies, and a fast-changing international division of labor. Neoliberal globalization also subtly encouraged growing nationalist assertiveness in nations such as Russia and China whose economies were strengthened by the shifting contours of global economic relations.

These wide-ranging changes accompanied, and contributed to, a situation where the "production of events" in international capitalism increasingly came to rival the more traditional making of things.[81] The promotion of events facilitated economic growth by expanding the sphere of exchange – the universalization of the market. It also provided a way for capital that is launched into circulation to be recuperated quickly. As David Harvey argues, echoing Marx: "the faster the capital launched into circulation can be recuperated, the greater the profit will be."[82] With their fixed and short time frames, the recuperation of capital investments in spectacular events is noticeably faster than, say, in the automobile, electronic, or aerospace industries. The growing capacity for global media to construct both larger and more focused audiences intensified the promotional value of those international events that were seen to have the highest status and the highest levels of global interest. According to Harvey, the 1980s ushered in a "new entrepreneurialism" centrally focused on remaking cities to take advantage of the cultural economy.[83]

In this context, predominant visions of urban revitalization and modernization began to emphasize the postindustrial construction of spectacular sites for consumption, meant to attract international tourists and convention-goers, and new cultural workers, into cities entering a late twentieth-century global competition to be viewed as "world class." Not only did this strategy involve upgrading urban infrastructure in transportation and communications, it was also built on real-estate speculation associated with the creation of gentrified housing and shopping spaces.[84] In an age of diminished city budgets, the huge scale of investment required in such projects entailed greater reliance on public debt at the local level and partnerships with outside groups, which resulted in the diffusion of some of the traditional powers of city governments.[85]

In combination with a more sophisticated approach to maximizing revenues on the part of international sports organizations, these trends over the past 30 years combined to create an immensely lucrative seller's market for the rights to host international sporting events and for the media and trademark rights associated with them. The 1984 Los Angeles Summer Olympics were a high-water mark in this transition.[86] In the turbulent economic times of the mid-1970s, the high levels of civic indebtedness incurred by the city of Montreal as a result of hosting the 1976 Summer Olympics had not been offset by major federal subsidies. With growing doubt about the affordability of the Olympics – and of the willingness of national governments to subsidize them – applications to host the 1984 Summer Olympic Games shrank to only two candidates, one of which ultimately withdrew. That left Los Angeles as the only bidder, giving the city's Olympic Organizing Committee unprecedented leverage with the IOC to pursue and retain media and private sponsorship revenues. In the absence of state subsidies, the Los Angeles Organizing Committee turned to the private sector to raise revenues, largely for pragmatic rather than overtly ideological reasons. Yet the success of a private-sector Olympics in 1984 resonated with the Reagan administration's self-consciously neoliberal agenda and provided Reagan's 1984 reelection campaign with a powerful ideological discourse, where Montreal's indebtedness could be utilized as a metaphor for the failures of the postwar welfare state in general and with the Los Angeles Olympics serving as a testament to the "common sense" of neoliberalism.[87]

The 1984 Los Angeles Olympics were the first and last Olympics to be financed almost exclusively through private-sector earnings, but they dramatized the new economic potential of all sporting mega-events and ushered in an era of rapidly escalating media rights fees and sponsorship income. For example, according to Giannoulakis and Stotler, sponsorship revenues to the IOC rose from US$95 million in 1986 to US$650 million in 2004.[88] By the same token, FIFA's revenues in 2007–10 were twelve times greater than in 1995–8, up from US$257 million to US$3.2 billion.[89] These global market dynamics also worked to give new economic value for sponsoring INGOs to "second-tier" international or regional sporting events, such as the Asian Games, the Commonwealth Games, and the Pan American Games. Yet, while media rights and sponsorship fees have increased markedly, the amounts that accrue to host cities have been declining since 1984. Over the past few decades, the IOC in particular has appropriated a greater share of such revenues for itself. According to recent research the IOC now retains "more than 70% of Olympic television revenue, compared with less than 4% between 1960 and 1980."[90] At the same time, the money that cites and countries have spent on staging sporting mega-events has escalated wildly.[91]

Escalating costs of the most prominent international sporting mega-events have narrowed the field of bidding nations and cities in recent years, prompting discussions about new ways to control costs, such as spreading events between different countries or cities. Since the early 2000s, these costs have also been driven upward by an increasing ambition to host such events in cities and countries found in the global South. As Robert Baade and Victor Matheson note: "Only 18 percent of the bids submitted for the Summer Games prior to 2000 came from the developing world or the former Soviet sphere of influence."[92] However, since that time, "half of all bids have come from this group, including applications by Istanbul, Bangkok, Havana, Doha, and Cape Town, as well as the successful bids from Beijing and Rio de Janeiro. For the Winter Olympics, the past decade has witnessed for the first time bids from Kazakhstan, Georgia, China, Slovakia, and Poland."[93]

Within such cities and countries, along with western cities such as London (host to the 2012 Summer Olympics), Glasgow (host to the 2014 Commonwealth Games), and Toronto (host to the 2015 Pan American Games), it has become conventional wisdom among booster coalitions that such investments are justified because sporting mega-events and related infrastructure projects can be leveraged as powerful engines of development, symbolic vehicles for the accumulation of prestige, and even as vehicles for the application of "soft power" by ambitious cities and nations in the South.

To cite just two recent examples, in Delhi the India Olympic Committee, the governing body for the 2010 Commonwealth Games, was emphatic in arguing that the 2010 Games "will be the catalyst for the development of the city of Delhi and its environs."[94] Even more ambitiously, as Ashwin Desai points out, South African elites saw the 2010 World Cup as "a dramatic shortcut into modernity:"

> The world's greatest show – and a spectacular South African capitalism would be unleashed to stage it. World-class transport systems and gigantic stadiums would need to be built. And they would show the world that South Africa was ready for large-scale investment. Tourists would flood the country. But to attract such capital it would be necessary to spend on an equally "world-class scale . . ."[95]

Neither the Delhi Commonwealth Games nor the South African football World Cup proved able to meet these lofty goals. Still, every bid committee for a major international sporting spectacle since the mid-1990s has put similar arguments forward.

Such claims also resonate with similar statements found in foundational policy documents associated with the promotion of NGO-based approaches to sport and development. A 2003 UN Inter-Agency Task Force report, *Sport for Development and Peace*, provides an instructive example because many of its suggestions about sport and economic growth are repeated without much elaboration in later policy documents. The report argues that sport can act as both a catalyst and an engine for economic growth through "the economic weight, resulting from activities such as the manufacture of sporting goods, sports events, sport-related services and the media," and by "providing employment opportunities," stimulating "demand for goods and services," and acting as "an important source of public and private expenditure such as that spent on infrastructure, during major events and on consumption."[96] In the early years of the twenty-first century, non-profit NGOs appear to share similar views with many of their potential public and private-sector "partners."

No reasonable person can deny that sporting mega-events generate substantial economic activity, particularly in the areas of construction, real-estate development, tourism, increased foreign investment, and trade. It is also clear that such events can be catalysts for public investment in civic infrastructure in areas such as transportation and communications, the environmental cleanup and revitalization of former industrial districts, and the construction of sporting facilities that leave a highly visible legacy for certain groups within the urban community. Still, there is a deep suspicion among economists, sociologists, and urban geographers about the extent to which major sporting events, and related large-scale facilities construction and infrastructure development projects, generate the kind of growth they promise and, more important, about whether the development that does occur is inclusive, sustainable, and worth high levels of public investment.[97]

Projections of the economic impact of investment in large sporting events, or accompanying sports facilities, are often speculative and prone to exaggeration by event promoters.[98] In addition, the booster coalitions who support and promote such events tend to downplay their cost. Bookkeeping around these events typically overlooks the full range of public subsidy involved, especially in situations where local or regional governments have been able to use the event to leverage infrastructure investments from higher levels of government. There is also never assurance that the economic returns associated with a major sporting event or facilities project in one city or region will be automatically similar to those in other cities and regions. Indeed, Flyvbjerg, Swyngedouw and their colleagues note that project-based or event-driven approaches to urban development tend to be so tied to volatile real-estate markets that they are filled with levels of risk that would never be accepted in any other form of public investment.[99]

Research has shown that the level of economic activity associated with large-scale sporting events can vary dramatically from city to city and is highly contingent on global events beyond the control of local promoters.[100] In addition to issues at the site of the actual event (such as labor shortages or labor unrest), incidences of corruption, and increases in oil prices or interest rates on the global stage can wreak havoc on budgets. If estimates or planning go even slightly wrong in the game of international event roulette, as in the case of the 2004 Athens Summer Olympics, the result can be a legacy of crippling debt and decaying facilities.[101] Yet the various partners involved in organizing and staging these activities do not similarly share the risk. International sports organizations such as the IOC and FIFA are guaranteed profit, while local taxpayers, along with the users of public services, carry a disproportionate part of virtually inevitable cost overruns.[102]

Furthermore, when civic boosters and event promoters make claims about the positive economic benefits of investing in major sporting events, they never compare them to the possible economic benefits that might flow from other types of large-scale public investments. How would the social and economic returns on investment in an international sporting event compare to the returns that would be generated if a city suddenly spent billions of dollars to upgrade sanitation and public health infrastructure, create affordable housing on a large scale, subsidize community arts and job retraining, as well as build new parks, community centers, affordable technical colleges, and public universities, along with smaller and more localized sport and recreational facilities? We do not know enough about such comparisons because the local and transnational coalitions of economic and political interests who push for investment in large-scale sporting events tend to view such alternative social investments as secondary and dependent upon the greater priorities of entrepreneurialism, wealth creation and, more recently, of geopolitical advantage. In western host cities and nations, wealth creation in particular is assumed to create employment, put money in people's pockets, and bring tax revenues into government coffers that can be used to strengthen social services, including support for the poor and the homeless. It is for this reason that supporters of so-called "world-class" sporting events and related urban development projects in the West argue that these truly are *public* events and projects with widespread benefits that accrue to the community as a whole.

Yet the suggestion that large international sporting events are part of the public domain, or serve democratically accountable public interests, is an ironic exaggeration on many levels. First, organizations such as the IOC or FIFA are not accessible to the public, and they are certainly not accountable to elected public bodies anywhere in the world. Similarly, while many of the corporate partners of international sporting associations are publicly traded companies, as private-sector organizations they are not subject to the traditions of democratic governance typically found in the public sphere of western democracies. None of the more than three thousand companies who signed the 1999 UNGC statement are legally responsible to any international body if the company fails to live up to its UN commitment to operate in a manner that helps build "a better world for all." Likewise, the IOC's 1999 commitment to sustainable development is not enforceable by any higher-level body, and the committee has only ever "invited" national Olympic associations to share in the commitment "to the best of their ability."[103]

By the same token, the essentially private local organizing committees that are formed to run large-scale international sporting events are not accountable to public bodies and are prone to operate in ways that are far less transparent than would be tolerated in any public institution in a democratic society.[104] Democratic governance is also challenged by the fact that sporting mega-events not only often require creative destruction as a requisite for "development," they require it on a fixed schedule, with little room for error. Transportation infrastructure must be well in place by the start of the event and land redevelopment completed, with pavilions, stadiums, arenas, and other venues finished to required standards. For these reasons, the run-up to staging mega-events is often put on an emergency footing with an accompanying relaxation of normal democratic oversight. In this sense, and virtually from the point at which bids from hosting nations or cities are accepted, mega-events occur as "states of exception" where normal rules of governance become suspended in deference to the needs of local organizing committees, sponsors, and the INGOs that have given them their blessing.[105]

For example, in an exhaustive study of thirteen large-scale urban development projects (including the 2004 Athens Summer Olympics) in twelve European countries Swyngedouw, Moulaert, and Rodriguez conclude that such projects have too often been used to establish exceptional measures in planning that are part of very selective "middle- and upper-class" interests associated with "new forms of governing." These forms of governance have entrenched inequalities in access to decision making that are not reflective of broader democratic public priorities.[106] While local grassroots movements have sometimes won concessions in the planning and staging of large-scale urban events and projects, local democratic mechanisms are not always respected or are used unevenly.

Swyngedouw and his colleagues argue that the project-based and event-driven forms of development so favored in recent years reveal a "new choreography of elite power" in major European cities, based partly on the desire of urban elites to elevate the international visibility of the city in the interests of economic growth, with a view to positioning the city better in global trade and financial networks as well as promoting it as a destination site for international tourists. However, in almost all of the cities studied, large-scale urban development projects were found to have accentuated rather than reduced social polarization. This occurred primarily through changes in the priorities of public budgets that were redirected from more traditional social objectives "to investments in the built environment and the restructuring of the labor market."[107] In addition, social polarization resulted from both price rises associated with gentrification and the physical displacement of lower-income urban residents in conjunction with project-based or event-driven development.

The conclusions drawn by Swyngedouw and his colleagues about the social and economic dimensions of large-scale urban development events and projects in Europe are similar to the conclusions reached about large-scale events and projects in other parts of the world.[108] Recent literature on the economic impact of international sporting events and the facility construction and infrastructure projects associated with them offers no substantial deviation from the social polarization thesis outlined in the analysis of World's Fairs, festival markets, and other forms of tourist-oriented urban revitalization.[109] Across many parts of the global South, in particular, the divisions are stark: gentrification, often of former slum areas, on the one hand, and the dramatic expansion of slums, barrios, shantytowns, and favelas on the other.

This does not mean in economically strong economies – such as the United States, some European societies, affluent oil-rich countries in the Middle East, as well as *some* of the BRIC and East Asian nations – that sporting mega-events can never contribute positively to local ambitions for global modernization. They provide a way of absorbing surplus capital while simultaneously creating additional stimulants to local economies by multiplying and accelerating connections to global circuits of capitalist production and circulation. The problem is that most of the benefits arising from such ambitions are experienced unevenly, with the most affluent groups feeling the majority of benefits and the least affluent receiving fewest of them. Slum dwellers are especially vulnerable because they are most likely to suffer from a diversion of public expenditures into the staging of urban spectacles, rather than the provision of social services in health, sanitation, and transportation.

More troubling is the fact that large-scale international sporting events and the development projects associated with them have frequently been accompanied by evictions and forced relocations of slum dwellers in an attempt to put the host city's best face forward to the world and to create attractive, gentrified, spaces in downtown areas.[110] In 2007, the Geneva-based Centre on Housing Rights and Evictions (COHRE) issued a devastating report on the numbers of evictions and forced relocations associated with past Olympic Games. The scale ranges from several hundred to thousands of people in Olympic cities in western nations, to even larger numbers in Olympic cities in the global South. For example, COHRE claims that more than 720,000 slum dwellers, including both squatters and property owners, were displaced through expropriation or forced eviction prior to the 1988 Seoul Summer Olympics in order to "beautify" the parts of the city that Olympic organizers thought would receive the greatest media attention.[111] The Asian Coalition for Housing Rights estimates that the number of forced evictions was even higher, exceeding a million people.[112]

The scale of evictions and slum demolition in recent Chinese urban redevelopment has been equally dramatic, despite the Chinese Communist Party's professed commitment to universal housing. Over the past three decades, China has emerged as a global economic powerhouse, based largely on a strategy of attracting investments in manufacturing through the creation of special economic zones.[113] A lessening of Communist Party restrictions has also created opportunities for ambitious cities to pursue so-called world-class events and projects to attract international attention, foreign investment, and tourism. In this context, several Chinese cities have responded to the challenge of slums simply by expropriating whole communities and removing their residents to high-rise complexes on the city's periphery. For example, in Guangzhou, where it is estimated that the city spent more than 122.6 billion yuan on the 2010 Asian Games, many slum dwellers were forced to move out to the city's periphery through evictions or an inability to pay newly inflated downtown real-estate prices.[114]

On an even larger scale, Beijing is said to have spent in excess of US$43 billion preparing for the 2008 Summer Olympic Games, with projections ranging in the hundreds of billions if security costs and related infrastructure projects are included.[115] COHRE has estimated that between 1.25 and 1.5 million people were displaced in the run-up to the Games, with many evicted forcibly. Of the total number of persons displaced in Olympics-related development, COHRE claims that each year between 2006 and 2008 "as many as 33,000 people with sustainable livelihoods were pushed into poverty, or into deeper poverty, because their homes and neighborhoods were demolished."[116]

A pattern in which event preparation, facility construction, and urban beautification schemes lead to the destruction of whole neighborhoods and to the forced relocation of residents has become the norm, especially in BRIC nations and many parts of the developing South. In Delhi, activists and former residents of the Yamuna Pushta slum settlement claim that 140,000 people were removed and 40,000 homes bulldozed to make way for the Commonwealth Games athletes' village, the Metrorail headquarters, and land slated for upmarket accommodation.[117] Yamuna Pushta was one of Delhi's oldest slum communities and contained schools, temples, and mosques, but many residents were squatters and were not offered compensation for lost homes or possessions. According to Samara, "less than a quarter of the residents were offered resettlement aid, while being relocated to a peripheral area with few public services. The rest were left to fend for themselves."[118] Like Beijing and Guangzhou, Delhi's approach to urban development through sport has involved a widespread relocation of the urban underclass.

All of this suggests a significant developmental paradox. International sporting organizations such as the IOC and FIFA endorse the United Nations Millennium Goal of poverty reduction and claim to be committed to the broader values of sustainability and inclusiveness. They support sport-for-development-and-peace initiatives and often form partnerships with well-intentioned NGOs that are making an effort to do good work in slums around the world. But the major events and projects that bring money into these international sporting organizations, and the forms of urban governance and public spending typically associated with their events, are implicated in deepening social polarization in many of the world's major cities, with an accompanying exacerbation of the problems of poverty and slums.

It is useful at this point to return to the conclusion reached in UN-Habitat's 2003 report *The Challenge of Slums*: there can be no solution to the growth in homelessness in many parts of the world, or to the spread of slums, without dramatic *direct* investment aimed at providing basic services for the world's urban poor. When they are asked, residents of the world's slums say they want to be empowered to run their own communities.[119] They want shelter on which they can count, clean water, and better sanitation, as well as work, personal security, and improved access to health care, transportation, and education. They want these things more than they want renovated airports, upmarket shopping malls, gentrified townhouse complexes, gorgeous hotels, and "world-class" sports events and facilities.

Yet, while there is typically public money available to fund sporting mega-events and related projects, there rarely seems to be enough to make the dramatic investments needed to meet the interrelated challenges of poverty, homelessness, and slum conditions. There is considerable rhetoric from international sporting associations, bid committees, and NGOs about making these kinds of investments but the results have been disappointing, to say the least.[120] Similarly, there is little evidence to support the claim that the money spent on such investments will create enough wealth to trickle down to improve the lives of people in slum neighborhoods. The gentrification of prime areas of urban real estate has been the more likely scenario.

There have traditionally been clear borders between slum dwellers and the residents of gentrified spaces in the world's major cities. However, an important part of the creative destruction and accumulation that has accompanied large scale international sporting events over the past two decades is the transgression of these borders by opening up favelas, ghettos, and slums to the combined interventions of real-estate investment and finance capital.[121] On the one hand, these areas can be emptied of their residents in the run-up to staging sporting spectacles in order to open up geographically desirable slum spaces to financial speculation and gentrification. On the other hand, large-scale sporting spectacles can also act as stimulants to open slums to the sale of internationally branded products by inundating poor communities with the advertising of event sponsors, encouraging a loosening of credit restrictions to encourage consumption and providing a rationale for a police clampdown on black-market activities.

Even if slum residents are not forcibly removed, huge capital investments in new spaces of spectacle have tended to hyper-inflate the importance of real estate, not only in established "global cities" but in many aspiring cities as well. For example, unprecedented rural in-migration in Chinese cities has made the construction of residential apartments a major factor in an economy that in turn has become "the main driver of the global economy since the worldwide crisis that began in 2007."[122] When you add in expenditure for creating factory, warehouse, and office spaces, along with investment in gentrified shopping and entertainment districts and large-scale infrastructure projects – including mega-events such as the Beijing Olympics or the Asian Games in Guangzhou – the scale of investment in Chinese cities over the past two decades has simply been overwhelming. Along with this urban boom, real-estate values in the "desirable" areas of Chinese "global" cities – Shanghai and Hong Kong are obvious examples – have increased significantly, while also being subject to volatile swings in market prices.

At least in China a socialist legacy has meant there have been attempts (although rarely at market rates) to compensate the large populations that have been displaced by mega-projects and mega-events.[123] As the regulatory climate in international economic development shifted in a neoliberal direction in many other parts of the world, there has been greater reliance on privatization in place of older state-centered models that operated on the notion that progressive taxation and rational planning could provide vital *public* amenities and services. Today, many self-defined global cities struggle with problems of housing unaffordability, homelessness, and reduced public services, while taxation rates for corporations and wealthy individuals continue to fall. Urban elites often view the staging of international sporting spectacles as vital strategies of wealth creation, but there is little evidence to suggest that the wealth they create trickles down to urban underclasses who face an erosion of public services and the challenge of finding affordable housing, health services, and transportation. In many of the world's most affluent Olympic cities, such as London or Vancouver, a combination of gentrification and land speculation has lent itself to housing shortages, frequently combined with surpluses of properties that sit empty as investors wait for property values to increase.

I want to raise one final aspect of sporting spectacles in the era of neoliberal globalization: the degree to which construction projects in some aspiring cities and nations recruit their labor forces from much poorer countries. An international division of labor has been characteristic of capitalism for hundreds of years, but as Sandro Mezzadra argues, the heterogeneity and mobility of contemporary global labor relations suggests "a different sort of globalization, what we could call a subaltern globalization, which accompanies capitalist globalization."[124] The migratory character of work in the early twenty-first century is an indication of this "subaltern globalization," indicating

192

that the critical analysis of "labor migration control regimes" is a vitally important topic in studies of global capitalist modernity.

It is only a short step from this general point to the argument that the critical analysis of mega-events must also engage with how the staging of mega-events is connected to these regimes of control, where what is at stake is not simply a wage but often the biopolitical control over life itself. The case of quasi-enslaved migrant workers building stadiums in Qatar for the 2022 men's football World Cup springs immediately to mind, but the globalization of subalternity is by no means limited to the Middle East, and it is necessary to extend this kind of analysis to other spaces and places and, especially, to the way that global capitalist modernity itself produces inequality on a dramatic and increasing scale.[125]

Conclusion

In an earlier chapter, I argued that western capitalist modernity was literally built on the "creative destruction" of earlier, and often culturally other, economic and social relations, including various forms of "dispossession by accumulation." Rather than the culmination of historical "progress," modernity is arguably better understood as the introduction of a state of constant and permanently disruptive change. According to Zygmunt Bauman, that is why "the society that entered the twenty-first century is no less 'modern' than the society that entered the twentieth": "What makes it as modern as it was a century ago is what sets modernity apart from all other historical forms of human cohabitation: the compulsive and obsessive, continuous, unstoppable, forever incomplete *modernization*; the overwhelming and ineradicable, unquenchable thirst for creative destruction ... [all for the sake of a greater capacity to enhance] productivity or competitiveness."[126]

Still, the association of modernity with creative destruction is neither random nor chaotic. In this chapter, I have tried to show that there *is* something qualitatively different about modernization over the past three decades in comparison to the modernization of industrial societies through the nineteenth and early twentieth centuries. There is also something qualitatively different today from the modernization that these societies and their colonial dependents underwent in the years immediately following World War II.

The differences lie in new phases of capitalist development and in related modes of political and institutional regulation that have their own distinctive logics of accumulation, institutional organization, and cultural form. Since the 1990s, Saskia Sassen argues, these "need to be distinguished from older imperial phases."[127] In Sassen's view, the late twentieth- and early twenty-first-century phase of capitalist modernity has involved the "geographic expansion and systemic deepening of capitalist relations of production," leading to a resurgence of "primitive accumulation" and the "most brutal sortings of winners and losers."[128] Global modernity is arguably shaped more by capitalism than by narrower civic or national interests, although there are signs in the last ten years that this may be changing somewhat as countries such as China and Russia try to carve out a modern world that best suits their national interests. Still, there is no indication that the strengthening of capitalist social relations on a global scale will end anytime soon, or that capitalist globalization will suddenly usher in greater equality between the world's "developed" and "developing" cities and nations. Similarly, the brutal "sorting of winners and losers" arguably threatens to become more pronounced than ever *within* many western cities and nations as they try to absorb and negotiate migrations from poor or war-torn nations in the South.

I have argued here that the staging of large-scale sporting spectacles has not only failed to make any substantial difference to this global sorting of winners and losers, it has been a significant part of the problem, even when such spectacles have been staged in countries outside the West. Modernity has always been more polyvalent and multi-hued in colonial, or formerly colonial, spatial situations than in the world's most advanced economies and powerful nations. For example, Brazil's enthusiasm for Euro-modernist artistic and architectural styles earlier in the century was less a matter of overt cultural imperialism from the West than it was a complex *appropriation*: a rejection of western classicism combined with an attempt to construct something distinctively Brazilian.[129] The construction of the Estádio de Maracanã for the 1950 World Cup is an obvious example.

But renovation of the Maracanã for FIFA's 2013 Confederation Cup and the 2014 World Cup took on radically different meanings than in 1950. The new conditions of co-presence with the West that they announced occurred in an age when the World Cup seemed more like an example of what Jules Boykoff calls "celebration capitalism" than an expression of any distinctively Brazilian sensibility.[130] For many Brazilians the key issues turned more on cynicism about the development capabilities of World Cup or Olympic mega-projects, including criticisms of the inadequacy of transportation, displacements of the poor, and widespread gentrification.[131] In this regard, the recent staging of major international sporting spectacles in Brazil created obvious rallying points for political opposition when they promoted actions contrary to local traditions and values, appeared to oppose hard-won democratic victories, or failed to live up to their own rhetoric of legitimation. Thus, as Mezzadra and Neilson argue, mass protests leading up to the 2013 Confederation Cup and the World Cup were able to mobilize around "the political legitimacy acquired in the years of the Lula governments and the social power manifest in an unprecedented access to consumer opportunities" deriving from previous income redistribution policies.[132]

In many respects, Brazilian opposition to its recent spate of large-scale international sporting spectacles is not unique. Since the turn of the twenty-first century, activism around such events has grown noticeably and now often has an international character, as evidenced by widespread international criticisms of Russia's stance on LGBTQ rights prior to the 2014 Sochi Winter Olympics or Qatar's mistreatment of migrant workers in the build-up to the 2022 men's football World Cup. I think there is much greater awareness today than ever before about the hypocrisy of INGOs such as the IOC and FIFA and their corporate and local NGO partners, who profess commitments to socially progressive goals of inclusivity but also participate in staging events and projects that are far from democratic or economically or politically inclusive.

In making this argument, I do not want to tar all smaller-scale sport and development initiatives with the same brush as large-scale sporting spectacles. There are certainly many NGOs and development organizations rooted deeply in the communities they serve. Many of these NGOs and agencies are involved in activist work, either by seeking to improve the daily lives of people who live in poor communities or, in some cases, by taking on a much more politicized and adversarial role in the struggles around economic development and land use. Harvey, Horne, and Safai have made an important first step in mapping and classifying the groups and movements associated with sport that claim to give priority to the "values of democracy, justice, environmental protection and human rights" over "purely economic concerns."[133] More recently, Jules Boykoff has developed a thorough analysis of activism prompted by the Olympics, using the recent examples of the Winter Olympics in Vancouver in 2010 and the London Summer Olympics in 2012.[134]

Still, it can be exceptionally difficult to distinguish the stated intentions of seemingly progressive groups and movements in sport from the economic or social consequences of their actions. This is especially true with organizations that have a mainstream global presence. For example, UN-Habitat began to work with sport and recreation organizations in slum areas in the early 2000s "to empower young people and help inform them about the challenges facing them as well as offering alternative life skills geared towards conquering life in informal settlements."[135] However, UN-Habitat has been unwilling to push organizations such as FIFA or the IOC to make the kinds of substantial investments in slums called for in *The Challenge of Slums*.

Solutions to such problems will surely require something more than informing young people about "the challenges facing them" or offering them "alternative life skills geared towards conquering life in informal settlements." Solutions may well lie in promoting decisions about property rights and the uses of urban space that are likely to be opposed by powerful economic interests. Similarly, making substantial investments in sanitation infrastructure or in the universal availability of health care in times of economic crisis, high public debt, and deficit may mean taking money away from projects such as stadiums and hosting large sporting events. Development programs always require judgments about priorities, and these inevitably involve questions of power. In the end, UN agencies have little power to make such judgments. Furthermore, UN agencies such as UNDP and UN-Habitat, which have sometimes shown resistance to neoliberalism, have been dragged into its political orbit, leading them to retreat from more politicized standpoints and toward the more impartial UNGC language of stakeholders and partnerships.

For example, Neuwirth notes that UN-Habitat has long claimed to take a progressive position regarding squatters but, whenever a situation has arisen in which the agency has had a chance to defend the rights of squatters in decision making, it has remained silent.[136] Furthermore, there has been a growing tendency for international development agencies and NGOs to adapt their vision of success to criteria adopted from the corporate sector in order to successfully integrate into the new international order typified by the UNGC.[137] By adopting corporate models of governance and evaluation, these agencies and NGOs tend to develop their own vested interests, resulting in a cascading proliferation of agencies all trying to do roughly similar things.

In making a case for including prominent INGOs as partners in the promotion of sport for development and peace Bruce Kidd argues that the idealistic rhetoric of Olympism can provide powerful leverage to make the IOC more accountable and more seriously committed to sustainability and economic inclusiveness.[138] Other reformist critics share this position, and it makes sense as a frontline political strategy. Inclusivity and sustainability will be enhanced if international sports associations and their corporate partners are held accountable, through various forms of public pressure, to honor the rhetoric of their UNGC commitment to build a better world for all.

However, there is good reason to be highly skeptical about how successful this public pressure has been, or can be. A great many people these days profess a commitment to some social cause or another, and it is often difficult to differentiate genuine commitment from marketing rhetoric. There is good business in philanthropy, and even in politically conscious activism, if it provides sources of self-identity and brand recognition, or satisfies consumers' desires to feel good about the products they purchase.[139] Social investments can also build audiences or markets for one's products. For example, over the past decade FIFA's expenditures in developing soccer programs, coaching, and facilities in poor communities around the world have increased at a rate that exceeds the rate of increase in the organization's profits.[140] These programs provide opportunities for many disadvantaged young people, but they appear to feed a culture of clientelism within the organization, as recent scandals have shown. They are also not purely altruistic insofar as they build attachments to global soccer culture, and to famous players and teams, and create larger markets for the sale of merchandise. Slums may be poor, but their sheer scale and the nature of their informal economies create substantial global markets for light consumer goods such as mobile phones, sunglasses, energy drinks, DVDs, inexpensive sports apparel, and equipment.

At the same time, contemporary politics have moved away from early and mid-twentieth-century socialist collectivism toward a hyper-individualistic version of politics. In many of the western nations, the game of politics is now played out in the media or expressed through acts of "ethical" individual consumption, such as drinking fair-trade coffee. The activist variant of this game may also involve signing online petitions or even volunteering to work with well-meaning NGOs for the provision of programs designed to meet local community needs, or perhaps supporting what appear to be progressive causes through online donations or signing online petitions. Yet digital activism in particular is also part of the systemic deepening of capitalist relations on a global scale. The commodification of new audiences in online platforms has enhanced capacities for an expansion – a further pushing back – of capital's frontiers. Social media such as Facebook and Twitter have become unprecedented

197

vehicles for creating new markets, commodities, synergies, forms of marketing, networks of publicity and, some argue, even new forms of immaterial labor.[141] They also play a key role in the acceleration of the recovery time of digital investments. But they simultaneously provide enhanced means to criticize the very markets, synergies, and networks they create. This invites the question of whether the possibilities for reflexivity and opposition that social media create can offer *effective* challenges to capitalist accumulation or whether, as Jodi Dean argues, these challenges are likely to be little more than democratic or participatory "fantasies."[142]

Samir Amin raises an important point when he argues that the highly mediated global politics of the twenty-first century – or as he calls it, "low-intensity democracy" – have a tendency to devolve into populist positions that are as likely to move in socially conservative directions as progressive ones. For every radical movement on the internet, there are reactionary alternatives that play to populist activism. When the criticisms of international sporting spectacles focus almost exclusively on local, regional, or national issues – such as transportation costs and housing availability – they downplay the current stage of international market-centered globalization.[143] According to Mezzadra and Neilson, the challenge is one of "translatability," of implementing effective articulations between local and global criticisms based on shared understandings of "the processes of dispossession and exploitation that crisscross the operations of capital."[144] This may mean linking up or coordinating criticism raised at different types of events, for example at WTO summits and World Cups or the Olympics. I share their view that the ultimate goal is the attempt to build "new transnational forms of democratic political organization capable of combining struggles and multiplying their affirmative aspects."[145]

NOTES

Introduction

1 For example, Thomas Scanlon argues that the ancient Egyptian word "*swtwt*" translates into the English word "sport." See his discussion in "Contesting Ancient Mediterranean Sport," *International Journal of the History of Sport* 26(2) (2009): 149. In contrast, Peter Keegan argues (more persuasively in my view) that "despite the existence of the word *swtwt* (technically "walk" but which might be loosely translated as "sport"), the ancient Egyptians had no specific term, and hence more than likely no concept corresponding to the modern notion of sports," *Graffiti in Antiquity* (London: Routledge, 2014): 186. In my reading of the classical historical literature, most historians appear to accept Keegan's view that there is "no equivalent" to the modern meanings of the term "sport" in the languages of ancient Mediterranean civilizations.

2 Henry Bradley, *The Making of English* (Mineola, NY: Dover Books, 2006 [1904]): 107.

3 Late nineteenth- and early twentieth-century examples include Thorstein Veblen's discussion of sports in *The Theory of the Leisure Class* (New York: Mentor Books, 1953 [1899]); Johan Huizinga's discussions of play, games and sports in *Homo Ludens: A Study of the Play Element in Culture* (Boston: Beacon Press, 1955 [1938]); and the early twentieth-century German scholars discussed in chapter 4 of this book.

4 For overviews of some of these attempts at definition and classification from the standpoint of the 1960s and 1970s, see Eric Dunning, "Notes on Some Conceptual and Theoretical Problems in the Sociology of Sport," *International Review of Sport Sociology* 2 (1967): 143–53; John Loy, "The Nature of Sport: A Definitional Effort," *Quest* 10 (1968): 1–15; Alan G. Ingham and John Loy, "The Social System of Sport: A Humanistic Perspective," *Quest* 19 (1973): 3–23; Richard S. Gruneau, "Sport as an Area of Sociological Study: An Introduction to Major Themes and Perspectives," in Richard S. Gruneau and John G. Albinson (eds), *Canadian Sport: Sociological Perspectives* (Don Mills, ON: Addison-Wesley, 1976): 8–43; and Klaus V. Meier, "On the Inadequacies of Sociological Definitions

of Sport," *International Review of Sport Sociology* 16(2) (1981): 79-102.
5 Scanlon, "Contesting Ancient Mediterranean Sport": 149.
6 Ibid.
7 *The Encyclopedia of Diderot and d'Alembert*, University of Michigan Collaborative Translation Project: http://quod.lib.umich.edu/cgi/t/text/text-idx?page=simple;c=did
8 Personal correspondence, January 1, 2016 from Dena Goodman, Lila Miller Collegiate Professor of History and Women's Studies and Co-director of the Diderot and D'Alembert Collaborative Translation Project, University of Michigan. I want to thank Dr Miller for providing this information and for conducting a search of the ARTFL–FRANTEXT database for the word "sport." The database lists the first appearance of the word in French, in Charles Fourier's *Théorie des quatre mouvements* (ARTFL electronic edn, 2009 [1808]).
9 Jon Hughes, "'Im Sport ist der Nerv der Zeit selber zu spüren': Sport and Cultural Debate in the Weimar Republic," *German as a Foreign Language* 2 (2007): 32.
10 Pierre Bourdieu, "Sport and Social Class," *Social Science Information* 17(6) (1978): 826.
11 E. H. Carr, *What is History?*, 2nd edn, edited by R. W. Davies (Harmondsworth: Penguin Books, 1964 [1961]): 9.
12 Bourdieu, "Sport and Social Class": 826.
13 Huizinga, *Homo Ludens*.
14 Ibid.: 192.
15 See John B. Thompson, *Ideology and Modern Culture: Critical Theory in the Age of Mass Communication* (Stanford: Stanford University Press, 1991).
16 Richard S. Gruneau, "Modernization or Hegemony? Two Views on Sport and Social Development," in Jean Harvey and Hart Cantelon (eds), *Not Just a Game: Essays in Canadian Sport Sociology* (Ottawa: University of Ottawa Press, 1988).
17 Ulrich Beck, Anthony Giddens and Scott Lash, *Reflexive Modernization* (Stanford: Stanford University Press, 1994).
18 Anthony Giddens, *The Consequences of Modernity* (Stanford, CA: University of California Press, 1990): 1.
19 Ibid.: 4.
20 For just a few examples see: Daniel Bell, *The Coming of Postindustrial Society* (New York: Basic Books, 1973); Jean-François Lyotard, *The Postmodern Condition: A Report on Knowledge*, trans. Geoff Bennington and Brian Massumi (Minneapolis: University of Minnesota Press, 1984); Fredric Jameson, *Postmodernism: Or the Logic of Late Capitalism* (Durham, NC: Duke University Press, 1981); Ben Agger, *Fast Capitalism: A Critical Theory of Significance* (Urbana, IL: University of Illinois Press, 1989); Ash Amin (ed.), *Post-Fordism: A Reader* (Hoboken, NJ: Wiley-Blackwell, 1995); Scott Lash and John Urry, *The End of Organized Capitalism* (Madison, WN: University of Wisconsin Press, 1987); Zygmunt Bauman, *Liquid Modernity* (Cambridge: Polity, 2000).
21 For early summaries, see: Andreas Huyssen, "Mapping the Postmodern," *New German Critique* 33 (1984): 5-52; David Harvey, *The Condition*

of Postmodernity: An Enquiry into the Origins of Cultural Change (Cambridge, MA: Blackwell, 1989); Steven Connor, *Postmodernist Culture: An Introduction to Theories of the Contemporary* (Oxford: Basil Blackwell, 1989). My discussion here draws from Nick Witheford and Richard Gruneau, "Between the Politics of Production and the Politics of the Sign: Post-Marxism, Postmodernism and 'New Times,'" in Ben Agger (ed.), *Current Perspectives in Social Theory*, Vol. 13 (Greenwich, CN: JAI Press, 1993): 69–92.

22 Marshall Berman, *All that is Solid Melts into Air: The Experience of Modernity* (Harmondsworth: Penguin Books, 1982).

23 Anthony Giddens, *The Consequences of Modernity*; David Harvey, *Paris: Capital of Modernity* (London: Routledge, 2003).

24 For a detailed discussion, see Jürgen Habermas, *The Philosophical Discourse of Modernity: Twelve Lectures*, trans. Frederick Lawrence (Cambridge, MA: MIT Press, 1990 [1985]). A more focused emphasis on what Habermas sees as the enabling aspects of the project of modernity can be found in his essay, "Modernity: An Incomplete Project," in Hal Foster (ed.), *The Anti-Aesthetic: Essays on Postmodern Culture* (Seattle: Bay Press, 1983): 3–15.

25 Arif Dirlik, "Global Modernity? Modernity in an Age of Global Capitalism," *European Journal of Social Theory* 6 (2003): 279.

26 See Samir Amin, "Imperialism and Globalization," *Monthly Review* 53(2) (June 2001): http://monthlyreview.org/2001/06/01/imperialism-and-globalization.

27 A useful early twenty-first-century survey of this tension can be found in Nagesh Rao, "New Imperialisms, New Imperatives: Taking Stock of Postcolonial Studies," *Postcolonial Text* 2(1) (2006): http://postcolonial. org/index.php/pct/article/view/386/816

28 For early examples see Andre Gunder Frank, *The Development of Underdevelopment* (New York: Monthly Review Press, 1966) and *Capitalism and Underdevelopment in Latin America* (New York: Monthly Review Press, 1967; as well as Immanuel Wallerstein's three volumes written between 1979 and 1989 and dedicated to analyzing "the modern world system." Wallerstein has published a useful summary of this work in *World Systems Analysis: An Introduction* (Durham, NC: Duke University Press, 2004).

29 Fredric Jameson, *A Singular Modernity: Essay on the Ontology of the Present* (London: Verso, 2002): 35.

30 See Fredric Jameson, *Postmodernism: Or the Logic of Capitalism* (Chapel Hill, NC: Duke University Press, 1992).

31 Allen Guttmann, *From Ritual to Record: The Nature of Modern Sports* (New York: Columbia University Press, 1978).

32 Eric Dunning and Kenneth Sheard, *Barbarians, Gentlemen, and Players: A Sociological Study of the Development of Rugby Football* (London: Martin Robertson, 1979): 33–4; and Melvin Adelman, *A Sporting Time: New York City and the Rise of Modern Athletics, 1820–70* (Urbana, IL: University of Illinois Press, 1986).

33 See the Introduction and several of the essays in S. W. Pope (ed.), *The New American Sport History: Recent Approaches and Perspectives* (Urbana, IL: University of Illinois Press, 1996); for more recent overviews of theoretical

growth in discussions of history and sport, see Richard Giulianotti (ed.), *Routledge Handbook of the Sociology of Sport* (London: Routledge, 2015), especially the chapter by Douglas Booth and Mark Falcous, "History, Sociology and Critical Sport Studies": 153–65; and the essays in S. W. Pope and John Nauright, *Routledge Companion to Sport History* (London: Routledge, 2010).

34 See Geneviève Rail, *Sport in Postmodern Times* (Albany, NY: SUNY Press, 1998).
35 Ibid.; and also see Ben Carrington, *Race, Sport, and Politics: The Sporting Black Diaspora* (Thousand Oaks, CA: Sage, 2010).
36 For example, Francis Fukuyama, *The End of History and the Last Man* (New York: Free Press, 1992).
37 Frank J. Lechner and John Boli (eds), *The Globalization Reader*, 5th edn (Chichester: Wiley Blackwell, 2015): 544.

Chapter 1 Athletics, Body Imagery, and Spectacle: Greco-Roman Practices, Discourses, and Ideologies

1 Walter Benjamin, *Selected Writings, Vol. 4, 1938–1940*, ed. Howard Eiland and Michael W. Jennings (Cambridge, MA: Belknap Press of Harvard University Press, 2003): 49.
2 Karl Marx, *The Eighteenth Brumaire of Louis Bonaparte*, trans. Saul Padover from the 1869 (German edn 1852): https://www.marxists.org/archive/marx/works/download/pdf/18th-Brumaire.pdf: 5.
3 Ibid.
4 Biases and influences of classicism in nineteenth-century English art and education are usefully discussed in John Hughson, "The Ancient Sporting Legacy: Between Myth and Spectacle," *Sport in Society* 12(1) (January 2009): 18–35.
5 See John MacAloon, *This Great Symbol: Pierre de Coubertin and the Origins of the Modern Olympic Games* (Chicago: University of Chicago Press, 1981); John E. N. Gardiner, *Athletics of the Ancient World* (Oxford: Clarendon Press, 1930); and H. A. Harris, *Sport in Greece and Rome* (London: Thames & Hudson, 1972).
6 Some of these characteristics are outlined in Anthony Mangan, "Preface: Swansong." *International Journal of the History of Sport* 27(1–2) (January/February 2010): 9–20.
7 Harold B. Segel, *Body Ascendant: Modernism and the Physical Imperative* (Baltimore, MD: Johns Hopkins University Press, 1998): 208.
8 Ibid.: 136–7.
9 For some early work on the romantic and "classicist" biases in nineteenth- and twentieth-century sport history, see David Young, *The Olympic Myth of Greek Amateur Athletics* (Chicago: Ares Publishers, 1984); and Donald Kyle, *Athletics in Ancient Athens* (London: E. J. Brill, 1987).
10 Useful histories of ancient Greece can be found in M. I. Finley, *The Ancient Greeks* (New York: Penguin, 1977); and Geoffrey Ernest Maurice de Ste Croix, *The Class Struggle in the Ancient Greek World: From the Archaic Age to the Arab Conquests* (Ithaca, NY: Cornell University Press, 1989).

11 David Hawkes, *Ideology: The New Critical Idiom*, 2nd edn (London: Routledge, 2003): 20.
12 On class and occupational structures in ancient Greek city-states, see M. M. Austin and P. Vidal-Naquet, *Economic and Social History of Ancient Greece: An Introduction* (Berkeley: University of California Press, 1977) and de Ste Croix, *The Class Struggle in the Ancient Greek World*. Practices and ideologies of gender in Greek antiquity are explored in Sarah B. Pomeroy, *Goddesses, Whores, Wives and Slaves: Women in Classical Antiquity*, new edn (New York: Schocken Books, 1995 [1975]).
13 On slavery, see de Ste Croix, *Class Struggle in the Ancient Greek World*; M. I. Finley, *Economy and Society in Ancient Greece* (London: Chatto and Windus, 1981); and Y. Garlan, *Slavery in Ancient Greece* (Ithaca, NY: Cornell University Press, 1988).
14 David M. Pritchard, "Sport, War and Democracy in Classical Athens," *International Journal of the History of Sport* 26(2) (February 2009): 217.
15 On Greek education, see Robert Gardner, *Daily Life of the Ancient Greeks*, 2nd edn (Westport, CN: Greenwood Press, 2009): 155–64.
16 Hannah Arendt, *The Human Condition* (Chicago: University of Chicago Press, 1958): 41n34.
17 Ibid.
18 Ibid.: 205–6.
19 For example, see Bhikhu Parekh, *Hannah Arendt and the Search for a New Political Philosophy* (London: Macmillan, 1981); and Chantal Mouffe, *On the Political* (London: Verso, 2005).
20 Patricia Springborg, "Hannah Arendt and the Classical Republican Tradition," in Gisela T. Kaplan and Clive S. Kessler (eds), *Hannah Arendt: Thinking, Judging, Freedom* (Sydney: Allen & Unwin, 1989): 8–17.
21 Bonnie Honig, "The Politics of Agonism," *Political Theory* 21(3) (1993): 528–33.
22 Arendt, *The Human Condition*: 26.
23 Ibid.: 26–7.
24 Also see Honig, "The Politics of Agonism."
25 Ryan Belot, *Courage in the Democratic Polis: Ideology and Critique in Classical Athens* (Oxford: Oxford University Press, 2014): 166.
26 Michel Foucault, *The Use of Pleasure: The History of Sexuality*, Vol. 2 (New York: Vintage Books, 1986): 78–82.
27 Ibid.: 82–93.
28 Gary Forsythe, *A Critical History of Early Rome: From Prehistory to the First Punic War* (Berkeley, CA: University of California Press, 2006): 28.
29 Louis A. Ruprecht Jr, "Greek Exercises: The Modern Olympics as Hellenic Appropriation and Reinvention," *Thesis Eleven* 93 (May 2008): 75.
30 Ibid.
31 Ibid.
32 Ibid.
33 Donald Kyle, *Athletics in Ancient Athens*: 12.
34 Useful overviews of Greek athletic festivals and the various meanings associated with them can be found in D. J. Phillips and D. Pritchard (eds), *Sport and Festival in the Ancient Greek World* (Swansea: Classical Press of Wales, 2003); and David Pritchard, *Sport, Democracy and War in Classical Athens* (Cambridge: Cambridge University Press, 2013).

35 Thomas Hubbard, "Contemporary Sport Sociology and Ancient Greek Athletics," *Leisure Studies* 27(4) (2008): 383.
36 Louis A. Ruprecht Jr, "Greek Exercises": 79.
37 Sofie Remijsen, "The So-Called 'Crown Games': Terminology and Historical Context of the Ancient Categories for *Agones*." *Zeitschrift für Papyrologie und Epigraphik* 177 (2011): 97–109.
38 On prizes awarded to Ancient Greek athletes, see H. W. Pleket, "Games, Prizes, Athletes and Ideology," *Stadion* 1 (1975): 49–89.
39 See Donald Kyle, "Greek Female Sport: Rites, Running and Racing," in Paul Christesen and Donald G. Kyle (eds), *Companion to Sport and Spectacle in Greek and Roman Antiquity* (Chichester: Wiley-Blackwell, 2014): 258–75.
40 Sue Blundell points to the difficulty of analyzing gender relations in Greek antiquity because knowledge of women in Greek antiquity has most often come from male commentators. In her book *Women in Ancient Greece* (Cambridge, MA: Harvard University Press, 1995), she argues: "Both as a group and as individuals, the women of ancient Greece are to a large extent creatures who have been invented by men": 10–11.
41 Robin Osborne, *The History Written on the Classical Greek Body* (Cambridge: Cambridge University Press, 2011): 35.
42 Ibid.; and Nigel Spivey, *Greek Sculpture* (Cambridge: Cambridge University Press, 2013).
43 Spivey, *Greek Sculpture*: 135.
44 Ibid.
45 On the complexity of gender and sexuality in Greek antiquity, and particularly on the issues of pleasure, homosexuality, and pederasty, see Foucault, *The Use of Pleasure*: esp. 187–225.
46 Robin Osborne, "Looking On – Greek Style: Does the Sculpted Girl Speak to Women Too?" in Ian Morris (ed.), *Classical Greece: Ancient Histories and Modern Archaeologies* (Cambridge: Cambridge University Press, 1994): 81–96.
47 Nigel James Nicholson, *Aristocracy and Athletics in Archaic and Classical Greece* (Cambridge: Cambridge University Press, 2005): 1.
48 Ibid.
49 Hubbard, "Contemporary Sport Sociology and Ancient Greek Athletics": 384.
50 Mark Pizzato, *Theatres of Human Sacrifice: From Ancient Rituals to Screen Violence* (Albany: SUNY Press, 2005): 2.
51 Ibid.: 21.
52 On the often excitable and violent spectatorship at the ancient Olympics, see M. I. Finlay and H. W. Pleket, *The Olympic Games: The First Hundred Years* (London: Chatto & Windus, 1976).
53 On homoeroticism and pederasty in Greek athletics, see T. F. Scanlon, *Eros and Greek Athletics* (New York: Oxford University Press, 2002).
54 On these differences of opinion, see Hubbard, "Contemporary Sport Sociology and Ancient Greek Athletics": 384–6; David Young, *The Olympic Myth of Greek Amateur Athletics* (Chicago: Ares Publishers, 1984); and Donald Kyle, "The First 100 Olympiads: A Process of Decline or Democratization?," *Nikephoros* 10 (1997): 53–75.
55 Remijsen, "The So-Called 'Crown Games'": 99–104.

56 Hubbard, "Contemporary Sport Sociology and Ancient Greek Athletics": 384.
57 Ibid.: 386.
58 Ibid.
59 Pritchard, "Sport, War and Democracy in Classical Athens": 234–5.
60 Remijsen provides a number of examples of competitors at the Panhellenic Games from outside the Greek Peloponnesus, as well as initiatives to stage localized athletic events in the competition for a city's status. See "Challenged by Egyptians: Greek Sports in the 3rd Century BC," *International Journal of the History of Sport* 26(2) (February 2009): 246–71.
61 Pritchard, "Sport, War and Democracy in Classical Athens": 224.
62 De Ste Croix, *The Class Struggle in the Ancient Greek World*; M. I. Finley, *Economy and Society in Ancient Greece*; and Austin and Vidal-Naquet, *Economic and Social History of Ancient Greece*.
63 Ellen Meiksins Wood. *Peasant-Citizen and Slave: The Foundations of Athenian Democracy* (London: Verso, 1988).
64 Donald Kyle, *Sport and Spectacle in the Ancient World* (Malden, MA: Wiley-Blackwell, 2007): 152–3.
65 Max Weber, *The Agrarian Sociology of Ancient Civilizations* (London: New Left Books, 1976): 27.
66 Hubbard, "Contemporary Sport Sociology and Ancient Greek Athletics": 387.
67 Nicholson, *Aristocracy and Athletics*: 9–10.
68 Ibid.
69 Ibid.
70 Cited in William J. Baker, "Organized Greek Games," in Eric Dunning and Dominic Malcolm (eds), *Sport: Critical Concepts in Sociology, Vol. 2, The Development of Sport* (London: Routledge, 2003): 85.
71 Pritchard, "Sport, War and Democracy in Classical Athens": 219.
72 Hubbard, "Contemporary Sport Sociology and Ancient Greek Athletics": 387.
73 My discussion here draws on Remijsen, "The Imperial Policy on Athletic Games in Late Antiquity," in Kaja Harter Uibopuu and Thomas Kruse (eds), *Sport und Recht in der Antike* (Vienna: Holzhausen Verlag, 2014): 334.
74 Patrick Brantlinger. *Bread and Circuses: Theories of Mass Culture as Social Decay* (Ithaca, NY: Cornell University Press, 1983): 54.
75 Ibid.
76 Hubbard, "Contemporary Sport Sociology and Ancient Greek Athletics": 387.
77 Cited in Baker, "Organized Greek Games": 86.
78 On Hippocrates and especially his influence on later writers in the Roman imperial period, see Jason König, *Athletics and Literature in the Roman Empire* (Cambridge: Cambridge University Press, 2005).
79 Pritchard, "Sport, War and Democracy in Classical Athens": 218–19.
80 Hawkes, *Ideology*: 24.
81 Ibid.
82 Hubbard, "Contemporary Sport Sociology and Ancient Greek Athletics": 387.
83 Hawkes, *Ideology*: 25.

84 Rex Warner, *The Greek Philosophers* (New York: Mentor Books, 1958): 112–14.
85 Sebastian de Grazia, *Of Time, Work and Leisure* (Garden City, NY: Anchor Books, 1964): 11.
86 Ibid., 12.
87 Norbert Elias, "Introduction," in Norbert Elias and Eric Dunning (eds), *Quest for Excitement: Sport and Leisure in the Civilizing Process* (Oxford: Basil Blackwell, 1986): 77–9.
88 Peter Sloterdijk, *Philosphical Temperaments: From Plato to Foucault*, trans. Thomas Dunlap (New York: Columbia University Press, 2013): 15.
89 Aristotle, *Politics VIII*, 6, 1341, b. 8–14.
90 Pritchard, *Sport, Democracy and War in Classical Athens*: 4.
91 Friedrich Nietzsche, *The Birth of Tragedy: Out of the Spirit of Music*, ed. Michael Tanner and trans. Shaun Whiteside (London: Penguin Classics, 1994 [1872]).
92 See Forsythe, *A Critical History of Early Rome: From Prehistory to the First Punic War*. A definitive nineteenth-century analysis of early Roman development can be found in Theodor Mommsen, *The History of Rome, Vols 1–5* (Oxford: Benedictine Classics, 2011 [1854]).
93 Forsythe, *A Critical History of Early Rome*: 1.
94 Mommsen, *The History of Rome, Vol. 2*, and Forsythe, *A Critical History of Early Rome*: chs. 8–10, 234–368.
95 Louis A. Ruprecht Jr, "Greek Exercises": 74.
96 Christian Mann, "Gladiators in the Greek East: A Case Study of Romanization," *International Journal of the History of Sport* 26(2) (February 2009): 272–3.
97 Ibid.: 277.
98 Ibid.: 273.
99 Ibid.: 278.
100 Ibid.: 285.
101 Ibid., 287.
102 Ibid.: 279.
103 Remijsen, "Imperial Policy": 335.
104 Ibid.: 336.
105 Alison Futrell, *Blood in the Arena: The Spectacle of Roman Power* (Austin, TX: University of Texas Press, 1997): 3.
106 Ibid.
107 Ibid.: 35.
108 Ibid.: 10.
109 Ibid.: 35.
110 Keith Hopkins, "Murderous Games: Gladiatorial Contests in Ancient Rome," *History Today* 33(6) (1983): http://www.historytoday.com/keith-hopkins/murderous-games-gladiatorial-contests-ancient-rome. Also see David S. Potter, *Life, Death, and Entertainment in the Roman Empire* (Ann Arbor, MI: University of Michigan Press, 1999).
111 Keith Hopkins and Mary Beard, *The Colosseum* (London: Profile Books, 2006).
112 Ibid.: 91–6.
113 Roger Dunkle, *Gladiators, Violence and Spectacle in Ancient Rome* (London: Routledge, 2008): ch. 2.

114 Ibid.: 15.
115 Ibid.
116 Mann, "Gladiators in the Greek East": 274.
117 Dunkle, *Gladiators, Violence and Spectacle in Ancient Rome*: 35–6.
118 On female gladiators see Steven Brunet, "Women with Swords: Female Gladiators in the Roman World," in Christesen and Kyle (eds), *Companion to Sport and Spectacle in Greek and Roman Antiquity*.
119 Ibid.: 489.
120 Expanded discussions of this point can be found in Futrell, *Blood in the Arena*; Hopkins and Beard, *The Colosseum*; and Dunkle, *Gladiators, Violence and Spectacle in Ancient Rome*.
121 Keegan, *Graffiti in Antiquity*: 213.
122 Dunkle, *Gladiators, Violence and Spectacle in Ancient Rome*: 35–6.
123 See Elizabeth Rawson, "Chariot Racing the Roman Republic," *Papers of the British School at Rome* 49 (Nov. 1981): 1–16; and John Humphrey, *Roman Circuses: Arenas for Chariot Racing* (Berkeley: University of California Press, 1986).
124 A useful summary of Roman values can be found in Donald Earl, *The Moral and Political Tradition of Rome* (Ithaca, NY: Cornell University Press, 1984).
125 Donald Kyle, *Sport and Spectacle in the Ancient World*: 274. Kyle adds that after the defeat at Cannae the "ideology of military virtue" was extended to the arena and prompted an increase in numbers of gladiatorial contests.
126 Julius Caesar, *The Gallic Wars*, trans. John Warrington (New York: Heritage Press, 1955 [approximately 50 BCE]): 3.
127 Thucydides, *History of the Peloponnesian War*, trans. Rex Warner (Baltimore: Penguin, 1954): Book II, 118.
128 Kathryn Mammel, "Ancient Critics of Roman Spectacle and Sport," in Christesen and Kyle (eds), *Companion to Sport and Spectacle in Greek and Roman Antiquity*: 607.
129 De Ste Croix. *The Class Struggle in the Ancient Greek World*, ch. VI: 337–63.
130 Juvenal, cited in Patrick Brantlinger, *Bread and Circuses: Theories of Mass Culture as Social Decay* (Ithaca, NY: Cornell University Press, 1983): 22; online original version, trans. G. G. Ramsay: http://www.tertullian.org/fathers/juvenal_satires_10.htm
131 Brantlinger, *Bread and Circuses*, 22. This negative view of arena-goers is by no means limited to Juvenal or Seneca. For example, the Roman historian Ammianus Marcellinus referred to the "people" as a "slothful commons," who "spend all their life with wine and dice, in low haunts, pleasures, and the games." See *The Roman History of Ammianus Marcellinus*. Book XXVII, 28, Loeb Classical Library Edition, 1939: http://penelope.uchicago.edu/Thayer/E/Roman/Texts/Ammian/28*.html
132 Cited in Brantlinger, *Bread and Circuses*: 49.
133 John Sellers, *Stoicism* (Berkeley, CA: University of California Press, 2006).
134 Seneca, cited in Brantlinger, *Bread and Circuses*: 75.
135 Juvenal, *Satire X* (final paragraph): http://www.tertullian.org/fathers/juvenal_satires_10.htm
136 Plutarch, cited in Mann, "Gladiators in the Greek East": 282–3.

137 Martial, *De Spectaculis Liber*, in *Epigrams* (trans. Walter Kerr), 2 vols (Cambridge, MA: Loeb Classical Library, 1919).
138 Keegan, *Graffiti in Antiquity*: 204.
139 John H. Humphrey, *Roman Circuses*: 1.
140 Keegan, *Graffiti in Antiquity*: 203.
141 Keith Hopkins, "Murderous Games."
142 "Cosmopolitanism." *Stanford Encyclopedia of Philosophy*: http://plato. stanford.edu/entries/cosmopolitanism/
143 For example, Janet Huskinson (ed.), *Experiencing Rome: Culture, Identity and Power in the Roman Empire* (London: Routledge, 1998).
144 De Ste Croix, *The Class Struggle in the Ancient Greek World*: 454–6.
145 Useful examples include Frank Snowden, *Blacks in Antiquity: Ethiopians in the Greco-Roman Experience* (Cambridge, MA: Belknap Press, 1970; and Loyd Thompson, *Romans and Blacks* (London, UK: Routledge, 1989).
146 Benjamin Isaac, *The Invention of Racism in Classical Antiquity* (Princeton: Princeton University Press, 2006). For a countering view, see Erich S. Gruen, *Rethinking the Other in Antiquity*, Martin Classical Lectures (Princeton: Princeton University Press, 2011).
147 James Rosbrook-Thompson, *Sport, Difference and Belonging: Conceptions of Human Variation in British Sport* (London: Routledge, 2013).
148 Ibid.: 18.
149 For a roughly parallel but somewhat different argument about the history of race and sport, see Ben Carrington, *Race, Sport and Politics* (Newbury Park, CA: Sage, 2010).
150 Jason König, "Conventions of Prefatory Self-Presentation in Galen's *On the Order of My Own Books*," in Christopher Gill, Tim Whitmarsh, and John Wilkins (eds), *Galen and the World of Knowledge* (Cambridge: Cambridge University Press, 2012): 37.
151 Ibid.: 39.
152 Ibid.
153 Jason König, "Training Athletes and Interpreting the Past in Philostratus's *Gymnasticus.*" In E. L. Bowie and J. Elsnor (eds), *Philostratus* (Cambridge: Cambridge University Press, 2009): 259.
154 Ibid.: 283.
155 For example, see Edward Gibbon, *Decline and Fall of the Roman Empire* (London: PRC Publishing, 1979 [1776–1789]): 35.
156 Christer Brun, "The Antonine Plague and the 'Third-Century Crisis,'" in Olivier Hekster, Gerda de Kleijn, and Danielle Slootjes (eds), *Crises and the Roman Empire: Proceedings of the Seventh Workshop of the International Network Impact of Empire* (Leiden/Boston: Brill, 2007): 201–18.
157 In this process, Marx remarks that "free peasants" were increasingly turned into "debtor slaves." Karl Marx, *Capital, Vol. III: The Process of Capitalist Production as a Whole* (Moscow: Progress Publishers, 1971): 599.
158 De Ste Croix, *The Class Struggle in the Ancient Greek World*, 453–61; and also see Weber's discussion of the importance of the diminishing supplies of slaves in the changing economy of early imperial Rome in *The Agrarian Sociology of Ancient Civilizations*: 390–403.
159 De Ste Croix, *The Class Struggle*: 494–500.
160 Ibid.: 465–74.
161 Futrell, *Blood in the Arena*: 7.

162 Remijsen, "Imperial Policy": 333.
163 Mann, "Gladiators in the Greek East": 277.
164 Remijsen, "Imperial Policy": 333.
165 Tertullian, *Apology and De Spectaculis*, trans. T. R. Glover (New York: Loeb Classical Library, 1931).
166 Cited in Brantlinger, *Bread and Circuses*: 261.
167 Ibid.: 78.
168 Ibid.: 79–80.
169 For a useful discussion of this event, see Michael Gaddis, *There is No Crime for Those who Have Christ: Religious Violence in the Christian Roman Empire* (Berkeley, CA: University of California Press, 2005): 204–6.
170 Brantlinger, *Bread and Circuses*: 77.
171 Alan Cameron, *Circus Factions: Blues and Greens at Rome and Byzantium* (Oxford: Oxford University Press, 1976). For a more contemporary and multifaceted view, see Sotiris Giatsis, "The Organization of Chariot Racing in the Great Hippodrome of Byzantine Constantinople," *International Journal the History of Sport* 17(1) (2000): 36–68.
172 Remijsen, "Imperial Policy": 333.
173 Ibid.: 344.
174 Ibid.: 345.
175 Ibid.: 340.
176 Ibid.: 345.
177 Ibid.
178 Ibid.: 344.
179 Ibid.: 345.
180 An alternative view is outlined in David Sansone, *Greek Athletics and the Genesis of Sport* (Berkeley, CA: University of California Press, 1988).
181 For some examples, see Allen Guttmann, *From Ritual to Record: The Making of Modern Sports* (New York: Columbia University Press, 1978: Henning Eichberg, *Body Cultures: Essays on Sport, Space and Identity* (London: Routledge, 1998); and Alan G. Ingham, "The Sportification Process: A Biographical Analysis Framed by the Work of Marx, Weber, Durkheim and Freud," in Richard Giulianotti (ed.), *Sport and Modern Social Theorists: A Plurality of Perspectives* (London: Palgrave Macmillan, 2004).
182 Anthony Mangan, "Preface: Swansong": 10.
183 Notable exceptions include Norbert Elias and Eric Dunning, *Quest for Excitement: Sport and Leisure in the Civilizing Process* (Oxford: Blackwell, 1986); and John Hughson, *Sport and Modernity*, Special Issue of *Sport in Society* 12(1) (January 2009).
184 See George Mosse, *The Nationalization of the Masses: Political Symbolism and Mass Movements in Germany from the Napoleonic Wars through the Third Reich* (New York: Howard Fertig, 1975).
185 Anna Makolkin, "Machiavelli's Roman Nostalgia and his Critique of Christianity." *E-Logos, Electronic Journal of Philosophy*, 2008: 12.
186 Edward Gibbon, in *The History of the Decline and Fall of the Roman Empire*, 12 vols, ed. J. B. Bury with an introduction by W. E. H. Lecky (New York: Fred de Fau, 1906), Vol. 1, April 18, 2016: http://oll.liberty-fund.org/titles/1365.
187 Francis Bacon, *The Essays of Sir Francis Bacon*, with an introduction by Christopher Morley (New York: Heritage Press, 1944 [1625]): 100.

Chapter 2 The Politics of Representation:
English Sport as an Object and Project of Modernity

1 See Perry Anderson, *Passages from Antiquity to Feudalism* (London: New Left Books, 1974) for a Marxian interpretation of these changes. A broader and more recent interpretation can be found in Peter Brown, *Authority and the Sacred: Aspects of the Christianization of the Roman World* (London: Routledge, 2012).

2 A. P. Kazhdan and Ann Wharton Epstein, *Change in Byzantine Culture in the Eleventh and Twelfth Centuries* (Berkeley: University of California Press, 1985): 3.

3 William D. Phillips, *Slavery from Roman Times to the Early Transatlantic Trade* (Manchester: Manchester University Press, 1985).

4 For example see Ernst Kitzinger, *Byzantine Art in the Making: Main Lines of Stylistic Development in Mediterranean Art, 3rd–7th Century* (Cambridge: Cambridge University Press, 1977).

5 Pierre Bourdieu, "Sport and Social Class," *Social Science Information* 17(6) (1978): 826.

6 Bourdieu's former student, Jacques Defrance, offers the most significant application of Bourdieu's ideas about the social development of modern sport. See Jacques Defrance, *L'Excellence corporelle: La formation des activités physique et sportives moderne, 1770–1914* (Rennes: Presses Universitaires de Rennes, 1987) and Defrance's chapter, "The Making of a Field with Weak Autonomy: The Case of the Sports Field in France, 1895–1955," in Philip S. Gorski (ed.), *Bourdieu and Historical Analysis* (Durham, NC: Duke University Press, 2013).

7 For example the eighth-century monk Nennius makes passing reference to ancient ball games in his *Historia Brittonum*: http://www.fordham.edu/Halsall/basis/nennius-full.asp. Joseph Strutt also makes reference to the ancient roots of English games in his nineteenth-century antiquarian work, *The Sports and Pastimes of the People of England: Including the Rural Domestic Recreations, May Games, Mummeries, Shows, Processions, Pageants and Pompous Spectacles from the Earliest Period to the Present Time* (London: Thomas Teg, 1845 [1801]).

8 For a social history of hunting in England, see Emma Griffin, *Blood Sport: Hunting in Britain since 1066* (New Haven, CT: Yale University Press, 2009).

9 My discussion here draws largely on Robert W. Malcolmson, *Popular Recreations in English Society, 1700–1850* (Cambridge: Cambridge University Press, 1973).

10 On oral tradition in late medieval and early modern England see D. R. Woolf, "The Common Voice: History, Folklore and Tradition in Early Modern England," *Past and Present* 120(1) (1988): 26–52. Songs sung by minstrels and troubadours were an especially important aspect of this oral tradition. For a compendium of themes in these songs, see *The British Minstrel and Musical and Literary Miscellany*, vols 1–3 (Glasgow: William Hamilton, 1843).

11 On the inclusion of images of popular recreations in medieval Books of Hours, see David Diringer, *The Illuminated Book, its History and Production* (New York: Frederick A. Praeger, 1967).

12 For detailed discussion and analysis of the Luttrell Psalter, see Michelle P. Brown, *The World of the Lutrell Psalter* (London: British Library, 2007).
13 Roger Longrigg, *The English Squire and His Sport* (London: St Martin's Press, 1977): 28.
14 David Cresey, "Literacy in Context: Meaning and Measurement in Early Modern England," in John Brewer and Roy Porter (eds), *Consumption and the World of Goods* (London: Routledge, 1993): 305–7.
15 Karen Hearn (ed.), *Dynasties: Painting in Tudor and Jacobean England, 1530–1630* (London: Tate Publishing, 1995).
16 Kevin Sharpe, *Selling the Tudor Monarchy: Authority and Image in Sixteenth-Century England* (New Haven, CT: Yale University Press, 2009).
17 George Turberville, *Booke of Hunting* (Oxford: Clarendon Press, 1908 [1576]): https://archive.org/details/turbervilesbook00turbgoog
18 Malcolmson, *Popular Recreations in English Society*: 5–14.
19 Ibid.: 11.
20 Mikhail Bakhtin, *Rabelais and His World*, trans. H. Iswolsky (Cambridge, MA: MIT Press, 1968).
21 Ibid.: 10.
22 Peter Stallybrass and Allon White (eds), *The Poetics and Politics of Transgression* (Ithaca: Cornell University Press, 1986): 9.
23 Ibid.: 9–20.
24 A similar argument is developed in greater detail in Burke, *Popular Culture in Early Modern Europe*, 3rd edn (Farnham: Ashgate Publishing, 2009).
25 The comment is by US lawyer and later Vice President John Adams, cited originally by Peter Linebaugh and quoted here from Paul Gilroy, *The Black Atlantic: Modernity and Double Consciousness* (London: Verso, 1995): 13.
26 Peter Linebaugh and Marcus Rediker, *The Many Headed Hydra: Sailors, Slaves, Commoners and the Hidden History of the Revolutionary Atlantic* (Boston: Beacon Press, 2000). Also see Paul Gilroy's discussion in chs 1 and 2 of *The Black Atlantic*.
27 Emma Griffin, "Wholesome Recreations and Cheering Influences," in Sharon Harrow (ed.), *British Sporting Culture: The Literature and Culture of Sport in the Long Eighteenth Century* (London: Routledge, 2016).
28 E. P. Thompson, *The Making of the English Working Class* (Harmondsworth: Pelican Books, 1968): 442.
29 P. B. Munsche, *Gentlemen and Poachers: The English Game Laws, 1671–1831* (Cambridge: Cambridge University Press, 1981).
30 Henriette Gram Heiny, *Boxing in British Sporting Art: 1730–1824* (PhD dissertation, University of Oregon, Department of Art History, 1987): 5.
31 More detailed discussion and examples of this tradition can be found in Ralph Nevill, *Old English Sporting Prints and Their History* (London: The Studio Limited, 1923); F. L. Wilder, *English Sporting Prints* (London: Thames & Hudson, 1974); and James Laver, *English Sporting Prints* (London: Ward Lock, 1970).
32 E. P. Thompson, *Customs in Common* (London: Penguin Books, 1993): 17.
33 On the status and symbolic nature of pigs in medieval and renaissance life in Europe, and their association with fairs, festivals and the European under-classes, see Stallybrass and White, *The Poetics and Politics of Transgression*: 27–79.

34 Stephen Deuchar, *Sporting Art in Eighteenth-Century England: A Social and Political History* (New Haven, CN: Yale University Press, 1988).
35 My discussion here adapts ideas from Thompson, *Customs in Common*: 44–5.
36 Roger J. P. Cain, John Chapman and Richard R. Oliver, *The Enclosure Maps of England and Wales, 1595–1918* (Cambridge: Cambridge University Press, 2004).
37 *Cambridge Group for the History of Population and Social Structure*: http://www.geog.cam.ac.uk/research/projects/earlymodernlondon/
38 Thompson, *Customs in Common*: 36.
39 See Rictor Norton, *The Georgian Underworld: A Study of Criminal Subcultures in Eighteenth-Century England*: http://rictornorton.co.uk/gu00.htm; and Dan Cruickshank, *London's Sinful Secret: The Bawdy History and Very Public Passions of London's Georgian Age* (New York: St Martin's Press, 2010).
40 Thompson, *Customs in Common*: 50.
41 John B. Thompson, *The Media and Modernity* (Cambridge: Polity Press, 1995): 67.
42 Ibid.: 67–8.
43 Benedict Anderson, *Imagined Communities* (London: Verso, 1983). Anderson later developed his ideas about simultaneity and nationalism in his essay on "Nationalism, Identity and the World in Motion," in Peng Cheah and Bruce Robbins (eds), *Cosmopolitics: Thinking and Feeling Beyond the Nation* (Minneapolis: University of Minnesota Press, 1998).
44 Peter Burke, *Popular Culture in Early Modern Europe*, 3rd edn (Farnham: Ashgate Publishing, 2009).
45 Cited in Stallybrass and White, *The Poetics and Politics of Transgression*: 32.
46 Harriet Ritvo, *The Animal Estate: The English and Other Creatures in the Victorian Age* (Cambridge, MA: Harvard University Press, 1987): 152.
47 Malcolmson, *Popular Recreations in English Society*: 68.
48 Deuchar, *Sporting Art in Eighteenth-Century England*: 63–5.
49 Thompson, *Customs in Common*: 44–5.
50 Terry Eagleton, *The Function of Criticism* (London: Verso, 1989): 9. Cited in Stallybrass and White, *The Poetics and Politics of Transgression*: 82.
51 See Jürgen Habermas, *The Structural Transformation of the Public Sphere: An Inquiry into a Category of Bourgeois Society* (Boston: MIT Press, 1991 [1962]). In his essay, "A Theory of the Evolution of Modern Sport," *Journal of Sport History* 35(1) (Spring 2008), Stefan Szymanski develops the argument that the invention and organization of sport in the nineteenth and twentieth centuries grew out of the expansion of free "associativity" within the bourgeois public sphere. In Szymanski's view, the genesis of the idea that sport should be "autonomous" lay in the emerging liberal idea that individuals should be free to create social networks and organizations outside the family and separate from the state. This set the idea of sport as a positive component of civil society against older ideas of physical education and training which were largely promoted and pursued through state institutions. This is a compelling argument, but it leaves far too much out of account, especially in respect to the emergence of rationality as a mode of

control, in addition to the importance of class structures and British imperial history.

52 Stallybrass and White, *The Poetics and Politics of Transgression*: 96.

53 Ibid.: 96.

54 Ibid.: 97.

55 Deborah Heller, "Bluestocking Salons and the Public Sphere." *Eighteenth-Century Life* 22(2) (1998): 59–92.

56 Rictor Norton, *The Georgian Underworld*: http://rictornorton.co.uk/gu00.htm/.

57 Stephen Hardy, Brian Norman, and Sara Sceery, "Toward a History of Sport Branding," *Journal of Historical Research in Marketing* 4(4) (2012): 486–7. Hardy et al. note that the British Museum claim the image reprinted here was actually created by another printmaker and engraver, Anna Maria Ireland.

58 Norton, *The Georgian Underworld*, ch. 14.

59 Timothy Mitchell (ed.), *Questions of Modernity (Contradictions of Modernity)* (Minneapolis: University of Minnesota Press, 2000): 17.

60 For example, Francis Willughby (Willoughby), a seventeenth-century English naturalist prepared a book-length manuscript analyzing English sporting and gaming pastimes that was not published in his lifetime. In the early parts of the manuscript, he discusses the growing "scientific" literature on game and sporting pastimes in Europe. See David Cram Jeffrey Forgeng and Dorothy Johnston (eds), *Francis Willughby's Book of Games: A Seventeenth-Century Treatise on Sports, Games and Pastimes* (Farnham: Ashgate Publishing, 2003).

61 Joseph Strutt, *The Sports and Pastimes of the People of England*.

62 Jürgen Habermas, "Modernity: An Incomplete Project," in Hal Foster (ed.), *The Anti-Aesthetic: Essays on Postmodern Culture* (Seattle: Bay Press, 1983): 9.

63 Daniel O'Quinn, "In the Face of Difference: Molineux, Cribb and the Violence of the Fancy," in Paul Younquist (ed.), *Race, Romanticism and the Atlantic* (Farnham: Ashgate Publishing, 2013).

64 Joel T. Helfrich, "Becoming British by Beating Black America: National Identity and Race in the Molineux–Cribb Prize Fights of 1810 and 1812," in Dawne Y. Curry, Eric D. Duke, and Marshanda A. Smith (eds), *Extending the Diaspora: New Histories of Black People* (Urbana, IL: University of Illinois Press, 2009): 205–24.

65 For example, see Armand Mattelart's discussion of changing conceptions of reason and time in eighteenth- and nineteenth-century Europe, *The Invention of Communication* (Minneapolis: University of Minnesota Press, 1996): 3–53.

66 Michel Foucault, *Power/Knowledge: Selected Interviews, 1972–1977* (New York: Random House, 1981): 55.

67 A more developed discussion of this point can be found in Richard Gruneau, "The Somatic/Linguistic Turn in Histories of Exercise and Sport," in Robert Edelman and Wayne Wilson (eds), *The Oxford Handbook in Sport History* (New York: Oxford University Press, 2017).

68 Cited in Clifford Geertz, "Deep Play: Notes on the Balinese Cockfight," *Daedalus* 134(4) (2005): 56–86.

69 A more detailed discussion can be found in James Anthony Mangan,

Athleticism in the Victorian and Edwardian Public School: The Emergence and Consolidation of an Educational Ideology (Cambridge: Cambridge University Press, 1981).

70 Walter Arnstein, "The Survival of the Victorian Aristocracy," in Frederic Cople Jaher (ed.), *The Rich, the Well Born and the Powerful* (London: Lyle Stuart, 1975).

71 For a more developed discussion of amateurism, see Richard Gruneau, "Amateurism as a Sociological Problem: Some Reflections Inspired by Eric Dunning," *Sport in Society: Cultures, Commerce, Media, Politics* 9(4) (2006): 559–82.

72 Ann McClintock, *Imperial Leather: Race, Gender and Sexuality in the Colonial Contest* (London: Routledge, 1995): 24.

73 My discussion here is influenced by Peter Bailey, *Leisure and Class in Victorian England: Rational Recreation and the Contest for Control, 1830–1885* (London: Routledge & Kegan Paul, 1978).

74 Mangan, *Athleticism in the Victorian and Edwardian Public School*: 136.

75 David Young, *The Modern Olympics: A Struggle for Revival* (Baltimore: Johns Hopkins University Press, 1996): 31.

76 Stallybrass and White, *The Poetics and Politics of Transgression*: 22.

77 Susan Brownell, "Bodies before Boas: Sport before the Laughter Left," in Susan Brownell (ed.), *The 1904 Anthropology Days and Olympic Games: Sport, Race and American Imperialism* (Lincoln, NB: University of Nebraska Press, 2008): 3.

78 My discussion here draws on the contrast between positive and negative classicism developed by Patrick Brantlinger in *Bread and Circuses: Theories of Mass Culture as Social Decay* (Ithaca, NY: Cornell University Press, 1985).

Chapter 3 "Staging" (Capitalist/Colonial) Modernity: International Exhibitions and Olympics

1 Timothy Mitchell, "The Stage of Modernity," in Timothy Mitchell (ed.), *Questions of Modernity (Contradictions of Modernity)* (Minneapolis: University of Minnesota Press, 2000): 18.

2 Ibid.: 19.

3 Ibid.

4 Ibid.: 23.

5 Building on Fernand Braudel's idea of the "long sixteenth century," Hobsbawm suggests that the fundamental institutional and cultural dynamics of the nineteenth century in Europe begin with the French Revolution in 1789 and end with World War I in 1914. Eric Hobsbawm, *The Age of Revolution, 1789–1848* (London: Weidenfeld & Nicolson, 1962).

6 This chapter is also influenced by Ben Carrington's discussion of colonialism in *Race, Sport and Politics: The Sporting Black Diaspora* (Thousand Oaks, CA: Sage, 2010).

7 Raymond Williams, *Marxism and Literature* (Oxford: Oxford University Press, 1977): 94.

8 Book 1, aphorism 29 of *Novum Organon* (1620). For a translated version,

see Francis Bacon, *The New Organon*, ed. Lisa Jardine and Michael Silverthorne (Cambridge: Cambridge University Press, 2000).

9 Krishan Kumar, *From Postindustrial to Post-Modern Society: New Theories of the Contemporary World* (Oxford: Blackwell, 1995): 75. Also see Fredric Jameson, *A Singular Modernity: Essay on the Ontology of the Present* (London: Verso, 2002): Part 1.

10 Kumar, *From Postindustrial to Post-Modern Society*: 76.

11 On clock time and modernity, see Gerhard Dohrn-van Rossum, *History of the Hour: Clocks and Modern Temporal Orders* (Chicago, IL: University of Chicago Press, 1997); the association between clock time and capitalist labor discipline is explored in E. P. Thompson, "Time, Work Discipline and Industrial Capitalism," *Past and Present* 38 (December 1967): 56–97.

12 This is not to say that a desire for mastery over the physical world was not present in places outside of Europe, only that the idea of achieving this mastery in Europe took a different form than in the most economically "developed" countries in Africa and Asia. On this point, see Walter Rodney, *How Europe Underdeveloped Africa* (Dar es Salaam: Bogle-L'Ouverture Publications, 1973), ch. 1. Cited from the transcript from 6th reprint, 1983: http://abahlali.org/files/3295358–walter-rodney.pdf/.

13 Armand Mattelart, *The Invention of Communication*, trans. Susan Emanuel (Minneapolis, MN: University of Minnesota Press, 1996): 16.

14 Kumar, *From Postindustrial to Post-Modern Society*: 77.

15 See John B. Thompson, *The Media and Modernity: A Social Theory of the Media* (Stanford, CA: Stanford University Press, 1995): 52–69.

16 See Mattelart, *The Invention of Communication*, ch. 3.

17 John Hobson, *The Eastern Origins of Western Civilization* (Cambridge: Cambridge University Press, 2004): 5.

18 Andre Gunder Frank, *ReOrient: Global Economy in the Asian Age* (Berkeley, CA: University of California Press, 1998).

19 Ibid.: 37.

20 Karl Marx, *Capital*, Vol. 1 (Moscow: Progress Publishers, 1971).

21 Marx, cited in Kevin B. Anderson, *Marx at the Margins: On Nationalism, Ethnicity and Non-Western Societies* (Chicago, IL: University of Chicago Press, 2010): 83.

22 Karl Marx and Frederick Engels, "Manifesto of the Communist Party," in Marx/Engels, *Selected Works, Vol. One*, trans. Samuel Moore in cooperation with Frederick Engels, 1888, and proofed against the 1888 version by Andy Blunden (Moscow: Progress Publishers, 1969), online version at: https://www.marxists.org/archive/marx/works/download/pdf/Manifesto.pdf: 15–16.

23 Marshall Berman, *All that is Solid Melts into Air: The Experience of Modernity* (New York: Penguin Books, 1988 [1983]).

24 Ibid., 49.

25 Joseph A. Schumpeter, *Capitalism, Socialism and Democracy* (New York: Harper Brothers, 1942).

26 Berman's analysis has drawn such diverse commentary that it is prudent to note one or two of the concerns raised by his work. Few people disagree with his description of nineteenth-century modern life as a "maelstrom" of change that often has a Faustian character. Dispute lies with his tendency to universalize, and in some instances romanticize, the experiences of

modernity in major European and North American cities. Critics argue that this imagined universal perspective tends to marginalize the unique experiences of modernity for women or subaltern racial or ethnic groups. See Rita Felski, *The Gender of Modernity* (Cambridge, MA: Harvard University Press, 1995): 2–4; and Paul Gilroy, *The Black Atlantic: Modernity and Double Consciousness* (London: Verso, 1995): 46–8.

27 Marx and Engels, "Manifesto of the Communist Party": 17.

28 David Harvey, *The Condition of Postmodernity: An Enquiry into the Origins of Cultural Change* (Oxford: Blackwell, 1989): 240–50.

29 Marx sees both "freedom" and "equality" as key aspects of the emergence of capitalism in Europe. See his discussion in *Grundrisse* (Harmondsworth: Penguin Books, 1973): 244–5; and in *Capital, Vol. I: The Process of Production of Capital* (Moscow: Progress Publishers, 1971), see ch. 6. More recently, Tom Brass has argued that "mature" capitalism actually requires an increase in "unfree" labor. See Tom Brass, *Labour Regime Change in the Twenty-first Century: Unfreedom, Capitalism and Primitive Accumulation* (Chicago, IL: Haymarket Books, 2013).

30 Harvey, *The Condition of Postmodernity*: 240–50.

31 The classic statement on these processes is Henri Lefebvre, *The Production of Space*, trans. Donald Nicholson-Smith (Hoboken, NJ: Wiley, 1992 [1972]).

32 On Condorcet, Turgot, Saint-Simon and Comte, see Mattelart, *The Invention of Communication*, chs 1–3. On links between the thinking of eighteenth-century French philosophers to industrialism and progress, see Krishan Kumar, *Prophecy and Progress: Sociology of Industrial and Postindustrial Society* (New York: Viking Books, 1978).

33 Mattelart, *The Invention of Communication*, 92–4. An edited collection of Saint-Simon's writing, including a useful introduction, can be found in Keith Taylor (ed.), *Henri Saint-Simon, 1760–1825: Selected Writings on Science, Industry and Social Organization* (Teaneck, NJ: Holmes & Meier, 1975).

34 Mattelart, *The Invention of Communication*, 66–8. Detailed discussion of Comte can be found in Mike Gane, *Auguste Comte* (London: Routledge, 2006).

35 John B. Thompson, *The Media and Modernity* (Stanford, CA: Stanford University Press, 1995): 46.

36 Walter Benjamin, "Paris, Capital of the Nineteenth Century," reprinted in Walter Benjamin, *The Arcades Project*, trans. Howard Eiland and Kevin McLaughlin, prepared from the German volume, ed. Rolf Tiedemann (Cambridge, MA: Belknap Press of Harvard University Press, 1999 [1935]): 26.

37 Mattelart, *The Invention of Communication*: 112.

38 This argument is developed in depth in Robert Rydell, *All the World's a Fair: Visions of Empire at American International Expositions, 1876–1917* (Chicago, IL: University of Chicago Press, 1984).

39 This view is also expressed in Roche, *Mega-Events and Modernity: Olympics and Expos in the Growth of Global Culture* (London: Routledge, 2000); A. Geppert, *Fleeting Cities: Imperial Expositions in Fin-de-Siècle Europe* (Basingstoke: Palgrave Macmillan, 2010); and P. Greenhalgh, *Ephemeral Vistas: The Expositions Universelles: Great Exhibitions and*

World's Fairs, 1851–1939 (Manchester: Manchester University Press, 1988).

40 Timothy Mitchell, "The World as Exhibition," *Comparative Studies in Society and History* 31(2) (April 1989): 217–36. Alexander Geppert also highlights the communicative/representational aspects of international exhibitions, calling them "meta-media." See his discussion in *Fleeting Cities*: 3.

41 Mattelart, *The Invention of Communication*: 112.

42 On these points, see Arthur Chandler, "Market, Fair, Festival and Exposition: Preludes to the National and International Expositions Held in Paris, 1798–1937": http://www.arthurchandler.com/market-fair-festival-and-exposition/; and Maurice Roche, *Mega-Events and Modernity*: 40.

43 Benjamin, "Paris, Capital of the Nineteenth Century": 18.

44 On the history of fairs and European trade, see Fernand Braudel, *Civilization and Capitalism, 15th to the 18th Century, Vol. 3: The Perspective of the World*, trans. Sian Reynolds (Berkeley, CA: University of California Press, 1994 [1974]).

45 N. J. G. Pounds, *An Economic History of Medieval Europe*, 2nd edn (New York: Routledge, 1994 [1974]): 357–8.

46 Janet Lippman Abu-Lughod, "The World System in the Thirteenth Century: Dead-End or Precursor?" in Michael Adas (ed.), *Islamic and European Expansion: The Forging of a Global Order* (Philadelphia: Temple University Press, 1993): 187.

47 Braudel, *Civilization and Capitalism*, Vol. 3: 98.

48 Chandler, "Market, Fair, Festival and Exhibition."

49 Mattelart, *The Invention of Communication*: 114; and Chandler, "Market, Fair, Festival and Exhibition."

50 Mattelart, *The Invention of Communication*: 114.

51 Ibid.: 115.

52 Samuel McKechnie, *Popular Entertainments through the Ages* (New York: Benjamin Blom, 1969), especially chs 2 and 8.

53 Mattelart, *The Invention of Communication*, 114. In his essay on "Market, Fair, Festival and Exhibition," Chandler states that the new post-revolutionary French Republic invented a number of new festival celebrations of the Republic and its secular ideals, including the Festival of Law (1792); the Festival of Unity (1793); the Festival of Reason (1793); and the Festival of the Supreme Being (1794), among many others.

54 Mattelart, *The Invention of Communication*: 114.

55 Ibid.

56 Walter Borgers, "From the Temple of Industry to Olympic Arena: The Exhibition Tradition of the Olympic Games," *Journal of Olympic History* 11(1) (January 2003): 9.

57 Ibid.: 115.

58 Ibid.

59 For example, Marina Muñoz Torreblanca points out that Spain held an industrial exhibition in 1827: "Barcelona's Universal Exhibition of 1888: An Atypical Case of a Great Exhibition," in Marta Filipova (ed.), *Cultures of International Exhibitions, 1840–1940* (Farnham: Ashgate Publishing, 2015): 45–67. John R. Davis has written a discussion of an industrial exhibition in Berlin in 1844, "A Marginal Exhibition? The All-German

Exhibition of 1844," in Filipova, *Cultures of International Exhibitions*: 69–90.
60 Roche, *Mega-Events and Modernity*: 44.
61 Ibid.: 48. Roche argues that the impetus to shift from a national to an international focus occurred largely as a result of Prince Albert's idea of staging "a peace festival of nations."
62 Joseph Paxton, cited in Mattelart, *The Invention of Communication*: 113.
63 Ibid., 128–9.
64 Ibid.: 87.
65 Ibid.: 128–9.
66 Ibid.: 129.
67 David Harvey, *Paris: Capital of Modernity* (London: Routledge, 2003).
68 Useful discussions of this transformation can be found in Benjamin, "Paris, Capital of the Nineteenth Century;" and T. J. Clark, *The Painting of Modern Life: Paris in the Art of Monet and his Followers* (Princeton, NJ: Princeton University Press).
69 Berman, *All that is Solid Melts into Air*: 151.
70 Clark, *The Painting of Modern Life*: 37.
71 Ibid.: 43.
72 Kenneth H. Tucker Jr, *French Revolutionary Syndicalism and the Public Sphere* (Cambridge, Cambridge University Press, 1996): 98.
73 Charles Baudelaire, *The Painter of Modern Life and Other Essays*, trans. and ed. Jonathan Mayne (London: Phaidon Press, 1964): 13. Baudelaire goes on to qualify this statement by suggesting that "every old master has had his own modernity," suggesting that modernity lies in the sensitivity and reflexivity of artists to the give and take of change and permanence, rather than something that emerges automatically out of the specific social characteristics of nineteenth-century Europe. But, in my view, it is precisely this focus on social reflexivity that seems so distinctly "modern" in Baudelaire's definition of modernity.
74 Harvey, *The Condition of Postmodernity*: 22.
75 Roche, *Mega-Events and Modernity*, 65–71, and also see Geppert, *Fleeting Cities*: 106–7.
76 Ibid.; 69–71.
77 Susan Brownell, "Bodies before Boas: Sport before the Laughter Left," in Susan Brownell (ed.), *The 1904 Anthropology Days and Olympic Games: Sport, Race and American Imperialism* (Lincoln, NB: University of Nebraska Press, 2008): 1–58.
78 W. E. B. Du Bois, "The American Negro at Paris," *The American Monthly Review of Reviews* 22(5) (November 1900): 575–7: http://www.webdubois.org/dbANParis.html.
79 David Levering Lewis and Deborah Wills, *A Small Nation of People: W. E. B. Du Bois and African American Portraits of Progress* (New York: Amistad, 2003): 24–49.
80 Mattelart, *The Invention of Communication*: 113; and Tony Bennett, "The Exhibitionary Complex," *New Formations* 4 (Spring 1988): 96.
81 For summaries of the growth of large urban international exhibitions from the mid-nineteenth century through the twentieth century, see Roche, *Mega-Events and Modernity*: 43; and Geppert, *Fleeting Cities*, 7–8 and the "Appendix": 250–80.

82 Mattelart, *The Invention of Communication*: 113.
83 Ibid.: 120.
84 Ibid.: 112.
85 See Roche's discussion in *Mega-Events and Modernity* (33–8) of the work of Benedict Anderson and Eric Hobsbawm on this point. Mattelart points out that during the 1870s British authorities moved away from internationalism in favour of a short-lived run of annual industrial exhibitions; *The Invention of Communication*: 116. British internationalism became focused on international trade agreements and non-governmental organizations, international sports, and on newly conceived "imperial" exhibitions.
86 Mattelart, *The Invention of Communication*: 119–20.
87 Roche, *Mega-Events and Modernity*: 8.
88 Ibid.: 67–71.
89 Benjamin, "Paris, Capital of the Nineteenth Century": 17.
90 Mattelart, *The Invention of Communication*: 131.
91 Roche, *Mega-Events and Modernity*: 38.
92 In *The Invention of Communication*: 124–6. A history of the international organizations often responsible for promoting these agreements can be found in Volker Barthes, "International Organisations and Congresses": http://ieg-ego.eu/en/threads/transnational-movements-and-organisations/international-organisations-and-congresses
93 Don Handelman, *Models and Mirrors: Toward an Anthropology of Public Events* (New York: Berghahn, Books, 1990): 15–19; Roche, *Mega-Events and Modernity*, ch. 2.
94 Tony Bennett, "The Exhibitionary Complex," *New Formations* 4 (Spring 1988): 73–102. In developing his argument, Bennett cites Foucault's suggestion that Greek and Roman antiquity were cultures of spectacle that were largely supplanted by a modern culture of surveillance. I agree to a point. However, I think this view underplays the ongoing importance of spectacle culture in modernity for political and economic reasons other than surveillance.
95 Mattelart, *The Invention of Communication*: 117–18.
96 Mitchell, "The World as Exhibition": 217.
97 For a brief history of racial science, see Martial Guedron "Panel and Sequence: Classifications and Associations in Scientific Illustrations of the Human Races (1770–1830)," in Nicolas Bancel, Thomas David, and Dominic Thomas (eds), *The Invention of Race: Scientific and Popular Representations* (London: Routledge, 2014): 60–7.
98 Mitchell, "The World as Exhibition": 218.
99 See the essays in Brownell (ed.), *The 1904 Anthropology Days*.
100 Greater detail on race and orientalism in international exhibitions and early international sport can be found in Roche, *Mega-Events and Modernity*; Mattelart, *The Invention of Communicatiion*; and Brownell (ed.), *The 1904 Anthropology Days and Olympic Games: Sport, Race and American Imperialism*.
101 John Horne and Garry Whannel, *Understanding the Olympics*, 2nd edn (London: Routledge, 2016): 132.
102 Borgers, "From the Temple of Industry": 9.
103 Bruce Kidd, "The Myth of the Ancient Games," in Alan Tomlinson and

Garry Whannel (eds), *Five Ring Circus: Money, Power and Politics at the Olympic Games* (London: Pluto Press, 1984): 71.

104 John Horne and Garry Whannel, *Understanding the Olympics*, 2nd edn (London: Routledge, 2016).

105 Borgers, "From the Temple of Industry": 12.

106 Ibid.

107 On this point, see Kidd, "The Myth of the Ancient Games"; David Young, *The Olympic Myth of Greek Amateur Athletics*, and *The Modern Olympics: A Struggle for Revival* (Baltimore: Johns Hopkins University Press, 1996).

108 Cited in David C. Young, *The Modern Olympics*: 25.

109 Horne and Whannel, *Understanding the Olympics*: 137–8.

110 Ibid.: 138.

111 I discuss this in greater detail in Richard Gruneau, "Amateurism as a Sociological Problem: Some Reflections Inspired by Eric Dunning," *Sport in Society: Cultures, Commerce, Media, Politics* 9(4) (October 2006): 559–82.

112 David C. Young, *A Brief History of the Olympic Games* (Oxford: Blackwell, 2004): 145.

113 See David Young, *The Modern Olympics: A Struggle for Revival*, especially chs 2–4.

114 John MacAloon, *This Great Symbol: Pierre de Coubertin and the Origins of the Modern Olympic Games* (Chicago: University of Chicago Press, 1981), chs 1 and 3. In addition to MacAloon's discussion of Coubertin, see David C. Young, *The Modern Olympics: A Struggle for Revival* (Baltimore: Johns Hopkins University Press, 1996); Allen Guttmann, *The Olympics: A History of the Modern Games* (Urbana, IL: University of Illinois Press, 1992), ch. 1; Christopher Hill, *Olympic Politics* (Manchester: Manchester University Press, 1992), ch. 1.

115 In addition to MacAloon's work, a useful overview of this intellectual context can be found in Sigmund Loland, "Coubertin's Ideology of Olympism from the Perspective of the History of Ideas." *Olympica: The International Journal of Olympic Studies* 4 (1995): 49–78.

116 See MacAloon, *This Great Symbol*, ch. 3; and Theodore Porter, "Reforming Vision: The Engineer Le Play Learns to Observe Society Sagely," in Lorraine Daston and Elizabeth Lunbeck (eds), *Histories of Scientific Observation* (Chicago, IL: University of Chicago Press, 2011): 281–302.

117 Mattelart, *The Invention of Communication*: 292.

118 Ibid.: 287.

119 Borgers, "From the Temple of Industry": 14.

120 Ibid.: 14–15.

121 The international rowing regatta was won by a team of virtual unknowns from the Canadian province of New Brunswick against highly favored English, German, and French crews and reveals the international scope of "representative" sport by the 1860s. Dubbed the "Paris crew" by French and English media, the team received extensive media coverage and returned home to huge fanfare and coast-to-coast media coverage. See Charles Dougall, "Samuel Hutton," *Dictionary of Canadian Biography* 11, 1891–1900 (Toronto, ON: University of Toronto Press, 1990): 461–2.

122 See Kristin Ross, *The Emergence of Social Space: Rimbaud and the Paris Commune* (London: Verso, 2008): 15.

123 Porter, "Reforming Vision": 297.
124 Jacques Rancière, "Going to Expo: The Worker, His Wife and Machines," in Adrian Rifkin and Roger Thomas (eds), *Voices of the People: The Politics and Life of "La Sociale" at the End of the Second Empire* (London: Routledge, 1988): 23–44.
125 Alan Pitt, "The Irrationalist Liberalism of Hippolyte Taine," *The Historical Journal* 41(4) (1998): 1035–53.
126 Horne and Whannel, *Understanding the Olympics*: 143.
127 Anthony Th. Bijkerck, "Appendix: Pierre de Coubertin," in John E. Findling and Kimberley D. Pelle (eds), *Encyclopedia of the Olympic Movement* (Westport, CT: Greenwood Press, 2004).
128 On a similar point, see Dikaia Chatziefstathiou, "Pierre de Coubertin: Man and Myth," in Helen Jefferson Lenskyj and Stephen Wagg (eds), *The Palgrave Handbook of Olympic Studies* (Basingstoke: Palgrave Macmillan, 2012): 28–9; and the discussion of Coubertin in D. Chatziefstathiou and Ian Henry, *Discourses of Olympism: From the Sorbonne 1894 to London 2012* (Basingstoke: Palgrave Macmillan, 2013): 70–144.
129 Chatziefstathiou, "Pierre de Coubertin: Man and Myth": 29–30; and Borgers, "From the Temple of Industry": 14.
130 Borgers, "From the Temple of Industry": 16.
131 Ibid.
132 On late nineteenth-century French colonialism and debates about colonial policy, see Raymond F. Betts, *Assimilation and Association in French Colonial Theory, 1890–1914*, 2nd edn (Lincoln, NB: University of Nebraska Press, 2005 [1960]).
133 See Anthony J. Mangan, *"Manufactured Masculinity": Making Imperial Morality, Manliness and Militarism* (London: Routledge, 2012).
134 Jean Harvey and Robert Sparks, "The Politics of the Body in the Context of Modernity," *Quest* 43 (1991): 164–89.
135 Ibid.: 182–3.
136 Cited in Mattelart, *The Invention of Communication*: 284.
137 Ibid.
138 D. R. Quanz, "Civic Pacifism and Sports-Based Internationalism Framework for the Founding of the International Olympic Committee," *Olympika: The International Journal of Olympic Studies* 2 (1993): 1–23; and Borgers, "From the Temple of Industry."
139 Betts, *Assimilation and Association*: 3.
140 Otto J. Shantz, "Pierre de Coubertin's 'Civilizing Mission,'" in Robert K. Barney, Michael K. Heine, Kevin B. Wamsley, and Gordon H. MacDonald (eds), *Pathways, Critiques and Discourses in Olympic Research: Ninth International Symposium for Olympic Research* (London, ON: International Centre for Olympic Studies, 2008): 57.
141 Ibid.
142 Ibid.
143 Patrick Clastres, "Playing with Greece: Pierre de Coubertin and the Motherland of Humanities and Olympics." *Histoire @ Politique* 12(3) (2010): https://www.cairn.info/revue-histoire-politique-2010-3-page-9.htm
144 Borgers, "From the Temple of Industry": 14.
145 Coubertin cited in Clastres, "Playing with Greece."

146 Coubertin, cited in Clastres, and also see Mattelart, *The Invention of Communication*: 126.
147 John Hoberman, "Toward a Theory of Olympic Internationalism," *Journal of Sport History* 22(1) (1995): 1–37.
148 On this point, see Allen Guttmann's discussion in *The Olympics*: 12.
149 Young, *The Modern Olympics*: 100–5.
150 William Fortescue, *The Third Republic in France: 1870–1940: Conflicts and Continuities* (London: Routledge, 2000): 108.
151 Horne and Whannel, *Understanding the Olympics*: 155.
152 Young, *The Modern Olympics*: 152–4.
153 Stefan Hübner, "Muscular Christianity and the Western Civilizing Mission: Elwood S. Brown, the YMCA and the Idea of the Far Eastern Championship Games," *Diplomatic History* 39(3) (2015): 532–57.
154 See Amanda Shuman, "Elite Competitive Sport in the People's Republic of China, 1958–1966: The Games of the New Emerging Forces (GANEFO)," *Journal of Sport History* 40(2) (Summer 2013): 258–83; and Scarlet Cornelissen, "The Geopolitics of Global Aspiration: Sport Mega-Events and Emerging Powers." *The International Journal of the History of Sport* 25(16–18) (November 2010): 3008–25.
155 Berman, *All that is Solid Melts into Air*: 24.
156 See Geppert, *Fleeting Cities*, ch. 7.
157 Ibid.: 204.
158 Ibid.: 206–16.
159 Borgers, "From the Temple of Industry," 20–21; Geppert, *Fleeting Cities*: 206–16.
160 On US influences on the Olympics, see Mark Dyreson, *Crafting Patriotism for Global Dominance: America at the Olympics* (London: Routledge, 2009).

Chapter 4 German Modernism, Anti-Modernism, and the Critical Theory of Sport

1 Richard D. Mandell, "Modern Criticism of Sport," in Donald Kyle and Gary Stark (eds), *Essays on Sport History and Sport Mythology* (College Station, TX: Texas A&M Press, 1990).
2 John Bale provides a useful survey of some of these critical arguments in the opening chapter of his book *Anti-Sport Sentiments in Literature: Batting for the Opposition* (London: Routledge, 2008).
3 Pierre de Coubertin sought to counter some of these criticisms throughout his involvement with the IOC and there are numerous "defenses" of sport in the pages of the journal that Coubertin initiated, *Revue Olympique*, which Douglas Brown suggests contains "an evolving cultural manifesto on sport." See "Modern Sport, Modernism, and the Cultural Manifesto: De Coubertin's *Revue Olympique*, International Journal of the History of Sport* 18(2) (2001): 78–109. More contemporary defenses of the beauty and abstract ideals of sport can be found in Michael Novak, *The Joy of Sports: Endzones, Bases, Baskets, Balls and the Consecration of the American Spirit*, rev. edn (Lanham, MD: Madison Books, 1994 [1976]); and Hans Ulrich Gumbrecht, *In Praise of Athletic Beauty* (Cambridge, MA: Belknap Press, 2006).

4 Dave Hickey, *Air Guitar: Essays on Art and Democracy* (Los Angeles: Art Issues Press, 1997): 188.

5 "A Contribution to the Critique of Hegel's Philosophy of Right," *Deutsch-Französische Jahrbücher* (February 7 and 10, 1844): https://www.marxists.org/archive/marx/works/1843/critique-hpr/intro.htm/

6 Stuart Hall, "Notes on Deconstructing the Popular," in Raphael Samuel and Gareth Stedman Jones (eds), *People's History and Socialist Theory* (London: Routledge & Kegan Paul, 1981): 227–8.

7 Some of these ideas are developed in greater detail in Richard Gruneau, *Class, Sports, and Social Development* (Amherst, MA: University of Massachusetts Press, 1983), and in the "Postscript" to the 2nd edn (Urbana, IL: Human Kinetics Press, 1999).

8 John Hoberman, *Sport and Political Ideology* (Austin, TX: University of Texas Press, 1984): 123.

9 Erik Jensen, *Body by Weimar: Athletes, Gender and German Modernity* (Oxford: Oxford University Press, 2010): 4–5. Also see Jon Hughes, "Im Sport ist der Nerv der Zeit selber zu spüren:' Sport and Cultural Debate in the Weimar Republic.'" *German as a Foreign Language* 2 (2007): 28–45.

10 Hughes, "Sport and Cultural Debate": 32.

11 Hoberman, *Sport and Political Ideology*: 100.

12 Jensen, *Body by Weimar*: 5–6.

13 Ibid. Examples of such cultural criticism include the highly influential work of Georg Simmel. See his discussion of the atrophy of individual culture in the modern city: "The Metropolis and Mental Life," in Richard Sennett (ed.), *Classic Essays on the Culture of Cities* (Englewood Cliffs, NJ: Prentice Hall, 1969 [1903]).

14 Jensen, *Body by Weimar*: 4.

15 Christiane Eisenberg, "Massensport in der Wiemarer Republik," cited in James van Dyke, "Max Beckmann, Sport and the Field of Cultural Criticism," in Rose-Carroll Washton Long and Maria Makela (eds), *Of Truths Impossible to Put in Words: Max Beckmann Contexualized* (Bern, Switzerland: Peter Lang, 2008): 199–228.

16 See W. L. Guttsman, *Workers' Culture in Weimar Germany: Between Tradition and Commitment* (Munich: Berg Publishing, 1990): 136.

17 Jensen, *Body by Weimar*: 9.

18 Ibid.

19 Ibid.: 5.

20 Ibid.: 5.

21 Scheler, "Preface" to Alfred Peters, *Psychologie des Sports*, cited in Hoberman, *Sport and Political Ideology*: 154.

22 Van Dyke, "Max Beckmann": 211.

23 Cited in Hoberman, *Sport and Political Ideology*: 90.

24 Ibid.

25 Cited in Van Dyke, "Max Beckmann": 213.

26 Scheler cited in Hoberman, *Sport and Political Ideology*: 155.

27 Van Dyke, "Max Beckmann": 214.

28 Hughes, "Sport and Cultural Debate": 31.

29 Ibid.

30 Anson Rabinbach, *The Human Motor: Energy, Fatigue and the Origins of Modernity* (New York: Basic Books, 1990).

31 See the discussion in Diego P. Roldán, "Discourses on the Body, the 'Human Motor' Energy and Fatigue: Cultural Hybridations in Fin-de-siècle Argentina." *História, Ciências, Saúde – Manguinhos*, 17(3) (2010). Available at: http: www.scielo.br

32 Jensen, *Body by Weimar*: 7.

33 A useful discussion of issues and debates around this issue can be found in Frank Becker, "Sportsmen in the Machine World: Models for Modernisation in Weimar Germany," *International Journal of the History of Sport* 12(1) (April 1995): 153–68.

34 Martin Heidegger, cited in Hoberman, *Sport and Political Ideology*: 147.

35 It is not clear where the idea that Risse was Adorno's student started. The claim is noted in many places. For just a few examples, see Eric Dunning and Kenneth Sheard, *Barbarians, Gentlemen, and Players*, 2nd edn (London: Routledge, 2005 [1979]): 302n45; and see Jay Coakley and Eric Dunning, "General Introduction," in Coakely and Dunning, *Handbook of Sports Studies* (Thousand Oaks, CA: Sage, 2000): xxii; and Ian Ritchie, "Sport and Social Class," in Richard Giulianotti (ed.), *Routledge Handbook of the Sociology of Sport* (London: Routledge, 2015): 214.

36 Cited in Hoberman, *Sport and Political Ideology*: 139.

37 For histories of the Frankfurt School, see Martin Jay, *The Dialectical Imagination: A History of the Frankfurt School and the Institute for Social Research, 1923–1950* (Berkeley: University of California Press, 1973); Zoltan Tar, *The Frankfurt School: The Critical Theories of Max Horkheimer and Theodor W. Adorno* (New York: Wiley, 1977); David Held, *Introduction to Critical Theory: Horkheimer to Habermas* (Berkeley: University of California Press, 1980); and Rolf Wiggershaus, trans. Michael Robertson, *The Frankfurt School: Its History, Theories and Political Significance* (Cambridge: Polity Press, 1994 [1986]).

38 Max Horkheimer, "Traditional and Critical Theory," in Max Horkheimer, *Critical Theory: Selected Essays*, trans. Matthew J. O'Connell and others (New York: Continuum, 1972): 188–243.

39 Max Horkheimer and Theodor Adorno, "Preface, 1944 and 1947," *Dialectic of Enlightenment*, ed. Gunzelin Schmid Noerr and trans. Edmund Jephcott (Stanford, CA: Stanford University Press, 2002 [1944]): xvii.

40 On reification, see György Lukács, "Reification and the Consciousness of the Proletariat," in *History and Class Consciousness: Studies in Marxist Dialectics*, trans. Rodney Livingstone (Cambridge, MA: MIT Press, 1971 [1923]): 83–222. Other useful interpretations can be found in Andrew Arato, *Lukács's Theory of Reification* (Candor, NY: Telos Press, 1972), and more recently in Axel Honneth, *Reification: A New Look* (Oxford: Oxford University Press, 2008); and Andrew Feenberg, *The Philosophy of Praxis: Marx, Lukács and the Frankfurt School* (London: Verso Press, 2014)

41 See John Abromeit, *Max Horkheimer and the Foundations of the Frankfurt School* (Cambridge: Cambridge University Press, 2011): 181–3; and Stephen Eric Bronner, *Of Critical Theory and its Theorists*, 2nd edn (New York: Routledge, 2002): 79–81.

42 Lukács, "Reification and the Consciousness of the Proletariat": 92–111.

43 On this point, Lukács cites Marx's comment that "it is not the textbooks

that impose this separation upon life . . . [but] life upon the textbooks": "Reification and the Consciousness of the Proletariat": 104.

44 For example, see Terry Eagleton's discussion of Lukács in *Ideology: An Introduction* (London: Verso, 1991): 95–107.
45 Held, *Introduction to Critical Theory*: 15.
46 Ibid.: 15–16.
47 Siegfried Kracauer, *The Mass Ornament: Weimar Essays*, trans. and ed. Thomas Y. Levin (Cambridge, MA: Harvard University Press, 1995).
48 Van Dyke, "Max Beckmann": 212.
49 On boxing, Brecht and Weimar Germany see David Bathrick, "Boxing as an Icon of Weimar Culture," *New German Critique* 51 (Fall 1990): 113–36.
50 Bertoldt Brecht, "Emphasis on Sport," in Stephen Duncombe (ed.), *Cultural Resistance Reader* (London: Verso, 2002 [1926]): 183–5.
51 Van Dyke, "Max Beckmann": 212.
52 Susan Sontag, "Fascinating Fascism," *New York Review of Books*, February 6, 1975.
53 Adolf Hitler, cited in Roger Griffin, *Modernism and Fascism: The Sense of a Beginning under Mussolini and Hitler* (Basingstoke: Palgrave Macmillan, 2007): 250.
54 Ibid.: 282–3.
55 Ibid.: 287.
56 See Steven Connor, "Sporting Modernism," an expanded version of a talk presented at the Centre for Modernist Studies, University of Sussex, January 14, 2009: http://stevenconnor.com/sportingmodernism/sportingmodern-ism.pdf
57 Faye Brauer, "Introduction," in Faye Brauer and Anthea Callen (eds), *Art, Sex and Eugenics: Corpus Delecti* (London: Routledge, 2008): 15.
58 Ibid.
59 On futurism, see Richard Humphreys, *Futurism* (Cambridge: Cambridge University Press, 1999). A useful history of Soviet constructivism can be found in Maria Gough, *The Artist as Producer: Russian Constructivism in Revolution* (Berkeley, CA: University of California Press, 2005).
60 Griffin, *Modernism and Fascism*: 287.
61 Ibid.: 291.
62 Brauer, "Introduction": 1.
63 Ibid.
64 Griffin, *Modernism and Fascism*: 291.
65 Overviews of the Berlin 1936 Olympics from somewhat different perspectives can be found in: Richard D. Mandell, *The Nazi Olympics* (New York: Macmillan, 1971); David Clay Large, *Nazi Games: The Olympics of 1936* (New York: W. W. Norton, 2007).
66 Large, *Nazi Games*: 156.
67 David Leonhardt, "Stimulus Thinking and Nuance." *New York Times*, March 31, 2009: http://www.nytimes.com/2009/04/01/business/economy/01leonhardt.html?_r=0/.
68 Nadine Rossol, "Performing the Nation: Sports, Spectacles, and Aesthetics in Germany, 1926-1936," *Central European History* 43 (2010): 616–38.
69 Ibid.: 625.
70 Ibid.

71 Ibid.: 638.
72 Franz Neumann, *Behemoth: The Structure and Practice of National Socialism, 1933–1944* (Oxford: Oxford University Press, 1942).
73 Benjamin, "The Work of Art in the Age of Mechanical Reproduction," in Hannah Arendt (ed.), *Illuminations: Essays and Reflections*, trans. Harry Zohn (New York: Schocken Books, 1968). On Brecht's influence on Benjamin (and vice versa), see Edmut Wizisla, *Benjamin and Brecht: The Story of a Friendship* (London: Verso, 2016).
74 Max Horkheimer, "Preface," *Studies in Philosophy and Social Science* 9(3) (1941): 365.
75 Theodor Adorno, "Veblen's Attack on Culture," in Theodor Adorno, *Prisms*, trans. Samuel and Shierry Weber (Cambridge, MA: MIT Press, 1981 [1941]): 79.
76 Ibid.: 80.
77 For an excellent summary discussion in reference to relations between "the culture industry" and leisure, see Chris Rojek, *Capitalism and Leisure Theory* (London: Routledge, 2014 [1985]): 112–22.
78 Horkheimer and Adorno, "Preface, 1944 and 1947," *Dialectic of Enlightenment*: xviii.
79 Herbert Marcuse, *Eros and Civilization: A Philosophical Inquiry into Freud* (Boston: Beacon Press, 1955); *One-Dimensional Man: Studies in the Ideology of Advanced Industrial Society* (London: Routledge & Kegan Paul, 1964).
80 Gerhard Vinnai, *Football Mania* (London: Orbach & Chambers, 1973); Paul Hoch, *Rip Off the Big Game* (New York: Doubleday, 1972); Jean-Marie Brohm, *Sport: A Prison of Measured Time* (London: Ink Links, 1978); Bero Rigauer, *Sport and Work*, trans. Allen Guttmann (New York: Columbia University Press, 1981 [1969]).
81 Adorno, "Veblen's Attack on Culture": 84.
82 Theodor Adorno, "Education after Auschwitz," (1966), available at http://www.heathwoodpress.com/education-after-auschwitz-theodor-w-adorno
83 Adorno, "Education after Auschwitz."
84 On Adorno's references to gratuitousness and autonomy in sport, see William Morgan, "Adorno on Sport: The Case of the Fractured Dialectic," *Theory, Culture and Society* 17 (1988): 813–38.
85 For example, Gruneau, *Class, Sports, and Social Development*.
86 György Lukács, "Preface," *The Theory of the Novel: A Historico-philosophical Essay on the Forms of Great Epic Literature*, trans. Anna Bostock (London: Merlin Press, 1978): https://www.marxists.org/archive/lukacs/works/theory-novel/preface.htm
87 Raymond Williams, *Towards 2000* (London: Chatto & Windus, 1983): 240.
88 For example, Dallas Smythe, *Dependency Road: Communication, Capitalism, Consciousness and Canada* (Norwood, NJ: Ablex Publishing, 1981).
89 For example, see Alan Swingewood, *The Myth of Mass Culture* (London: Macmillan, 1977).
90 For example, Tony Bennett, "The Politics of the Popular and Popular Culture," in Tony Bennett, Colin Mercer, and Janet Woolacoatt (eds), *Popular Culture and Social Relations* (Milton Keynes: Open University Press, 1986).

91 Hannah Arendt, "Preface," *Illuminations*: x.
92 Theodor Adorno, "Music and Mass Culture," in Richard Leppert (ed.), *Essays on Music*, trans. Susan H. Gillespie (Berkeley: University of California Press, 2002): 466.
93 Information on the Guerrilla Girls can be accessed at: http://www.guerrillagirls.com/#open Also see the history of the Guerrilla Girls in Dustin Kidd, *Legislating Creativity: The Intersections of Art and Politics* (London: Routledge, 2012): 130–2.
94 For example, see Horkheimer, "Authority and the Family," in *Critical Theory: Selected Essays*: 47–128.
95 In his essay "The Frankfurt School Revisited: A Critique of Martin Jay's 'The Dialectical Imagination,'" *New German Critique* 4 (1973): 131–52, Douglas Kellner criticizes Martin Jay for failing to stretch the meaning of "critical theory" beyond the Institute to include other Marxist writers of the era and for overstating the influence of the Jewish backgrounds of many of the Institute's members. Somewhat similarly, in his book, *The Frankfurt School*, Zoltan Tar makes a distinction between the work of the Institute itself and the broader, albeit related, project of "critical theory," which involved people who may have had little association with the Institute.
96 For example, Richard Gruneau, "Leisure, Freedom and the State," in Alan Tomlinson (ed.), *Leisure, Politics, Planning and People* (Brighton: British Leisure Studies Association, 1985). For a somewhat similar argument, see Alan G. Ingham, "From Public Issue to Personal Trouble: Well Being and the Fiscal Crisis of the State." *Sociology of Sport Journal* 2(1) (1985): 43–55.
97 Ulrich Beck, *Risk Society: Towards a New Modernity*, trans. Mark Ritter (Thousand Oaks, CA: Sage, 1992 [1986]).
98 Inspired largely by Max Weber and Herbert Marcuse, Alan Ingham was discussing some of these ideas as early as 1975. See his discussion of "rationalization" in Alan G. Ingham, "Occupational Subcultures and the Work World of Sport," in Donald Ball and John Loy (eds), *Sport and Social Order: Contributions to the Sociology of Sport* (Reading, MA: Addison-Wesley, 1975).
99 Michel Foucault, cited in James Miller, *The Passion of Michel Foucault* (Cambridge, MA: Harvard University Press, 1993): nn52, 457.
100 See John B. Thompson, *Ideology and Modern Culture: Critical Social Theory in the Era of Mass Communication* (Cambridge, UK: Polity Press, 1991); David Hawkes, *Ideology*, 1st edn (London: Routledge, 1996); Slavoj Žižek, *The Sublime Object of Ideology* (London: Verso Books, 1989).
101 This point is made strongly by Ian McDonald in a short essay in 2007, which draws on Marcuse. See "One-Dimensional Sport": http://idrottsforum.org/articles/mcdonald/mcdonald071212.pdf
102 Theodor Adorno, "Late Capitalism or Industrial Society," Opening Address to the 16th German Sociological Congress (1968), trans. Dennis Redmond in 2001, original German from Suhrkamp Verlag as: Theodor Adorno, *Collected Works, Vol. 4*: https://www.marxists.org/reference/archive/adorno/1968/late-capitalism.htm

Chapter 5 A Savage Sorting of "Winners" and "Losers":
Modernization, Development, Sport, and the Challenge of Slums

1 Mike Davis, *Planet of Slums* (London: Verso, 2006): 1.
2 *Demographic World Urban Areas*, 12th annual edition (2016): http://www.demographia.com/db-worldua.pdf/.
3 Davis, *Planet of Slums*: 7; and *Demographic World Urban Areas*: 110.
4 Davis, ibid.: 2.
5 *Demographic World Urban Areas*, 12th annual edition (2016): 19.
6 Davis, *Planet of Slums*: 16–17.
7 "China Encourages Mass Urban Migration," *People's Daily Online*, November 28, 2003, en.people.cn/200311/28/eng20031128_129252.shtml
8 Robert Neuwirth, *Shadow Cities: A Billion Squatters, a New Urban World* (New York and London: Routledge, 2005): 9.
9 *Demographic World Urban Areas* (2016): 50.
10 See *Homes, Not Handcuffs: The Criminalization of Homelessness in US Cities* (Washington, DC: The National Law Center on Homelessness and Poverty and the National Coalition for the Homeless, July 2009); Laszlo Andor and Martin Summers, *Market Failure: Eastern Europe's "Economic Miracle"* (London: Pluto Press, 1998); Joseph Stiglitz, *Globalization and Its Discontents* (New York: Norton, 2002).
11 Examples include: J. Harvey and F. Houle, "Sport, World Economy, Global Culture, and New Social Movements," *Sociology of Sport Journal* 11(4) (1994): 337–55; Toby Miller, Geoffrey Lawrence, Jim McKay, and David Rowe, *Globalization and Sport: Playing the World* (Thousand Oaks, CA: Sage, 2001); Richard Giulianotti and Roland Robertson (eds), *Sport and Globalization* (London: Blackwell, 2009); James Mills (ed.), *Subaltern Sports: Politics and Sport in South Asia* (London: Anthem Press, 2005); D. L. Andrews and A. D. Grainger, "Sport and Globalization," in George Ritzer (ed.), *The Blackwell Companion to Globalization* (Malden, MA: Blackwell Publishing, 2006): 478–97; and Lucie Thibault, "Globalization of Sport: An Inconvenient Truth," *Journal of Sport Management* 23 (2009): 1–20.
12 For an early literature review, see Peter Donnelly and Jay Coakley (with Simon Darnell and Sandy Wells), *Literature Reviews on Sport for Development and Peace* (Sport for Development and Peace International Working Group (SDP IWG) Secretariat, Faculty of Physical Education and Health, University of Toronto, October 2007). Also see Roger Levermore and Aaron Beacom (eds), *Sport and International Development* (London: Palgrave Macmillan, 2009); Simon Darnell, *Sport for Development and Peace: A Critical Sociology* (New York: Bloomsbury, 2012): and Brian Wilson, *Sport and Peace: A Sociological Perspective* (Toronto: Oxford University Press, 2012).
13 Examples include: S. J. Greene, "Staged Cities: Mega-Events, Slum Clearance and Global Capital," *Yale Human Rights and Development Journal* 6(1), Article 6 (2003): 161–87; L. K. Davis, "International Events and Mass Evictions: A Longer View," *International Journal of Urban and Regional Research* 35(3) (2011): 582–99; UN-Habitat, *Forced Evictions: Global Crisis, Global Solutions* (Nairobi: UN-Habitat, 2012); Jacqueline Kennelly, *Olympic Exclusions: Youth Poverty and Social Legacies* (London:

Routledge, 2016); and Richard Gruneau and John Horne (eds), *Mega-Events and Globalization: Capital and Spectacle in a Changing World Order* (London: Routledge, 2016).

14 Neuwirth, *Shadow Cities*: 16.
15 Ibid.
16 Ibid.: 249.
17 UN-Habitat, *The Challenge of Slums: Global Report on Human Settlements* (London, 2003): 167: http://mirror.unhabitat.org/pmss/listItemDetails.aspx?publicationID=1156
18 See United Nations *Millennium Declaration Resolution*, adopted by the General Assembly, September 18, 2000: http://www.un.org/ga/search/view_doc.asp?symbol=A/RES/55/2
19 UN-Habitat, *The Challenge of Slums*: 167.
20 Robert Skidelsky, *Keynes: The Return of the Master* (London: Allen Lane, 2009): 75–100.
21 David Harvey, *A Brief History of Neoliberalism* (Oxford: Oxford University Press, 2005): 10.
22 UN-Habitat, *The Challenge of Slums*: 36.
23 David Harvey, *The Condition of Postmodernity: An Enquiry into the Origins of Cultural Change* (Oxford: Blackwell, 1989): 132.
24 Ibid.
25 Harvey, *A Brief History*: 10.
26 Ibid.
27 Mass society theory was kept alive in US modernism in the 1950s, largely in literary theory and art criticism. In sociology, the best example of mass society theory as an alternative to pluralist triumphalism can be found in the chapter "The Mass Society," in C. Wright Mills's book, *The Power Elite* (New York: Oxford University Press, 1956). The influence of the Frankfurt School on Mills's work is significant. Eight years later, Herbert Marcuse refined and proposed an even more critical version of the United States as a mass society in his book, *One-Dimensional Man: Studies in the Ideology of Advanced Industrial Society* (London: Routledge & Kegan Paul, 1964).
28 Daniel Bell, "America as a Mass Society: A Critique," in Bell, *The End of Ideology: On the Exhaustion of Political Ideas in the Fifties* (New York: Free Press, 1960). Bell shared this view with a growing number of social scientists, who embraced a liberal and pluralist view of US society. See Nils Gilman's discussion of this point in the opening chapter of *Mandarins of the Future: Modernization Theory in Cold War America* (Baltimore, MD: Johns Hopkins University Press, 2003).
29 Bell, *The End of Ideology*: 373.
30 Gilman, *Mandarins of the Future*: 1–23.
31 Armand Mattelart, *The Invention of Communication*, trans. Susan Emanuel (Minneapolis, MN: University of Minnesota Press, 1996): 73.
32 This point, as well as the phrase "general theory of industrial society," comes from Anthony Giddens, *Studies in Social and Political Theory* (New York: Basic Books, 1977): 15.
33 Gilman, *Mandarins of the Future*: 3.
34 See especially W. W. Rostow, *The Stages of Economic Growth: A Non-Communist Manifesto* (Cambridge: Cambridge University Press, 1960).

35 Gilman, *Mandarins of the Future*, 3. Gilman (13–15) also notes rough similarities between liberal capitalist and socialist visions of modernization by virtue of their shared faith in industrialism and technology. Some writers went so far as to suggest a future "convergence" between capitalist and socialist visions of modernization.

36 This discussion is modified and expanded somewhat from Gilman, *Mandarins*: 4–5.

37 Ibid.: 6.

38 Ibid.: 14.

39 Simon C. Darnell and Rob Millington, "Modernization, Neoliberalism, and Sports Mega-Events: Evolving Discourses in Latin America," in Gruneau and Horne, *Mega-Events and Globalization*: 65–80.

40 Ibid.: 68.

41 A more detailed discussion of these expenditures can be found in F. Zarnowski, "A Look at Olympic Costs," *International Journal of Olympic History* 1(2) (1993): 16–32.

42 This brief definition of *civil society* works for my purposes here; however, in modern political philosophy the concept is far more complex. See the essays in Virginia A. Hodgkinson and Michael Foley (eds), *The Civil Society Reader* (Lebanon, NH: University Press of New England, 2003).

43 *The Challenge of Slums*: 36–8.

44 Sam Chege, "Donors Shift More Aid to NGOs," *Africa Recovery* 13(1) (June 1999).

45 David Lewis and Nazneen Kanji, *Non-Governmental Organizations and Development* (London: Routledge, 2009): 2.

46 *A Better World for All* (New York and London: United Nations, Organization for Economic Cooperation and Development; World Bank; and International Monetary Fund, 2000). See the United Nations Global Compact page on new 2015–2030 initiatives and principles at: https://www.unglobalcompact.org/what-is-gc

47 Bruce Kidd, "A New Social Movement: Sport for Development and Peace," *Sport in Society* 11(4) (2008): 371.

48 Ibid.: 374.

49 Ibid.

50 Ibid.

51 Overviews of ongoing IOC-sponsored projects for sport and development and for sport and peace can be found on the IOC's official website, http://www.olympic.org/olympism-in-action.

52 *Sport for Development and Peace: Towards Achieving the Millennium Development Goals*, Report from the United Nations Inter-Agency Task Force on Sport for Development and Peace (Geneva: United Nations, 2003); https://www.unicef.org/spanish/sports/reportE.pdf

53 Annual reports for 2013 and 2014 are available from the UNOSDP website: https://www.un.org/sport/

54 *Sport for Development and Peace: From Practice to Policy*, Preliminary Report of the Sport for Development and Peace International Working Group, Toronto, Canada, June 2006.

55 *Sport for Development and Peace: From Practice to Policy*: 9.

56 Ibid.

57 On the failures of IMF structural adjustment policies, see R. Peet, *Unholy*

Trinity: The IMF, World Bank, and WTO (London: Zed Press, 2009). By the early twenty-first century, many mainstream social institutions, and even some sectors within the World Bank, were beginning to have concerns about the failures of the IMF emphasis on debt reduction and free-market principles in development policy. See *The Policy Roots of Economic Crisis and Poverty: A Multi-country Participatory Assessment of Structural Adjustment* (Washington, DC: Structural Adjustment Participatory Review International Network, 2001).

58 *Sport for Development and Peace: From Practice to Policy*: 10.
59 In addition to the critical analysis developed in the UN-Habitat report *The Challenge of Slums*, see the more trenchant critiques in R. Peet, "Madness and Civilization: Global Financial Capitalism and the Anti-poverty Discourse," *Human Geography* 1(1) (2008): 82–9, and the more developed analysis in Peet, *Unholy Trinity*. Also see J. Brohman, *Popular Development: Rethinking the Theory and Practice of Development* (Oxford: Blackwell, 1996).
60 The SDP IWG also remarks on a partnership with the UNDP to survey the extent to which sports figure in the poverty-reduction strategies in twenty-six different nations. The 2006 *From Practice to Policy* report summarizes the UNDP results (p. 10) and suggests that to be successful in poverty-reduction strategies, sport would have to be "positioned as a cross-cutting tool in national development strategies for achieving the MDGs"; that countries need more information on the way in which sport can be used to advance their development objectives; and that national governments and NGOs need "advocacy and support" from the United Nations. There is nothing new in these pronouncements. However, the UNDP concluded that the effective use of sport poverty-reduction programs would need to ensure "local ownership," as well as an understanding of "local contexts." Unfortunately these latter ideas are not developed significantly.
61 My description of the MYSA draws from Fred Coulter, "Sport in Development: Accountability or Development," in Levermore and Beacom, *Sport and International Development*: 59–60, and from the MYSA website, http://www.mysakenya.org/
62 John Sugden, cited in Donnelly, Coakley, Darnell, and Wells, *Literature Reviews on Sport for Development and Peace*: 186: http://www.righttopl ay.com/moreinfo/aboutus/Documents/Literature%20Reviews%20SDP.pdf
63 Kidd, "A New Social Movement": 370. The International Platform on Sport and Development can be found at http://www.sportanddev.org/.
64 Issa G. Shivji, "The Silences in the NGO Discourse: The Role and Future of NGOs in Africa." *Pambazuka Special Report* 14 (Nairobi: Fahamu, 2006): 10–11.
65 Ibid.: 10.
66 Ibid.: 11.
67 Ibid.: 14. A link to the website of the Make Poverty History coalition can be found at http://www.makepovertyhistory.org/takeaction/
68 UN-Habitat, *The Challenge of Slums*: 36.
69 Ibid.
70 Ibid.: 36–8. For a more developed analysis, see Giovanni Arrighi, *The Long Twentieth Century: Money, Power, and the Origins of Our Times* (London: Verso, 1994).

71 *The Challenge of Slums*: 36.
72 Ibid. There was some dispute about this point during the 1990s, with both the World Bank and the UNDP claiming that overall economic growth in the world was contributing to a reduction in world poverty. However, the sheer volume of evidence suggesting the contrary has made such assertions increasingly untenable. By the early twenty-first century, for example, UN-Habitat had taken a position counter to the earlier UNDP position. See Peet, "Madness and Civilization": 82–9.
73 *The Challenge of Slums*: 36.
74 Ibid.
75 Ibid.
76 David Harvey, *The Condition of Postmodernity*: 141–88; and *A Brief History of Neoliberalism*.
77 *The Challenge of Slums*: 36.
78 Harvey, *A Brief History of Neoliberalism*: 64–86.
79 Nick Witheford and Richard Gruneau, "Between the Politics of Production and the Politics of the Sign: Post-Marxism, Postmodernism, and 'New Times,'" in Ben Agger (ed.), *Current Perspectives in Social Theory*, Vol. 13 (Greenwich, CT: JAI Press, 1993): 82–4.
80 More developed discussion of this point can be found in Nick Dyer-Witherford, *Cyber-Marx: Circuits of Struggle in High Technology Capitalism* (Urbana: University of Illinois Press, 1999); and Michael Hardt and Antonio Negri, *Empire* (Cambridge, MA: Harvard University Press, 2001).
81 Harvey, *The Condition of Postmodernity*: 179.
82 Ibid.
83 On these late twentieth-century trends, see Harvey, "From Managerialism to Entrepreneurialism: The Transformation in Urban Governance in Late Capitalism," *Geografiska Annaler* 71B, 1989: 3–18; Sharon Zukin, *Landscapes of Power: From Detroit to Disney World* (Berkeley: University of California Press, 1991); J. Hannigan, *Fantasy City: Pleasure and Profit in the Postmodern Metropolis* (New York: Routledge, 1998); and the essays in Dennis R. Judd and Susan S. Fainstein (eds), *The Tourist City* (New Haven, CT: Yale University Press, 1999).
84 See Neil Smith, "New Globalism, New Urbanism: Gentrification as Global Urban Strategy," *Antipode* 34(3) (2002): 427–50. Brief but excellent summary discussions of many of these points can be found in Timothy A. Gibson, *Securing the Spectacular City: The Politics of Revitalization and Homelessness in Downtown Seattle* (Lanham, MD: Lexington Books, 2004); and Mark Lowes, *Indy Dreams and Urban Nightmares: Speed Merchants, Spectacle and the Struggle over Space in the World-Class City* (Toronto: University of Toronto Press, 2002).
85 Erik Swyngedouw, Frank Moulaert, and Arantxa Rodriguez, "Neoliberal Urbanization in Europe: Large-Scale Urban Development Projects and the New Urban Policy," *Antipode* 34(3) (2002): 545–82.
86 See Richard Gruneau and Robert Neubauer, "A Gold Medal for the Market: The 1984 Los Angeles Olympics, the Reagan Era and the Politics of Neoliberalism," in Helen Jefferson Lenskyj and Stephen Wagg (eds), *The Palgrave Handbook of Olympic Studies* (London: Palgrave Macmillan, 2012): 134–62; and Alan Tomlinson, "Twenty-Eight Olympic Summers,"

in Lawrence A. Wenner and Andrew C. Billings (eds), *Sport, Media and Mega-Events* (London: Routledge, 2017): 51–68.

87 Gruneau and Neubauer, "A Gold Medal for the Market": 153–6.

88 C. Giannoulakis and D. Stotlar, "Evolution of Olympic Sponsorship and Its Impact on the Olympic Movement," in Nigel B. Crowther, Robert K. Barney, and Michael K. Heine (eds), *Cultural Imperialism in Action: Critiques in the Global Olympic Trust* (London, ON: International Centre for Olympic Studies, University of Western Ontario, 2006): 182.

89 Kevin Fylan, "FIFA Reveals Billion Dollar Equity, Big Profits," *Reuters*, June 10, 2010.

90 "Just Say No: Hosting the Olympics and the World Cup is Bad for a City's Health," *The Economist*, February 28, 2015: http://www.economist.com/news/books-and-arts/21645114–hosting-olympics-and-world-cup-bad-citys-health-just-say-no

91 For example, see the detailed comparative analysis of Olympic expenditures prepared by Bent Flyvbjerg, Allison Stewart, and Alexander Budzier, "The Oxford Olympics Study 2016: Cost and Cost Overrun at the Games," Working Paper, Saïd Business School, Oxford University, July 2016: https://www.academia.edu/26964093/The_Oxford_Olympics_Study_2016_Cost_and_Cost_Overrun_at_the_Games

92 Robert A. Baade and Victor A. Matheson, "Going for Gold: The Economics of the Olympics," *Journal of Economic Perspectives* 30(2) (2016): 202–3.

93 Ibid. Also see Gruneau and Horne (eds), *Mega-Events and Globalization*: 6–7.

94 Cited in Tony Samara, "Paving the Way for Neoliberal Development: Urban Transformation and the Mega-Event," *Global Studies Review* 5(1) (Spring 2009): 1: http://www.globality-gmu.net/archives/14. Discussions of the costs and failures of the 2010 Commonwealth Games to live up to these expectations can be found in: Mitu Sengupta, "The Price of Being World Class," *CounterPunch* (August 1, 2010); and Amita Baviskar, "Demolishing Delhi: World Class City in the Making," *Mute* 2(3) (2006): http://www.metamute.org/editorial/articles/demolishing-delhi-world-class-city-making

95 Ashwin Desai, "Between Madiba Magic and Spectacular Capitalism: The FIFA World Cup in South Africa," in Gruneau and Horne, *Mega-Events and Globalization*: 83. Desai proceeds to argue that these ambitions proved to be little more than "a conjurer's dream": 90. Also see Kate Manzo, "Visualizing Modernity: Development Hopes and the 2010 FIFA World Cup." *Soccer & Society* 13(2) (2012): 173–87; and Scarlett Cornelissen, "'Our Struggles are Bigger than the World Cup': Civic Activism, State–Society Relations and the Sociopolitical Legacies of the 2010 FIFA World Cup," *British Journal of Sociology* 63(2) (2012): 328–48.

96 UN Inter-Agency Task Force on Sport for Development and Peace, *Sport for Development and Peace*: 4.

97 Useful overviews can be found in Bent Flyvbjerg, Nils Bruzelius, and Werner Rothengatter, *Megaprojects and Risk: An Anatomy of Ambition* (Cambridge: Cambridge University Press, 2003); Maurice Roche, *Mega-Events and Modernity* (London: Routledge, 2000); Flyvbjerg, Stewart, and Budzier, "The Oxford Olympics Study 2016: Cost and Cost Overrun at the Games;" and Baade and Matheson, "Going for Gold."

98 On this point, see Andrew Zimbalist, *Circus Maximus: The Economic*

Gamble behind Hosting the Olympics and the World Cup (Washington, DC: Brookings Institution Press, 2015). The tendency toward speculative and exaggerated economic impacts also extends to North American major league sports franchises and sports arenas. See J. Siegfried and A. Zimbalist, "The Economics of Sports Facilities and Their Communities," *Journal of Economic Perspectives* 14(3) (2000): 95–114.

 99 See Flyvbjerg, Bruzelius, and Rothengatter, *Megaprojects and Risk*; and Swyngedouw, Moulaert, and Rodriguez, "Neoliberal Urbanization in Europe."

100 For example, see Zimbalist, *Circus Maximus* and the summary in *The Economist*, "Just Say No: Hosting the Olympics and the World Cup is Bad for a City's Health."

101 See S. Giorgiakis and J. Nauright, "Creating the Scarecrow: The 2004 Athens Olympic Games and the Greek Financial Crisis," George Mason University: Centre for the Study of Sport and Leisure in Society Working Papers: https://www.academia.edu/1922581/Creating_The_Scarecrow_The_2004_Athens_Olympic_Games_and_the_Greek_Financial_Crisis.

102 On the frequency of Olympic cost overruns, see Flyvbjerg, Stewart and Budzier, "The Oxford Olympics Study 2016: Cost and Cost Overrun at the Games."

103 See Helen Jefferson Lenskyj, "The Olympic (Affordable) Housing Legacy and Social Responsibility," in Crowther, Barney, and Heine (eds), *Cultural Imperialism in Action: Critiques in the Global Olympic Trust*: 196.

104 Greg Androvich, Matthew J. Burbank, and Charles H. Heying, "Olympic Cities: Lessons Learned from Mega-event Politics," *Journal of Urban Affairs* 23(2) (2001): 123–4.

105 For an application of the concept of a "state of exception" to a sporting bid city, see Carlos Vainer, "Mega-Events and the City of Exception: Theoretical Explanations of the Brazilian Experience," in Gruneau and Horne, *Mega-Events and Globalization*: 97–112.

106 Swyngedouw, Moulaert, and Rodriguez, "Neoliberal Urbanization in Europe": 547.

107 Ibid.: 547–8.

108 For some North American examples, see David Whitson, "World Class Leisure and Consumption: Social Polarization and the Politics of Place," in C. Andrew, P. Armstrong, and A. Lapierre (eds), *World Class Cities: Can Canada Play?* (Ottawa: University of Ottawa Press, 1999): 303–20; Mark Levine, "Tourism, Urban Redevelopment, and the 'World Class' City? The Cases of Baltimore and Montreal," in Andrew et al., *World Class Cities*: 421–50; P. K. Eisinger, "The Politics of Bread and Circuses: Building the City for the Visitor Class," *Urban Affairs Review* 35(3) (2000): 316–33. Although the social context is very different, the polarization argument is also made in countries outside Europe and North America: S. J. Greene, "Staged Cities: Mega-Events, Slum Clearance and Global Capital"; He Shenjing, "State-Sponsored Gentrification under Market Transition: The Case of Shanghai," *Urban Affairs Review* 43(2): 171–98; R. Forest, A. La Grange, and N. Yip, "Hong Kong as a Global City? Social Distance and Social Differentiation," *Urban Studies* 41(1) (January 2004); Hyun Bang Shin, "Unequal Cities of Spectacle and Mega-Events in China," *City* 16

(2012): 728–44; and "Urban Spatial Restructuring, Event-Led Development and Scalar Politics," *Urban Studies* 51 (2014): 2961–78.

109 See M. J. Burbank, G. D. Andranovich, and C. H. Heying, *Olympic Dreams: The Impact of Mega-events on Local Politics* (Boulder, CO: Lynne Rienner Publishers, 2001); H. J. Lenskyj, *The Best Olympics Ever? Social Impacts of Sydney 2000* (New York: State University of New York Press, 2002); B. Surborg, R. VanWynsberghe, and E. Wyly, "Mapping the Olympic Growth Machine," *City* 12(3) (2008): 341–55; and Anne-Marie Broudehoux, "Mega-Events, Urban Image Construction and the Politics of Exclusion," in Gruneau and Horne (eds), *Mega-Events and Globalization*: 113–30.

110 This point is developed in greater detail in Broudehoux, "Mega Events, Urban Image Construction and the Politics of Exclusion."

111 *Fair Play for Housing Rights: Mega-events, Olympic Games, and Housing Rights* (Geneva: Centre on Housing Rights and Evictions [COHRE], 2007): 42.

112 Cited in Lenskyj, "The Olympic (Affordable) Housing Legacy": 193.

113 On China's economic ascendancy, see Giovanni Arrighi, *Adam Smith in Beijing: Lineages of the Twenty-First Century* (London: Verso, 2007).

114 Wei Liming, Xie Liangbing, and Yang Xingyun, "Chinese Migrant Workers in Transition: Part 1," *Economic Observer News* (2008): http://www.eeo.com.cn/ens/feature/2008/08/04/109335.html. Also see Hyun Bang Shin, "China Meets Korea: The Asian Games, Entrepreneurial Local States and Debt-Driven Development," in Gruneau and Horne (eds), *Mega-Events and Globalization*: 187–205.

115 Steven Towns, "China's Massive Infrastructure Spending for the 08 Olympics and Beyond," *Wall Street Journal*, October 16, 2006.

116 *Fair Play for Housing Rights*: 154.

117 Samara, "Paving the Way for Neoliberal Development": 3.

118 Ibid.

119 This is a major theme in Neuwirth, *Shadow Cities*; see his summary in ch. 10.

120 On these failures and on the IOC's historical lack of interest in such investments, see *Fair Play for Housing Rights* and Lenskyj, "The Olympic (Affordable) Housing Legacy": 195–7.

121 Sandro Mezzadra and Brett Neilson, "Extraction, Logistics, Finance: Global Crisis and the Politics of Operations," *Radical Philosophy* 178 (March/April 2013): 12.

122 See David Harvey, "The Crisis of Planetary Urbanization," in Pedro Gadanho (ed.), *Uneven Growth: Tactical Urbanisms for Expanding Cities* (New York: Museum of Modern Art, 2014): http://post.at.moma.org/content_items/520–the-crisis-of-planetary-urbanization

123 See Ying-Fen Huang's discussion in *Spectacular Post-Colonial Cities: Markets, Ideology, and Globalization in the Making of Shanghai and Hong Kong* (PhD dissertation, School of Communication, Simon Fraser University, 2008): http://summit.sfu.ca/item/9072

124 Sandro Mezzadra, "How Many Histories of Labor? Toward a Theory of Postcolonial Capitalism," *Postcolonial Studies* 14(2) (2011): 166.

125 Samir Amin, "Capitalism, Imperialism, Globalization," in R. M. Chilcote (ed.), *The Political Economy of Imperialism* (Dordrecht, Netherlands: Kluwer Academic Publishers, 1999): 158.

126 Zygmunt Bauman, *Liquid Modernity* (Cambridge: Polity Press, 2000): 28.
127 Saskia Sassen, "A Savage Sorting of Winners and Losers: Contemporary Versions of Primitive Accumulation," *Globalizations* 7(1–2) (March–June 2010): 24.
128 Ibid.
129 In his article "Mega-Events and Socio-Spatial Dynamics in Rio di Janeiro 1919–1926," *Journal of Latin American Geography* 9(1) (2010): 7–29, Chris Gaffney suggests that significant public investments in football stadiums have been an important part of the history of Rio de Janeiro from the early twentieth century. The self-conscious architectural modernism of the Estádio de Maracanã is also no accident. On the role of modernism as an alternative to European classical styles in twentieth-century Brazilian culture, see Styliane Philippou, "Modernism and National Identity in Brazil, or How to Brew a Brazilian Stew," *National Identities* 7(3) (2005): 245–64.
130 Jules Boykoff, *Celebration Capitalism and the Olympic Games* (London: Routledge, 2014).
131 See David Zirin, *Brazil's Dance with the Devil: The World Cup, the Olympics and the Fight for Democracy* (Chicago, IL: Haymarket Books, 2014); Jake Blumgart, "Making Sense of Brazil's World Cup Protests," *NextCity*, (June 19, 2014): https://nextcity.org/daily/entry/brazil-world-cup-protests-why
132 Mezzadra and Neilson, "Extraction, Logistics, Finance": 12.
133 Jean Harvey, John Horne, and Parissa Safai, "Alterglobalization: Global Social Movements and the Possibility of Political Transformation through Sport," *Sociology of Sport Journal* 26 (2009): 383.
134 Jules Boykoff, *Activism and the Olympics: Dissent at the Games in Vancouver and London* (New Brunswick, NJ: Rutgers University Press, 2014).
135 UN-Habitat's use of sport in their programs is found listed on the UNODP website: https://www.un.org/sport/content/resources/publications
136 Neuwirth, *Shadow Cities*: 249.
137 Shivji, "The Silences in the NGO Discourse": 10.
138 Kidd, "A New Social Movement": 376–7.
139 See Matthew Bishop and Michael Green, *Philanthrocapitalism: How the Rich Can Save the World* (New York: Bloomsbury Press, 2008).
140 Fylan, "FIFA Reveals Billion Dollar Equity."
141 For example, see Christian Fuchs, *Digital Labour and Karl Marx* (London: Routledge, 2014).
142 Jodi Dean, *Democracy and Other Neoliberal Fantasies: Communicative Capitalism and Left Politics* (Chapel Hill, NC: University of North Carolina Press, 2009).
143 Amin, "Capitalism, Imperialism, Globalization": 158.
144 Mezzadra and Neilson, "Extraction, Logistics, Finance": 17.
145 Ibid.

INDEX